BARNS

OF THE

MIDWEST

Photo by Ingolf Vogeler

BARNS
OF THE
MIDWEST

Edited by

Allen G. Noble

and

Hubert G. H. Wilhelm

OHIO UNIVERSITY PRESS
ATHENS

Ohio University Press, Athens, Ohio 45701
© 1995 by Ohio University Press
Printed in the United States of America
All rights reserved

99 98 97 96   5 4 3 2

Ohio University Press books are printed on acid-free paper ∞

Library of Congress Cataloging-in-Publication Data

Barns of the Midwest / edited by Allen G. Noble and Hubert G. H.
   Wilhelm.
        p.   cm.
     Includes bibliographical references and index.
     ISBN 0-8214-1115-2 (cloth). — ISBN 0-8214-1116-0 (pbk)
     1. Barns—Middle West—History.   2. Vernacular architecture—
Middle West.   I. Noble, Allen George, 1930-   .   II. Wilhelm,
Hubert G. H.
NA8230.B27   1995
728'.922'0977—dc20   94-44659
                                                       CIP

CONTENTS

3

The Three-bay Threshing Barn 40
Charles Calkins and Martin Perkins

4

Midwestern Barns and their Germanic Connections 62
Hubert G. H. Wilhelm

5

Affordable Barns for the Midwest: Beginnings 80
Lowell J. Soike

ACKNOWLEDGEMENTS

THE BARN IS a building we have become so used to seeing in the countryside that we tend to ignore it. Yet, if it were to be totally removed somehow, the landscape, and our perception of it, would be dramatically altered. Imagine New England without small, red barns, the Shenandoah Valley without the immense grey stone barns, and the Corn Belt without plain, but neat, white barns. Most books which have been written about barns focus upon the picturesqueness of the structures and their inherent beauty. Not much scholarly attention has been directed to why the barns are built as they are, or what kinds of barns occur where, or what functions each one performs.

The Midwest is a good place to try to answer these questions. In the Midwest both early and later ethnic structures mingle with larger, improved design and special function barns. Because of the basic fertility of Midwest soils, agriculture continues to be a key activity and barns remain important structures, not just relics of the past.

For the most part, the authors of the different chapters of this book are specialists, who over years of study have developed insights which allow them to successfully interpret the particular barn types they discuss. Each author approaches the barn from a different, and sometimes unique, perspective. As editors, we have encouraged their diversity rather than attempting to enforce rigidity of form. After all, the barns of the Midwest are a collection of interestingly varied types.

Many individuals in addition to the authors have contributed to this work. The distinctive sketches by M. Margaret Geib provide a particularly attractive flavor to the volume. These drawings are scattered through almost all of the chapters. Hilda Kendron and Dorothy Tudanca supervised the typing, proof-reading, and assembly of the manuscript. Christa Anderson, Julie Dohner, Lauren Downs, and Audra Wixom, all students at the University of Akron, produced the type-written copy. Claudia James assisted with the final cartographic work. All of these people receive our thanks and appreciation.

Allen G. Noble
Hubert G. H. Wilhelm

1

The Farm Barns of the American Midwest

Allen G. Noble and Hubert G.H. Wilhelm

FEW OBJECTS ARE as visible or striking as the midwestern barn. Indeed, for many of us, the barn is *the* symbol of the Midwest. It conveys stability, hard work, stewardship, solid citizenship and "rural values"—never mind the stereotypes or our stereotypical ideals.

The barn stores a series of traditions, and not just those brought into middle America by conservative English and German farmers from the east. Settlement in the Midwest, although primarily of Anglo-Saxon origins, was never homogeneous. So, there never has been *a* midwestern barn. The barn of the Midwest was—and is—*many* barns common enough to be recognizable as midwestern. Of course, even the term *Midwest* has many definitions and interpretations.

Defining the Midwest

Everyone knows there is a Midwest, but few can agree on its precise boundaries. Geographers have been among the leaders in attempting to identify the limits of the Midwest (fig. 1.1), but even they do not agree. Much of the reason for such lack of accord is that the Midwest is a concept that can be approached from a number of equally valid viewpoints.

Charles B. Hunt (1974), a geologist, did not examine the Midwest *per se*, but he did define three physiographic areas which make up the interior of the United States: the Central Lowland, the Interior Low Plateaus, and the Great Plains (fig. 1.1a). His orientation was entirely toward physical conditions, but, taken together, those physical areas make up a unified interior region. Each of these physiographic units has its own particular character, but all share certain traits, providing an underlying physical unity. All possess an interior, continental location and, partly as a result of this, have a stronger inward than outward focus. Such a focus is also partly the result of general homogeneity of land-form surface. No lofty mountain ranges or extensive hill lands interrupt the generally smooth to rolling plains. Of

1

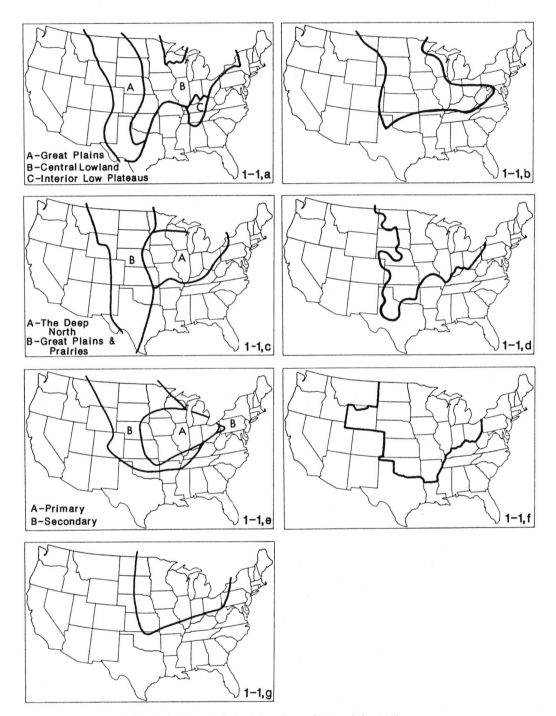

Fig. 1.1. Maps giving various boundaries of the Midwest

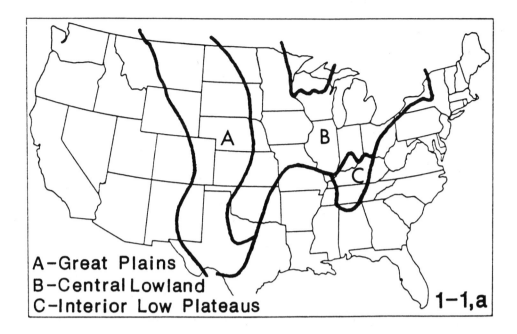

A—Great Plains
B—Central Lowland
C—Interior Low Plateaus

1–1,a

course, some areas are hillier than others; the Flint Hills of Kansas, the Driftless Area of Wisconsin, the Salem Plateau of Missouri, southern Indiana, southeastern Ohio, and the Pennyroyal of Kentucky are certainly areas of dissected surface. It may be significant that virtually all of these areas lie on the margins of the Midwest. They also share a history of nonglaciation. Throughout most of the rest of the Midwest recent glaciation has provided a mantle of soils that helps sustain surplus agricultural production.

Geographers J. Wreford Watson and Stephen Birdsall and John Florin approached the Midwest from this agricultural perspective. Watson (1967) identified an *agricultural Midwest region* which extends eastward to include all of West Virginia, an extension which would seem difficult to defend (fig. 1.1b). Equally problematic is the northeastern boundary which roughly bifurcates Wisconsin, Indiana, and Ohio. Watson's western boundary appears to be more logical in dividing the Great Plains, roughly excluding areas of irrigated cultivation, but including the extensive, dry grain farming areas of the Plains.

Birdsall and Florin (1981) identified an *agricultural core region* (fig. 1.1c). Its boundaries were rather restricted on the north, west, and south, but extended eastward to include northwestern Pennsylvania and the extreme western edge of New York. Although Birdsall and Florin admitted that the term "Middle West (or Midwest) will probably continue to be the most widely used and understood name for the U.S. portion of the continent's agricultural core region," they hesitated to use the term itself (271). Instead they invented the term *Deep North*, which is meaningless and confusing to virtually everyone except the authors. They rather weakly defended their term by noting that "'Deep North' refers to an area of particular cultural intensity and pervasiveness, but it does *not* refer to an area that is farther north than other places (271).

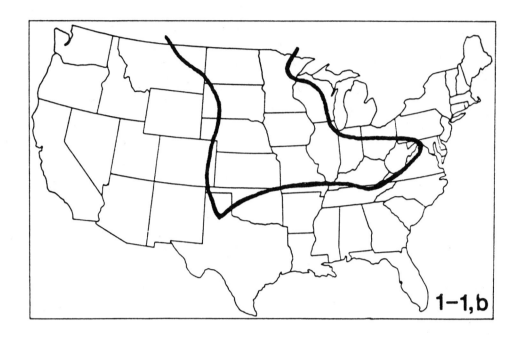

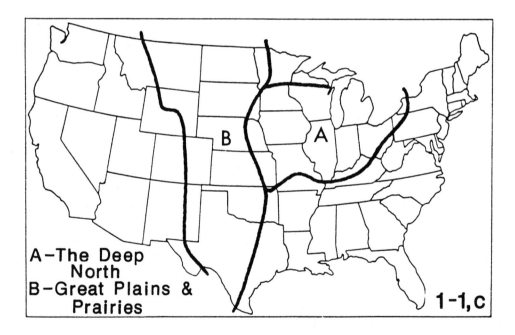

A–The Deep
North
B–Great Plains &
Prairies

Westward of the agricultural core region is another region of primarily agricultural activity which Birdsall and Florin (1981) labeled *The Great Plains and prairies* (297–323). This area is differentiated from the agricultural core essentially because of its more extensive agricultural systems, lower productivity per acre, sparser water resources, and lesser urbanization and manufacturing emphasis.

Alfred J. Wright (1948), an economic geographer, acknowledged the Middle

4

West to be "indefinitely defined." He recognized that it was perhaps the premier American economic region, but he added that it had "achieved a regional character which transcends the economy and involves the cultural and political attitude of the people" (239). Wright extended his boundaries of the Middle West to include portions of the eastern Great Plains (fig. 1.1d). Although sketched out almost a half century ago, Wright's limits of a midwestern region are surprisingly appropriate today, a tribute to his careful scholarship and perception.

The concept of the Middle West has been examined by both Wilbur Zelinsky (1980) and James Shortridge (1985) from the standpoint of the vernacular, a people's everyday perception and usage. Zelinsky's *vernacular Middle West*, relying on the use of the region's name in local city directories, consists of two parts: a core extending from eastern Ohio to central Kansas and from central Wisconsin to southern Missouri; and a periphery of small extensions—East to include Pittsburgh, South to incorporate western Kentucky and northern Arkansas, and West, and North, Montana, Wyoming and eastern Colorado (fig. 1.1e).

Shortridge (1985), basing his definition on respondents' perceptions, primarily agrees with Zelinsky's vernacular Middle West but includes all of Arkansas and most of Wyoming, and leaves out the high plains states (fig. 1.1f).

Finally, Zelinsky (1992), in another study, defines the Midwest from the perspective of cultural evolution, from the meshing of migration streams from the New England, the Middle Atlantic, and, possibly, Chesapeake Bay "hearth" areas. From extreme western New York and Pennsylvania, the region fans out westward as far as the central Dakotas, Nebraska, and Kansas (fig. 1.1g).

Considering all these delineations of the "Middle West," the veracity of Zelinsky's statement that, "Everyone within or without the Middle West knows of its existence, but no one seems sure where it begins or ends," is evident (1992, 128). In point of fact, some agreement does exist. Beginning in the vicinity of the Penn-

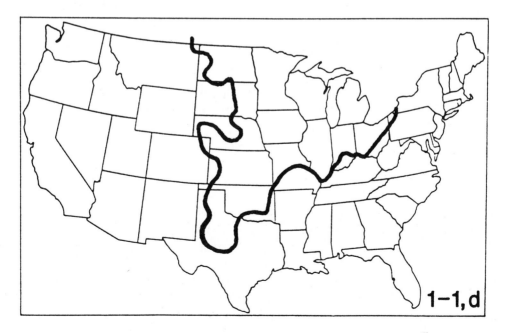

1–1,d

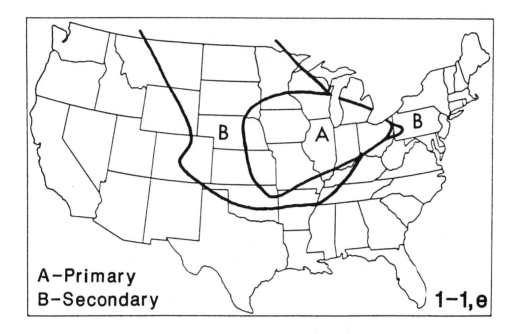

A-Primary
B-Secondary

1-1,e

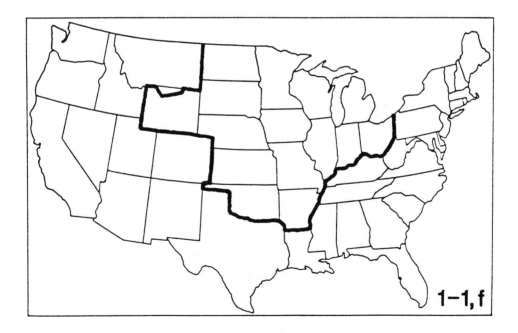

1-1,f

sylvania panhandle, the eastern boundary of the consensus Midwest excludes southeastern Ohio, but includes northern Kentucky. Farther west, southern Missouri and southeastern Oklahoma are excluded.

Also outside the designation of Midwest is the northern half of Minnesota and Wisconsin, which lies on the sterile Canadian Shield, and the northern half of Michigan, an area of boreal forest also with little agriculture. Within these areas

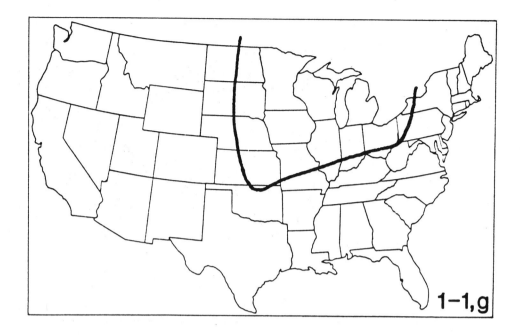

1–1,g

the landscape has a distinctive logged-over appearance that has little in common with the Midwest. Furthermore, the economy here is based upon extractive industries and tourism, and the settlement groups differ culturally from those further south.

The western boundary of the Midwest enjoys no such unanimity of definition. Some authors extend the region entirely across the Great Plains to the foothills of the Rocky Mountains, a convenient and easily defined physical boundary. Others prefer to use the eastern boundary of the Great Plains as a limit. For the purposes of this study, we have chosen a western boundary roughly through the middle of the Great Plains (fig. 1.2). Such a boundary effectively divides the cultivated Great Plains from those areas in which livestock grazing is the predominant agricultural activity.

DEFINING THE BARN

Grazing activities normally do not require an investment in barns, other than those used as machinery sheds or for equipment storage. Crop agriculture, on the other hand, normally has a barn as its central focus. The same is also true of agriculture in which the focus is primarily upon dairying or animal raising aside from grazing. Thus, across the various farming areas of the Midwest, the barn, or a main structure with similar function, dominates each farmstead.

August Meitzen (1882), a well-known nineteenth-century German settlement geographer, wrote that "the house is the embodiment of a people's soul" (*Das Haus ist die Verkoerperung des Volksgeistes*) (3). One can hardly argue with this observation of rural, vernacular, or folk houses. But, if the house reflects the soul of its owners, what about the barn? Although often structurally integrated with the house in Europe, the barn nevertheless represented a different image, one of

7

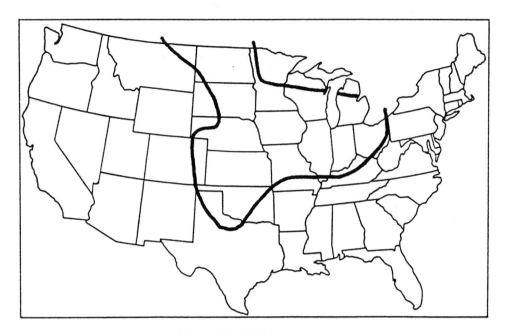

Fig. 1.2. The Midwest region

work, surpluses, income, thrift, and risk-taking. To rephrase Meitzen, the barn then is the embodiment of a people's economic worth. It is, to use Calkins and Perkins' analogy from chapter 3, the "farmer's bank." In America, and especially so in the Midwest with its specialized, commercial agriculture, that image and function translated into extraordinary architectural forms, often appearing like veritable castles upon the rural landscape.

The word *barn* is defined in Webster's as "a building for storing farm produce and/or stabling livestock." Its origins in England refer more to the first function. The word is derived from a combination of two Anglo-Saxon words, *bere*, meaning barley (or subsequently any grain), and *ern*, meaning place of storage. "Cow house," "stable," or some other term, is used to signify those structures providing animal shelter, although in the relatively mild climate of Great Britain animals are frequently left in the open during the entire year.

However, in North America, because of the harsher winter climate, the barn quickly assumed the functions both of animal shelter and crop storage. This was especially true for the earliest, simple barns in New England and elsewhere along the eastern seaboard, and along the advancing frontier as settlement pushed westward into the continent's interior. Under these conditions, yeoman farmers could afford only a single barn that did double duty. Even the simple three-bay barns, which had evolved in England primarily to permit storage and processing of grains, were adapted in North America by introducing animal stalls on one side of the central threshing floor.

The barn, then, is defined in the American Midwest by the functions it performs, either originally or currently. These functions include animal shelter, crop storage, crop processing, equipment storage, and machinery repair. *The barn* refers

8

to the place on the farm where any, or several, of these activities regularly takes place. However, if the building is specialized in function, its designation may carry an adjective, such as "sheep" barn or "horse" barn. Similarly, in some instances a substitute term, such as smoke house, machine shed, or sheep fold, may be used for the specialized-function structure, especially if a larger multipurpose "barn" is also on the farm.

FARMSTEAD PATTERNS AND THE POSITIONING OF THE BARN

The pattern of farmsteads and the relationship of the barn to the farmhouse and to other farm buildings have not been extensively analyzed. A few excellent studies do exist of individual farmsteads and very localized areas (Kiefer 1972), but these have not resulted in generalized studies applicable to larger areas and groups of barns. One highly impressionistic study by Robert Riley (1985) addresses the changing rural landscape of Illinois.

At least five factors—topography, weather, convenience or labor efficiency, land survey systems, and tradition—come into play in determining the arrangement of barns and other farmstead buildings. Most of the time, the various factors act in concert with one another, so that it is difficult or impossible to determine the extent of influence of a particular one.

Topography and other associated physical concerns, such as drainage and soil quality, act both negatively and positively. For example, slopes too steep or, conversely, too flat, promoting poor drainage, are avoided. However, a modest slope may encourage location of a bank barn (Kiefer 1972). A south-facing orientation secures maximum light, especially for stable areas underneath forebays. An orientation toward the east allows a barn to place its back against prevailing westerly winds. Local snow-accumulation tendencies also can influence barn locations. The effect of both topographical and weather conditions may be offset somewhat by how the land is marked off and divided up.

In much of the Midwest, the General Land Office survey system divides the surface geometrically. Roads run true and straight and in concert with compass directions. Barns and other farm buildings often line up in rigid conformity with survey lines, and the farmstead has an order imposed by the land division system. Riley (1985) notes that even the small country cemetery follows such an order with "its plots and marker stones . . . lined up so that even the dead are settled on the grid system" (79).

Riley also observes that, in level areas where the General Land Office survey system was employed, the siting of farmsteads obeyed just two general rules: They were square to the road (e.g., the survey lines), and, because of the prevailing westerly winds, hogs were housed to the east of the farmstead.

In some other areas, where topography is more rugged, such uniformity is absent and farmsteads follow the contours of the land. However, regularity still may be imposed by the hand of tradition. The original settlers of the land frequently laid out their farmsteads and positioned their barns in a way that seemed natural to them because they had seen farmsteads laid out this way all their lives. They instinctively followed their cultural guidelines, usually without even realizing they were doing so. The widespread occurrence of the courtyard plan among German-derived farmsteads is one example. Such an arrangement is widely recognized in the Midwest, but has not been closely studied.

The final factor governing barn positioning is convenience or labor efficiency. The barn did not need to be close to the house, except in areas of long, cold winters, but it was desirable to locate the barn closer to the fields than the house. Hence, barns are usually farther back from roads than are houses. Close proximity of the barn to outbuildings also was desirable.

Taking these factors into consideration, midwestern farmers usually laid out their farmsteads in one of three patterns. Most common are the farmsteads where all buildings have exactly the same orientation usually to compass directions. A second pattern can be termed the courtyard arrangement. In these cases, the house and barn form two sides of an open square. Smaller outbuildings define the remaining two sides. The third pattern is a more free-form arrangement, in which buildings vary in alignment, but generally follow the contour of a slope. Further study may reveal additional farmstead patterns.

The chapters which follow represent a premier undertaking, the comprehensive treatment of a long-overdue subject, the Midwestern Barn. These two elements, *Midwest* and *barn*, are inextricable related, forming the underpinning of a people's spatial perception of the American heartland. Neither East nor West, but rather in the center, where the combination of level land, grass-covered and dark, fertile soils, an ideal climate, and usually abundant water from lakes and rivers offered, to all those who dared, a panacea for settlement and development.

As the barriers to westward migration fell, American migrants and foreign immigrants alike converged onto the central parts of the country guided by the spirit of manifest destiny, which included natural routeways, and, most importantly, the unfailing attraction of cheap and plentiful land. There were New Englanders and Easterners, including large numbers of Pennsylvania-Dutch and, of course, Southerners, especially Virginians, who came by way of the hills of Appalachia and rivers of Kentucky. The immigrants were a varied lot, but prominent among them were the Scots-Irish and the Germans. Within a time period of little more than a generation, however, these traditions would give way to new influences. In part, these changes resulted from acculturation, but, more importantly, they were caused by urbanization and industrialization, and the impact that these processes had on agriculture.

Log Crib Barns

As the frontier of settlement passed into the Midwest, many early barns were constructed of log by advancing farmers, who either possessed log-building skills as part of their cultural baggage, or had perfected such techniques by association with other groups through a process of cultural transference in eastern United States (Jordan and Kaups 1989). The eastern margins of the Midwest were well-forested, so that log materials were readily available. However, as settlement progressed westward, suitable forest resources greatly diminished and logs disappeared as a common building material.

A second factor explaining the lack of log building in much of the Midwest was the relatively fertile soils covering large sections of the region, soils sufficiently rich to support prosperous agriculture that required larger and more elaborate barns. Thus, log structures were inadequate almost from the beginning of European settlement. The rolling hill lands of the southern fringes of the Midwest did not share in such agricultural prosperity. Hence, log crib barns continued to be built in these areas well into the twentieth century. Some, perhaps, are even being built today in isolated locations there. Log crib barns, especially in Dubois County, Indiana, are discussed in greater detail by Warren Roberts in chapter 2 as relicts of the initial waves of Middle Atlantic settlement.

SCANDINAVIAN LOG BARNS

In a few areas along the northern fringes of the Midwest region, a different range of log barns occurs. These are extensions of the Scandinavian-Finnish settlements which characterize the northcentral parts of the United States. Most of these settlements lie outside our region of interest, but in Chisago County, Minnesota, a large Swedish community evolved in the latter half of the nineteenth century, introducing elongated half-log barns to the Midwest (fig 1.3). These distinctive structures are comprised of two parts—a cow barn and a hay storage facility joined together side by side (A:son-Palmqvist 1983). Typical dimensions are twenty-seven to twenty-eight feet wide and sixty to sixty-two feet long, with the hay barn occupying somewhat more than half of the total area of the building.

Fig. 1.3. Swedish barn, Chisago County, Minnesota
Sketch: M. Margaret Geib

The cow barn, divided into stalls and calving pens, is essentially separate from the other part of the barn, connected through an interior partition by a single small door.

The cow barn section of the building is typically constructed of tightly fitted hewn logs, or occasionally of field stone. The hay storage part of the barn consists of a timber frame covered by vertical boards or planks. Each gable also is covered by vertical planks. The roof frame, extending across the entire building as a single unified structure, is of timber and was originally sheathed by wooden shakes. Many of these original roofs now have been replaced by asphalt composition shingles and other modern materials.

The Swedish settlement of Chisago County is an excellent example, not just of Scandinavian settlements, but of many other immigrant groups who transferred their traditional building forms from Europe to the Midwest, and established a unique ethnic landscape. Elsewhere in the Midwest, distinctive traditional barns have been described for several important but scattered communities, including Czechs in southeastern South Dakota (Rau 1992), Waloonian Belgians in Door County, Wisconsin (Laatsch and Calkins 1992), Dutch in southwestern Michigan (Durand 1951), and Welsh in Allen County, western Ohio (Brown 1989). Dozens of other immigrant communities still await documentation of their particular types of barns.

TRADITIONAL TIMBER-FRAME BARNS

At a much different scale are the German and English groups. These two peoples came in such numbers that they left their clear imprint over vast sections of the Midwest. Furthermore, they came not only as immigrant groups directly from Europe, but also as descendants of earlier settlers who had established themselves in eastern seaboard hearths.

The English (Yankee, or New England) stream of migration introduced the three-bay threshing barn (see fig. 3.1 p. 41). The characteristics and influence of this barn in the Midwest are discussed by Charles Calkins and Martin Perkins in chapter 3. Its ancient roots are in both continental Europe and the British Isles. In America, it became the barn of choice among the majority of early settlers. It fit well into the small-scale, mixed agriculture of New Englanders and many from the Middle Atlantic area. Today, these barns survive mostly in the eastern areas of the Midwest, and often where agriculture has not proven to be particularly prosperous, so that more modern and larger replacement barns were never erected. One should not assume, however, that traditional barns were static; they did change in response to altering agricultural and climatic conditions. One such change was the popularization of basement barns, either banked or raised, to supplement and ultimately replace the one-and-a-half story English barn as a more efficient structure.

The basement structures quickly became accepted barn forms in many parts of the Midwest (fig. 1.4). Rueber (1974), notes that such barns were constructed upon commencement of agricultural settlement in Fayette County, Iowa. Durand (1943, 1951) has commented on the structures in Wisconsin and Michigan, and Noble (1977) has documented them across Ohio. Although Ridlen (1972) com-

Fig. 1.4. Typical raised/basement barn, Crawford County, Ohio.
Photo: A. Noble, February 1991

pared them with German bank barns in Cass County, Indiana, and Hartman (1976) briefly reviewed them as "the most common type of timber-framed barn found in Michigan," hardly anyone has examined them in much detail.

The three-bay threshing barn was the kind of building that could be relatively easily adapted when substituting plank or balloon framing for its orginal, hand-hewn, heavy frame, by raising and extending it, or by adding a new kind of roof because of its full-frame construction. All of these changes happened to this little, inconspicuous farm building. These processes of change are discussed by Lowell Soike in chapter 5.

The other early stream of migration into the Midwest introduced the German bank barn, originally brought to North America via southeastern Pennsylvania. A more elaborate building than the English three-bay barn, the German bank barn provided for both crop storage and processing on the one hand, and for animal storage on the other (see fig. 4.3 p. 68). Large-scale German settlement ensured that the German barn would be the most popular traditional type of barn in the eastern Midwest. LaRock and Yeck (1956) estimated Wisconsin to have between sixty thousand and seventy thousand banked barns, a majority of which probably were German. Such barns remain widely scattered throughout Ohio, Indiana, Michigan, and Missouri, and in isolated locations elsewhere. Of course, in the level lands of the interior, "banking" of this barn was replaced by using an earthen ramp.

Simply because the terrain no longer suited the traditional way of building did not automatically mean that the building was altered accordingly. In general, human culture is conservative, and it was especially so among the Germanic settlers from the East. These were not a people inclined to change because it was fashionable. Because the barn has survived in both time and space, it has been possible to trace its diffusion paths out of the Middle Atlantic states into the Midwest (Ensminger 1992).

In the prairie grassland sections of the Midwest, especially western Ohio, northcentral Indiana, Illinois, and Iowa, a very different traditional German barn survives: these Saxon or North German Plain barns (Noble 1984) took a quite different form from the German bank barn (fig. 1.5). They were squarish in plan and had their doors on the gable wall rather than on the side. They rose only a single story above the ground and were generally smaller than the bank barns. Both of these German-derived barns are discussed further by Hubert Wilhelm under the rubric of Germanic traditions in chapter 4.

MIDWESTERN AGRICULTURE

Several types of farming operate in the Middle West and each dominates in particular sections of the larger region (fig. 1.6). Along the windward shores of Lakes Michigan and Erie, where specialized fruit farming predominates, the farm buildings are uniformly small. If a barn is present on the farmstead it is often non-

Fig. 1.5. Typical Saxon or North German plain barn, Dallas County, Iowa.
Photo: A. Noble, October 1984

14

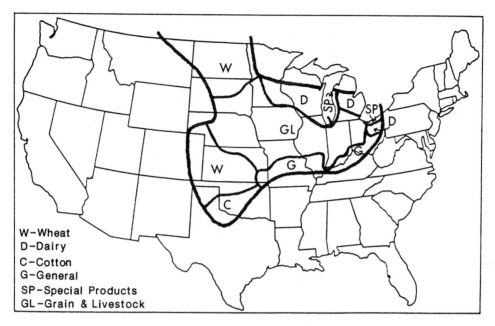

W—Wheat
D—Dairy
C—Cotton
G—General
SP—Special Products
GL—Grain & Livestock

Fig. 1.6. The Midwest: Types of farming

descript and used merely for machinery or equipment storage. Barns in these areas do not have the visual impact characteristic of other areas. In any event, these areas do not make up a very large segment of the Midwest.

A much larger area is given over to dairying. Located in three separate sections—southern Minnesota/Wisconsin, southern Michigan, and eastern Ohio—farm barns are larger, with the more recently built barns scattered throughout the dairy farming area. Although many basement barns and German bank barns characterize the dairy belt, the most typical farm building is the large barn called the Wisconsin dairy barn. Ingolf Vogeler discusses, in chapter 6, the evolution of the specialized function of dairying and the various barns associated therewith.

Another widespread, but even more specialized, type of agriculture is the cultivation of tobacco. Much of this occurs along the southern margins of the Midwest, but certain localized occurrences such as in Dane County, Wisconsin, and Darke County, Ohio, have persisted from the nineteenth century. In many areas, tobacco cultivation has been on the decline for some time. Hence, tobacco barns are steadily becoming obsolete structures, and they may have been converted to other agricultural uses. The tobacco barn as an element of midwestern agriculture is discussed in chapter 7 by Karl Raitz.

The largest part of midwestern farmland is devoted to raising field crops, such as wheat, corn and soybeans, sold as cash crops or used as animal feed. Within this area, the raising of livestock also has been historically important, although not as significant today as formerly. A liberal scattering of traditional barns remains throughout these crop areas, especially toward the East, but the dominant type of barn is one of lighter frame, dimension lumber or sawn planks. Often called "feeder barns," they are normally smaller than the traditional barns

15

and usually have gambrel or gothic roofing systems rather than gable. Lowell Soike in chapter 8 traces the popularization of these barns as midwestern agricultural prosperity was realized in the latter part of the nineteenth century and the first two decades of the twentieth century.

Throughout this "grain belt" the constant demand was for more and better facilities to store the field crops produced in ever larger quantities. Specialized structures, first as extensions of barns, and later as replacements for some of the storage and processing functions of the barn, were needed. Corncribs and granaries, often combined in the same building, came to be as characteristic of the midwestern farmstead as the barn itself. In McLean County, Illinois, as late as 1975, a survey counted corncribs on 192 of 200 farmsteads (Kruckman and Whiteman 1975). On some farms, the corncrib grew to enormous size, larger even than the barn or the house (fig. 1.7). All this was a reflection of the great productivity of most midwestern soils. The development of corncribs, corn-processing systems, granaries, and grain elevators as western extensions of the basic midwestern barn is discussed in chapter 9 by Keith Roe.

BARN ADDITIONS AND EXTENSIONS

Another consequence of growing agricultural productivity was that many barns were expanded, sometimes more than once. Sheds were added to one or both gable walls and the barn's main roof line was extended to incorporate a rear

Fig. 1.7. Masonry corn crib in Guthrie County, Iowa. Note how its size compares with that of the house.
Photo: A. Noble, October 1984

16

addition. Some German bank barns had the open areas beneath their forebays enclosed. A common modification was the addition of a large straw shed at right angles to the main barn. As herds grew, the shed housed more straw for bedding and additional hay for feed. The basement of the straw shed also could house additional cows.

In Fulton County, Ohio, barn expansion followed a different direction. Here, a second barn with the same dimensions and orientation as the original barn was erected beside the earlier one (fig. 1.8), and sometimes an intervening structure was built to connect the two. These twin barns, a distinctive feature of Fulton County since just after the turn of the century, did not spread much beyond the county boundaries.

THE MODERNIZATION OF MIDWESTERN BARNS

As the proliferation of grain storage facilities demonstrates, barn functions constantly have changed. Farmers were steadily searching for different solutions as they encountered new problems in the evolving agricultural systems of the Midwest. Some attempted to introduce innovative forms and materials for their barns. The use of lighter frames and preformed trusses was one important innovation. Of less permanent impact, but no less interesting, was the flirtation of many farmers and builders with nonorthogonal plans. Keith Sculle and H. Wayne Price, in chapter 10, look at these curiosities for what they tell us about the revo-

Fig. 1.8. Example of a twinned barn, Fulton County, Ohio. Note the elaborate door decoration.
Photo: A. Noble, March 1992

17

lutionary ideas permeating midwestern agriculture in the mid-nineteenth century. Round barns, or those of six or eight sides, were touted as "scientific" and hence modern. For a variety of reasons, explored by Sculle and Price, these innovative designs were ultimately rejected by midwestern farmers. Modernization took other directions.

One such direction was simply to replace a traditional barn roof with its heavy timber frame with a more commodious, lighter-framed structure. The visual change was usually that from gable roof to gambrel roof. Other new construction materials also began to be used. Concrete was favored over the earlier stone, brick or wood, for floors and foundation.

Changes in sanitation laws and attitudes, improvements in barn equipment, and enforcement of building codes had an impact on barn design. Increased mechanization radically changed the function of barns. Changes in farming practices, such as the adoption of baled and rolled hay, also contributed to modifications. Finally, barns of a radical new design appeared after World War II. The processes of modernization which brought about all these changes are examined by Glenn Harper and Steve Gordon in chapter 11.

Despite the changes in barn design, certain minor features seemed to persist and to be incorporated in newer barns. Perhaps this reflected the farmers' desire to hold onto some traditions, even as the new replaced the old in larger aspects of barn design. Of course, as Harper and Gordon point out, not all farmers rushed to adopt the new. Such conservatism is clearly seen among the Amish, who still erect barns, for the most part, according to their time-honored traditions.

Minor Architectural Features

A feature found on some barns in the eastern Midwest is the entry porch (fig. 1.9). It appears on a wide variety of barn types and does not seem to be associated with any particular ethnic group. Probably introduced to North America from west-central England, entry porches came into the Midwest from their hearth area of the lower Mohawk and Schohaire valleys in eastern New York state.

Another architectural feature characteristic of many barns in the Midwest is the unsupported pent roof. It is usually considered a German feature, although some evidence exists for an English Quaker origin (Fisher 1989). Regardless of whether English Quakers or German Protestants (i.e., Pennsylvania Dutch) introduced pent roofs, southeastern Pennsylvania was the apparent hearth area for this feature. Constructed over doorways, pent roofs offer entry protection from rain and snow. On many barns, however, the pent located on the gable wall acts to extend the protected area of the barn. This may have been an alternative to costly rebuilding of the structure in order to expand the interior area of the barn. It is not surprising that most gable-wall pent roofs in the Midwest occur on the small three-bay threshing barns.

Side-wall pents are less common, usually found on basement barns, particularly in southeastern Wisconsin. They resemble German bank barn overhangs and may be attempts to gain the perceived advantages of the German forebay without actually building it.

Fig. 1.9. Typical entry porch on a raised/basement barn, Mahoning County, Ohio.
The double entry is not common.
Photo: A. Noble, April 1985

Decorated doors are a third architectural feature, found mostly on traditional barns in the eastern Midwest. The kinds of decoration encompass a wide range of rounded arches, gothic frames, filled-in corners, geometric patterns, silhouettes of flowers, decorative drops, and a few other quite elaborate forms. These decorations seem to be outgrowths of the simple practice of giving doors more care and attention than the rest of the barn. Painting of the entire barn is a recent development.

The rounded arch is the basic form from which the other decorative devices appear to have evolved. The details of decoration, as well as other, wider aspects of barn decor, are considered by David Stephens in chapter 12.

Also examined by Stephens are decorative roofs. The geographical pattern of slate roofing material is explained by the location of slate deposits in the East and by the location of railroads. More recently, asphalt shingles have been used to create often impressive roof decorations.

In other parts of the Midwest, local availability or absence of various building materials explains much of the current pattern of barns. Foundation materials vary widely. In northcentral Ohio precisely cut blocks of Berea sandstone support many nineteenth-century barn buildings; in western Ohio, Devonian limestones replace the sandstone. Similar patterns reoccur throughout the Midwest. In glaciated areas, subangular to rounded glacial boulders often form the foundation. From Sanilac County to Macomb County in eastern Michigan, for example, particularly distinctive and attractive glacial boulders characterize the basement barns.

19

Along the Kettle moraine in southeastern Wisconsin, small boulders were so plentiful that the entire building was often made of them (Cetin 1969).

In unglaciated areas, clusters of stone barns are apt to be found whenever softer limestones occur as bedrock. Two factors encourage such construction. First, the bedrock is easily quarried and dressed, producing a desirable and attractive stone. Second, the presence of limestone bedrock ensures that the soils will support agriculture productive enough to warrant the farmer's considerable investment in a stone structure. One of the best-known concentrations of such stone barns is that built by German settlers in the second half of the nineteenth century in Gasconade County, Missouri (van Ravenswaay 1977).

Another area strongly influenced by the availability of local building materials was along the Kansas Flint Hills, from Wabaunsee County to Chautauqua County (fig. 1.10). Irregular fieldstones were combined with quarried and dressed limestone blocks to create solidly built barns that reflected the builders' European heritage (Scott 1967). Generally constructed between 1870 and 1880, they often possess arched doorways, stone quoining and tooled stone lintels (Hall 1972), raising them from mere utilitarian structures to the level of architectural creations.

Fig. 1.10. Stone barn typical of the Kansas Flint Hills area.
Sketch: M. Margaret Geib

20

PRESERVING MIDWESTERN BARNS

The modern-day observer is not the first to appreciate the architecturally satisfying barns of the Midwest. Nevertheless, it is only recently that momentum has been gained to mount efforts to preserve some of these fast-disappearing structures. Perhaps, this is because we are now an urban people and the barn is rapidly becoming an object of nostalgia, a pleasant but receding memory from our childhood. The growing strength, scope, and acceptance of preservation activities hold out hope that some portion of these barns can be salvaged and protected, so that future generations may better understand the early history and earlier cultural landscape at the Midwest. Hemalata Dandekar and Eric MacDonald review in chapter 13 the preservation strategies available to achieve these ends.

These forlorn, decaying buildings suggest that a way of life, one in which we may have participated, is passing forever. Jack Matthews, in the concluding essay of chapter 14, reflects on the symbolism and imagery that barns possess for many people.

CONCLUSION

Few Americans would miss the close relationship of two words. Midwest and barn. Indeed, here in the "middle" of the country where glaciers had flattened the land and left deep deposits of glacial sediment, where rainfall, although less than farther east, came during the right time or growing season of the year, where dense stands of trees gave way to tall grasses, and soils grew increasingly dark, even black, in appearance, American settlers carved out a region where commercial agriculture would be "the order of the day" and farms would give character to the landscape.

Yet, this American heartland, while part of our collective psyche, is difficult to pin down. Geographers have attempted it and have enclosed the Midwest with their boundaries, reflecting individual, spatial interpretation based, in part, on varying regional criteria. The latter, however, usually include measures or symbols of agriculture whether that be acreage in corn or soybeans, the distribution of rail links and market centers, or farmstead layout and composition, etc. In the end, of course, the Midwest is where we believe it is, a place in the middle of the country where people, land, farms, highways, rails, waterways, cities, and industries are linked into an American regional reality.

Foremost among the identifying regional features of the Midwest is the barn. Not just a white or red, rectangular, gabled structure, but one of great diversity in form and function. It is at once representative of surviving traditional regional building influences brought into the Midwest by American migrants from the Northeast, East, and South, and the construction peculiarities of immigrant ethnic groups. Most of all, however, it remains as a landscape element symbolic of specialization in American agriculture and the incorporation of science and technology in farming. The following chapters should greatly enhance our appreciation for a humble and now so rapidly disappearing landscape feature, the Midwestern barn.

REFERENCES CITED

A:son-Palmqvist, Lena. 1983. *Building traditions among Swedish settlers in rural Minnesota.* Stockholm: Nordiska Museet/ The Emigrant Institute.

Birdsall, Stephen S. and John W. Florin. 1981. *Regional landscapes of the United States and Canada.* 2d ed. New York: John Wiley.

Brown, Mary Ann. 1989. Barns in the Black Swamp of northwestern Ohio. *PAST— Pioneer America Society Transactions.* 12:47–54.

Cetin, Frank. 1969. Those beautiful barns. *Wisconsin Tales and Trails* 10(Spring): 25–30.

Durand, Loyal, Jr. 1943. Dairy barns of south-eastern Wisconsin. *Economic Geography* 17:37–44.

———. 1951. The lower peninsula of Michigan and the Western Michigan dairy region: A segment of the American dairy region. *Economic Geography.* 27(April): 163–83.

Ensminger, Robert F. 1992. *The Pennsylvania barn: Its origin, evolution, and distribution in North America.* Baltimore: Johns Hopkins Univ. Press.

Fisher, David H. 1989. *Albion's seed: Four British folkways in America.* New York: Oxford Univ. Press.

Glassie, Henry. 1974. The variation of concepts within tradition: Barn building in Otsego County, New York. *Geoscience and Man* 5:177–235.

Hall, Charles L. 1972. Stone barns of the Flint Hills. *Kansas Country Living* 17:12a–12d.

Hartman, Lee. 1976. Michigan barns: Our vanishing landmarks. Michigan Natural Resources 45(April/May): unpaged.

Hunt, Charles B. 1974. *Natural regions of the United States and Canada.* San Francisco: W. H. Freeman.

Jordan, Terry G., and Matti Kaups, 1989 *The American backwoods frontier.* Baltimore: Johns Hopkins Univ. Press.

Kiefer, Wayne E. 1972. An agricultural settlement complex in Indiana. *Annals of the Association of American Geographers* 62(3): 487–506.

Kruckman, Laurence, and Darrell L. Whiteman. 1975. Barns, buildings, and windmills: a key to change on the Illinois prairies. *Journal of the Illinois State Historical Society* 68:257–66.

Laatsch, William G., and Charles F. Calkins. 1992. Belgians in Wisconsin. In *To build in a new land,* edited by Allen G. Noble, 195–210. Baltimore: Johns Hopkins Univ. Press.

22

LaRock, Max J., and Robert G. Yeck. 1956. *Bank barns compared with aboveground barns*. Washington: U.S. Department of Agriculture, Production Research Report No. 2.

Meitzen, August. 1882. *Das Deutsche Haus in Seinen Volkstuemlichen Formen*. Berlin: Verlag von Dietrich Reimer.

Noble, Allen G. 1984. *Wood, brick and stone: The North American settlement landscape*. Vol. 2, *Barns and Farm Structures*. Amherst: Univ. of Massachusetts Press.

————., and Albert J. Korsok. 1977. Barn variations in Columbiana County, Ohio. *The East Lakes Geographer* 12:98–111.

Rau, John E. 1992. Czechs in South Dakota. In *To build in a new land*, edited by Allen G. Noble, 285–306. Baltimore: Johns Hopkins Univ. Press.

Ridlen, Susanne S. 1972. Bank Barns in Cass County, Indiana. *Pioneer America*. 4(2): 25–43.

Riley, Robert B. 1985. Square to the road, hogs to the east. *Places: A quarterly journal of environmental design*. 2(4): 72–80. (Also published with slightly different wording in *Illinois Issues* 11(7): 22–26).

Rueber, Bruce. 1974. *Factors influencing barn styles in Layette County, Iowa*. Master's thesis, San Diego State University.

Scott, Laura. 1967. Timeless barns of stone. *K-stater*. 17 (November): 8–11.

Shortridge, James R. 1985. The vernacular middle West. *Annals of the Association of American Geographers*. 75 (1): 48–57.

van Ravenswaay, Charles. 1977. *The arts and architecture of German settlements in Missouri*. Columbia: Univ. of Missouri Press.

Watson, J. Wreford. 1967. *North America: Its countries and regions*. New York: Frederick A. Praeger.

Wright, Alfred J. 1948. *United States and Canada*. New York: Appleton-Century-Crofts.

Zelinsky, Wilbur. 1980. North America's vernacular regions. *Annals of the Association of American Geographers*. 70(1): 1–16.

————. 1992. *The cultural geography of the United States*. Rev. ed. Englewood Cliffs, NJ: Prentice-Hall.

2

EARLY LOG-CRIB BARN SURVIVALS

Warren E. Roberts

THE HISTORY OF farming in the Midwest includes a watershed of great importance, the change during the nineteenth century from self-sufficient farming to cash-crop farming. Although southern Indiana is the focus of this chapter, virtually everything here concerning southern Indiana also applies to much of the rest of the Midwest.

The first settlers in southern Indiana came from the region commonly recognized as the Upland South, (North Carolina, Tennessee, and Kentucky), terrain remarkably similar to that in Indiana. They encountered no mountains nor even high hills, but they did find a countryside of countless deep hollows, steep ridges, and very little level land.

What level land they did find was along creeks and rivers, "bottom land" as they called it. They shunned this bottom land, knowing full well that anyone who built a house there would almost certainly suffer from the ague, and also perhaps from a dim perception of the risk of floods. They took up land, if at all possible, between the ridge tops, which they knew to be dry and infertile, and the potentially dangerous river and creek bottoms.

A typical farmstead before the midpoint of the nineteenth century would have had probably fewer than ten acres under the plow. The farmer and his wife were concerned primarily with raising enough food for their family. What would have been the point in raising more? A lack of transportation ensured that no bulky loads of farm produce could be taken to market by most farmers. An examination of maps made during the first half of the last century reveals few roads in the countryside and no access to most farms. In the drier seasons, creek beds were used as roads of a sort, hence the saying, "I'll be there if the Lord is willing and the creek don't rise." In addition to the few acres under the plow, there would have been some pasture for the animals, and lots of forest as a source of firewood and a place for the pigs to roam in search of acorns and beechnuts.

The changeover in farming was accompanied by changes of other sorts, some helping to bring about the revolution in farming, and some the result of it. Because of the necessarily limited scope of this chapter, it is possible to touch on

24

only two topics: the changes in farming itself, and the rebuilding of America that ensued.

FARMING CHANGES AND THE REBUILDING OF AMERICA

The growth of a network of railroad lines, and a frenzy of road building in the countryside in the latter half of the nineteenth century, made it possible for farmers to bring their produce to market. Consequently, farmers began putting more and more land under the plow. As some families left farms to move into towns and cities in search of those economic opportunities which would produce a "better life," remaining farmers staying in the countryside bought more land to raise production and increase their income and living standards, or at least to keep even. Instead of raising a wide variety of crops merely to satisfy the needs of their own families, farmers began concentrating on one crop or commodity—corn or dairy products, for example—and raising as much of it as they possibly could in order to sell as much as possible. New methods of farming and farm machinery were introduced to enable the farmer to reach bigger yields.

The impact of the socioeconomic changes in the United States in the second half of the nineteenth century and the early decades of the twentieth century is complex. Changes such as the explosive growth of many towns and cities, the settling of much of the West (making railway building profitable), the vast expansion of manufacturing, and the mushrooming numbers of immigrants characterize the era. They, and other factors, all of great importance, brought about what I call the "Rebuilding of America." In the process, forests were literally destroyed to provide lumber for an almost endless array of new buildings of all types in the burgeoning cities and towns, while countless old buildings were abandoned or torn down to make way for the new.

The countryside also took part in the Rebuilding of America. At least two forces were at work. The abandoning of farms and the consolidation of smaller farms into larger ones resulted in many buildings being razed or abandoned, while many new ones were built. Moreover, changes in farming meant that many old farm buildings were too small, or unsuitable for other reasons. They had to be replaced in one way or another by larger, more suitable and flexible structures. Thus, farm buildings, including barns, differed in many ways before and after the changeover in farming.

Some obvious differences in barns can be identified:

1. Size: The large barns that have become so familiar a feature of the American rural landscape almost always were built after the changeover in farming took place. Earlier, the self-sufficient farm family needed only a few dairy cows to supply its needs, plus a yoke of oxen, perhaps, and a horse. While a barn had many other uses, among its primary purposes were housing the animals and storing the hay needed during the winter.

2. Function: The early barns, while small, nonetheless had many uses. Housing animals and storing hay were the most space-consuming uses, but many early

barns also incorporated a corn crib, a grain bin, a workshop, a threshing floor, and storage for a wide variety of implements.

On the other hand, the large barns built after the changeover in farming devoted almost all their space to a single enterprise. In southern Indiana that enterprise is dairying, and while there are, of course, exceptions, most large barns are dairy barns, their size required to house large herds and to store huge quantities of hay.

3. Significance to Folklife Studies: A study of the buildings of the self-sufficient farms of southern Indiana reveals a way of life that existed there and elsewhere for hundreds of years. The patterns of self-sufficient farming, and the family and community life associated with them, were brought from Europe, flourished along the East Coast of the United States, and were then transferred into the Midwest by people who had inherited a strong tradition, including a knowledge of how to build houses, barns, and other farm buildings. They knew how to work with wood, how to hew logs, how to split shingles, how to lay out the floor plan for a house or barn; in short, they knew how to build and what to build, for all this knowledge and all these skills were part of their inherited lore.

Consequently, by studying their buildings, we can learn about a way of life characteristic of the overwhelming majority of the population for an immeasurably long period of time. Early barns can tell us much about ethnic and regional origins, paths of migration, routes of diffusion, traditional farming practices, subsistence patterns, and traditional building techniques. It is for these reasons that early barns and other farm buildings are one of the most valuable sources of information for the student of folklife, the life of most of the population in the preindustrial era.

However, as we look at the late nineteenth- and early twentieth-century barns, we must keep in mind that in many cases they were constructed by professional builders following plans derived from some "scientific" farm journal and using mass-produced lumber from some nearby lumber yard or sawmill.

Different kinds of farming, different terrain, and different climates caused different kinds of barns to be built in different parts of the country. Certainly, an Ohio tobacco barn is not the same as a Wisconsin dairy barn, although both fit under the rubric of Midwest barns. It is also true that the builders of barns and the farmers who had the barns built often were innovative. They sometimes included traditional features of early barns and they sometimes tried out new ideas. Yet, in a grander number of cases the designs of barns after the changeover in farming came mainly from the land-grant agricultural colleges or from "scientific" farm journals which were themselves often influenced strongly by the agricultural colleges (see chapters 8 and 11).

Consequently, a study of late nineteenth- and early twentieth-century barns often tells us little about the people who used them. They tell us little about ethnic origins, patterns of migration, routes of diffusion, or longstanding, traditional agricultural practices. The student of folklife will gain only limited important information from the study of these barns.

The study of preindustrial farm buildings has to be closely connected with an awareness of the building of railroad lines in the Midwest. Railroad lines fostered the changeover from the self-sufficient farm to the cash-crop farm. Farmers, usually for the first time, could get their crops, animals, and produce to markets. The cash-crop system in turn encouraged—indeed, required—the construction of new farm buildings, including barns.

Railroads were built mostly through and into terrain that was reasonably level. Bridges, tunnels, and trestles necessary in mountainous or rugged terrain were financially unfeasible unless some mineral deposit or other natural resource was to be tapped. Railroad lines sometimes had to be built through rough topography to connect one large population center to another, but, on the whole, railroad builders preferred, whenever possible, to by-pass rugged terrain.

It is for these reasons that self-sufficient farming practices persisted longest in areas where terrain is rugged. Indeed, buildings associated with self-sufficient farming may still be found in these areas. Large parts of southern Indiana fit this pattern.

Farms in southern Indiana were generally small. Much woodland remained, although most of the forests were logged off in the twentieth century by large commercial lumbering operations, and fields were relatively small and of irregular shape. In short, large-scale cash-crop farming simply could not develop in most of southern Indiana. In the twentieth century many farms were abandoned. Others became part-time farms when farmers found themselves unable to make an adequate livelihood from the farm itself and were forced to work off the farm.

The Log Barns of Southern Indiana

Let us now turn to a consideration of the barns themselves. The following discussion is based primarily on the log barns of southern Indiana. The collection of information on folk buildings is a time-consuming task. Information on log barns of some localities is very hard to come by and, with certain exceptions, very little has been published (Roberts 1984). Some data are beginning to be accumulated in the files of state historic preservation offices, but they are still sketchy, and no overall study has yet been made.

The log barns of southern Indiana are relatively small. The primary purpose of these barns was to provide space for a few farm animals, oxen, horses, and milk cows, with space for quantities of loose hay. Sometimes there was space provided for grain storage or for a threshing floor, but the basic size and shape of the structures, especially the large loft for storing hay, were dictated by their primary use. Such barns were adequate for self-sufficient farming operations. Indeed, the presence of these barns throughout southern Indiana proves—if proof were needed—that the self-sufficient farm was the norm in the preindustrial era. Many log barns still survive, and there is evidence on many other farms that log barns once stood there.

It is very difficult to determine the exact age of a log barn, indeed of any log structure. If written records of any kind are available, they usually deal only with the house on a farm, making little or no mention of the barn. I can recall only one instance where a date was carved into a log in a barn. That date, August 17, 1871, probably was the date of construction (fig. 2.1). Usually, the owners of standing

Fig. 2.1. Date carved into a log from a log barn (now destroyed) in Clear Creek
Township, Monroe County, Indiana
Photo: W. E. Roberts, February 1969

log barns have only vague notions about the age of the structures; they just know
that the barn has always been on their farm. Hence we are left to examine the
structure itself if we hope to gain any information as to when it was built.

All too often nothing in the examination will point to a specific year. The
skill of hewing logs was common in the early decades of the last century, it is true,
but that skill has persisted right down to the present time. I have talked to many
farmers or retired farmers who had earned money in the recent past by felling
trees and hewing the trunks into railroad ties, a process that uses exactly the same
skills as are needed to hew the logs for a barn. So, a log barn could have been built
in southern Indiana anytime within the last 150 years.

As a practical matter, the appearance of the logs in a log barn where the logs
have been protected from the weather, as is usually the case, indicates that they
were hewn long ago, but whether that means 75, 100, or 150 years ago, it is impossible to say, without dendrochronological analysis. This process involves a consideration of the growth patterns of the trees which provided the logs, based upon
an examination of the annual growth rings. The analysis involves comparing and
matching the pattern of growth rings in a cross-section of a wall log with those
already established as an index record. The matching process permits the estab-
lishment of two *approximate* dates, one the germination time of the tree from which
the log was cut, and the year in which the tree was cut and thus ceased growth. It

28

must be emphasized that these dates are likely to be only approximate, especially if the log was hewn. The process is time consuming and complicated. Although it appears that no such analyses have been done on Indiana barns, it is quite possible that dendrochronology could reveal the age of many log structures in southern Indiana.

The hardware found on log barns—hinges, latches, and the like—also cannot be relied upon to indicate exact age. Often the hardware has been handmade by a blacksmith but, after all, some blacksmiths are still at their forges in southern Indiana and the hardware in question might have been forged at any time. Most of the hardware could not be salvaged and used on newly built buildings. For instance, twentieth-century barn builders overwhelmingly preferred barn doors that slide on tracks to the old-style doors that swing on long strap hinges. Consequently, the old strap hinges and latches were not reused.

Cut nails (often called "square" nails because they are square in cross-section) are what one usually finds driven into the wood in log barns. Cut nails were used throughout the nineteenth century and well into the twentieth, however. Indeed, if one wants to drive a nail into a seasoned hardwood such as oak, one is still well advised to use a cut nail, far stiffer than the modern, round in cross-section, wire nail which would almost surely bend.

In the last analysis, then, there is usually no sound basis upon which to form a judgment as to the date of construction of any specific barn. Most log barns in southern Indiana, however, probably were built in the pre-Civil War period.

SINGLE-PEN BARNS

The most common log barn consists of a single pen of logs, often surrounded by sheds of frame construction (fig. 2.2). Fifty-nine barns of this type have been located in southern Indiana. The average length of the log pen is twenty-one feet, six inches, the smallest being sixteen feet long and the largest, forty feet. The average width is eighteen feet, six inches, with the smallest thirteen feet and the largest thirty feet. Because most barns have frame sheds on all four sides their overall dimensions are considerably larger.

The construction of these log pens is relatively simple when compared to a house, for they almost always have a dirt floor and few openings cut into the logs (fig. 2.3). The log portion of the walls of a barn are usually about twenty-one feet high, about six feet higher than the walls of a typical one-and-a-half story log house. Animals probably were stabled in the frame sheds, while the central log portion of the barn was used for the storage of grain and hay. The interstices between the logs normally were not filled with chinking, but were left open to facilitate the circulation of air.

Abandoned log houses often have been turned into barns, but the presence or absence of an opening for a fireplace cut into the end log wall indicates the original use of the structure. That is, if there is a fireplace opening, the structure probably originally was a house. In the totals cited above, abandoned houses have not been considered to be barns.

Fig. 2.2. Barn from Harbison Township, Dubois County, Indiana
Photo: W. E. Roberts, May 1969

Fig. 2.3. Barn from Lawrence County, Indiana. Moved and reerected in Spring Mill
State Park, Mitchell, Indiana
Photo: W. E. Roberts, June 1961

DOUBLE-PEN BARNS

Many barn builders must have considered the single-pen barn to be inadequate for their needs. They built barns consisting of two separate log pens with a central passageway between. At a height of about twelve feet, the two pens are joined together by two or three logs and a plate which span the entire structure (fig. 2.4). These barns are often of imposing dimensions. Of thirty-five examples located, the average overall length of the log portions is forty-nine feet, but one is as long as seventy-two feet, while five are over sixty feet long. The average width is twenty-two feet, six inches; the largest twenty-six feet. With the wooden sheds on all four sides extending the total length and width by as much as thirty feet,

Fig. 2.4. Double-crib log barn. Sheds on all four sides not shown. Main doors and other details omitted to show log portions more clearly
Sketch: W. E. Roberts

some of these barns are truly large. In many barns, too, the four or six logs and the two plates that run the entire length of the barn are in unbroken lengths. The longest timbers I have seen came from a barn that had been pulled down a few years before, but the two plates that were still lying on the ground were seventy-two feet long without a knot, meaning that the trees from which they were cut had no branches for at least that distance. The virgin forests in Indiana must have contained many remarkable specimens (fig. 2.5).

Most double-pen barns have a dirt floor in the passageway between the two log pens. The farmer was able to drive his loaded hay wagon into this passageway and to pitch the hay up into the large lofts over the log pens. When these areas were full, he could move timbers across the top of the passageway and use that area for hay storage as well. Six of the thirty-five barns, however, have wooden floors in the passageway. These floors, sometimes called "tramping floors," could be used for threshing. Wheat and other grain stored in one of the log pens could be pitched out onto the wooden floor and threshed as needed. Usually one of the log pens was used for stabling animals and the frame sheds surrounding the log portions of the barn were used for miscellaneous storage. In almost two-thirds of these barns the log pens are of about equal size, but in about a third of them one of the pens is quite small, seemingly built as a corn crib.

Fig. 2.5. Detail of heavy floor joists supporting the threshing floor in a log barn from Harbison Township, Dubois County, Indiana
Photo: W. E. Roberts, May 1969

German-American Log Barns of Dubois County, Indiana

In the 1840s and 1850s large numbers of immigrants from Germany began arriving in the United States. Many ended up in southern Indiana. Most of these people were Roman Catholics. One of the many areas in which they settled was Dubois County, whose county seat is Jasper. As one might expect, the actual boundaries of the county are of little significance in this connection, for the area where German immigrants settled extends well outside the county, while in both the northeastern and northwestern corners of the county there were relatively few Americans of German descent.

Fifteen log barns have been measured in the Dubois County area. All are of the double-pen type; that is, on the ground level, two log pens are separated by a driveway (fig. 2.6). The largest log barn is sixty feet long, not counting frame sheds attached to the log portions.

Most of what has been said elsewhere about the British-American barns applies to the German-American barns. There is, however, one distinctive feature that all German-American barns shared, but which no British-American barn had.

Fig. 2.6. Barn of the type common in the German-American area of Marion Township, Dubois County, Indiana. Note the overhanging "porch" roof on the front of the barn.
Photo: W. E. Roberts, May 1971

On every barn, one log in each side wall of each pen extends forward to support an overhang, or "porch" roof, that stretches across the front of the barn. There are four side walls, two in each pen, so there are four projecting logs. The average depth of the front extension is six feet (fig. 2.7).

Most of the barns also have logs extending from the same side walls to support a roof at the rear for a shed-like lean-to. The walls of this shed are of simple frame construction. In some of the barns the same log that extends from the front of the barn also extends at the rear, while in others, one log protrudes at the front while the log below it protrudes at the back. The typical rear extension measures twelve feet in depth. The overall size of the average barn, including both the front and the rear extensions, is fifty-by-forty-two feet. The actual log pens and driveway at floor level cover an area fifty-by-twenty-four feet. (For other Germanic barns in the Midwest, see chapter 4.)

LOG CONSTRUCTION TECHNIQUES

Whether the barns were built by people of British or German ancestry, the logs were shaped and joined at the corners in much the same way. First of all, the "logs" used in the walls might better be called "timbers," because they were invariably hewn. The logs chosen were normally between one and two feet in diameter,

Fig. 2.7. Log barn from Dubois County, Indiana. Details omitted to show logs clearly.
Sketched: W. E. Roberts

reasonably straight, and free of branches for the needed distance. They were hewn flat on two sides to a fairly uniform thickness of seven inches (fig. 2.8). The top and bottom surfaces, however, were left with the natural curvature of the log.

The logs were joined at the corners most commonly with a half-dovetail joint (as seen in fig. 2.8). Much less common was the so-called V-notch. Substantial lengthwise gaps, or interstices, were left between the logs. In house construction, these interstices were usually filled with chinking of some sort, but in barns they were left open to allow for the circulation of air. Spontaneous combustion in hay was an ever-present danger and efficient circulation of air around the hay was

Fig. 2.8. Detail from barn shown in Fig. 2.2. Note the plank-shaping of the logs, the half-dovetail corner notching, the interstices between the logs without chinking, and the foundation consisting of a cornerstone.
Photo: W. E. Roberts, April 1969

35

the best preventive measure. For a detailed discussion of log construction techniques, see Roberts (1984), chapter 4.

LOG BARNS IN OTHER MIDWESTERN STATES

Log barns are rare today throughout the Midwest, and they occur most often in marginal or peripheral areas (see fig. 1.3 page 11).

Donald Hutslar (1986) makes brief mention of log barns in Ohio. Although he gives no details, he does state that there is "a large number of double-pen log barns throughout Ohio" (300). He makes no mention of single-pen log barns, although some exist, especially in the southeastern section of the state.

H. Wayne Price (1988) has done yeoman service in providing data on log barns in two counties of Illinois. In Calhoun County, which is primarily German-American, he found at least eleven double-pen log barns. Their average size is forty-three-by-sixteen feet. Eight are of hewn logs, while three use round logs. Although all were seemingly built by German-Americans, none has the "front porch" roof feature used elsewhere by German-Americans. In Jersey County, Illinois, Price found six single-crib and two double-crib barns. Some of these were built as late as the 1930s. No dimensions are given.

Some useful information on log barn construction by German-Americans in Gasconade and Warren counties in Missouri has been provided by Charles van Ravenswaay (1977). He identified three double-pen log barns whose average dimensions are forty-eight-by-twenty-six feet. In addition, he implies that such barns had been present in these counties in large numbers.

One of the barns van Ravenswaay shows from Warren County has the front-porch roof supported by a cantilevered log in each short wall. This feature, so common in the log barns of German-Americans of Dubois County, Indiana, region and unlike the log barns of their Anglo-American neighbors, would appear to be an importation from Germany.

ON THE SOURCES OF MIDWESTERN
LOG-CRIB BARNS

Historically, many English farmers with small, self-sufficient farms did not build barns (Mason 1988–89). It was, of course, mostly these farmers who migrated to America in the colonial period. The same generalization about the absence of barns applies to Ireland, Scotland, and Wales. It is, therefore, impossible to make any statements with certainty concerning the British sources of log barns in the eastern United States. One statement is possible, however: the immigrants from Great Britain could not have brought with them a knowledge of how to build log barns, for there are no barns of log construction known to have existed anywhere in Great Britain.

At a very early date, however, the "English" barn, or three-bay threshing barn, was common in the eastern United States (see chapter 3). This barn is virtually identical to the double-crib log barn in its general layout and in the uses to which the spaces are put. However, in the eastern parts of the Upland South, in North Carolina, Tennessee, and Kentucky, log barns identical in all important respects to those of the Midwest must have existed before the people from those areas settled southern Indiana. Certainly, many existing log barns in the eastern Upland South closely resemble those in southern Indiana.

Henry Glassie's (1965, 1969–70) extensive fieldwork on log barns in the Upland South has preserved data on double-crib log barns in central and western Pennsylvania, western Maryland, the northern Alleghenies of Virginia and West Virginia, the Blue Ridge and the North Carolina Piedmont, northern Georgia and Alabama, and eastern Kentucky, indeed, throughout the Southern Mountains. Glassie (1970, vol. 2) also shows that single-crib log barns are found in Maryland, the Blue Ridge in Virginia, and throughout the Deep South.

In the Dubois County area, the log double-crib barns built by German-Americans closely resemble those of British-Americans in other parts of southern Indiana. Either a double-crib barn was introduced from both England and Germany to North America, or the immigrants from Germany learned to build double-crib log barns from their neighbors of British ancestry.

No barns of the so-called Pennsylvania-German bank barn types exist in the Dubois County area. Pennsylvania Germans who moved into northern and central Indiana in substantial numbers in the second half of the nineteenth century built bank barns, but those who moved into southern Indiana with the first wave of settlement, between about 1815 and 1835, apparently did not.

This leads to two implications. The first is that the bank barn was neither common nor preferred in those sections of Germany from which came the immigrants who flooded into the Midwest in such great numbers in the 1840s and 1850s. The second implication is that the bank barn was neither common nor preferred in those parts of Pennsylvania from which migrated the early German-American settlers to Indiana.

CONCLUSION

Log barns built in southern Indiana and in many other midwestern states in the nineteenth century are a valuable testimonial to a vanished way of life. They were built at a time when careful craftsmanship and cooperative labor were parts of daily life. The log barns were intimately connected with, and part of, a self-sufficient farming way of life which had existed in Europe for millennia before European settlers came to this country. These new Americans immediately established the same self-sufficient farming patterns on these shores that they had known and followed in Europe. Later, as the tide of settlement moved westward and reached the Midwest, these patterns still persisted. This is not to say, however, that the pattern was completely rigid and unchanging.

In actual practice constant changes occurred as the settlers encountered new conditions, new plants, and new animals. Changes took place over time and in reaction to new environments. Yet, the basic pattern remained essentially the same. Nothing could change the great seasonal round of plowing, planting, and harvesting. No technical innovation could alter the need to concentrate on foods that could be preserved over the long winter until the next harvest. Nothing could change the need to provide some shelter for farm animals during the harsh winter and a commodious place to store the hay and other foods the animals required.

So it was that the settlers who moved into the Midwest built barns of a type with which they were thoroughly familiar. The great forests provided the wonderfully straight tree trunks needed to build log barns, and the inherited and honed skills the settlers possessed preadapted them to use these tree trunks to build log barns.

These barns were of appropriate size to shelter the animals and to provide the storage space needed by a typical family. Moreover, they could be built almost entirely from the timber on the farm itself and with the skills that most farmers and their neighbors possessed. The logs could be hewn and notched and raised into place with the help of neighbors, rafters and floor joists could be prepared from smaller logs and poles, and shingles for the roof could be split or "rove out" from straight-grained oak. Some nearby water-powered sawmill could supply boards, and a blacksmith could supply hinges and latches. Probably the only purchase made at a store would have been nails, for by 1800 factory-made cut nails had pretty well supplanted the earlier handmade nails. More primitive ways of building—weight poles used to hold shingles on roofs, for instance—may conceivably have been used since some early engravings purport to show such features, but there are no surviving traces of them.

The second half of the nineteenth century brought dramatic changes in farming. The ancient self-sufficient system was replaced by the modern cash-crop system. The old barns became obsolete. Too small for large dairy herds, inadequate in size and shape to store modern farm machinery, they were replaced by larger structures built of modern materials by specialized barn builders. Plans for these new barns came not from the inherited wisdom of countless generations of farmers who had followed essentially the same methods of farming. Instead, plans came from agricultural colleges, from farm journals, and from governmental agencies.

It is only in isolated areas where the terrain is largely unsuitable for large-scale modern farming that remnants of the older patterns still persist. Old log barns can occasionally still be found there. These barns tell us, if we are willing to listen carefully, of a way of life of immense antiquity, a way of life that adapted itself to a new environment, and a way of life that shaped our modern world in every way. Let us hope that some of these barns will survive for future generations to study and to appreciate.

REFERENCES CITED

Glassie, Henry. 1965. The old barns of Appalachia. *Mountain Life and Work* 40(Summer): 21–30.

———. 1969–70. The double-crib barn in south-central Pennsylvania. *Pioneer America* 1(1): 9–17; 1(2): 40–46; 2(1): 47–52; 2(2): 23–34.

Hutslar, Donald A. 1986. *The architecture of migration.* Athens: Ohio Univ. Press.

Mason, Kate. 1988–89. Laithes: The barns of Craven. *Folk Life* 27:85–94.

Price, H. Wayne. 1980. The double-crib log barns of Calhoun County. *Journal of the Illinois State Historical Society* 73:140–60.

———. 1988. The persistence of tradition: Log architecture of Jersey County, Illinois. *PAST—Pioneer America Society Transactions* 11:54–62.

Roberts, Warren E. 1984. *Log buildings of southern Indiana.* Bloomington, IN: Trickster Press.

van Ravenswaay, Charles. 1977. *The arts and architecture of German settlements in Missouri.* Columbia: Univ. of Missouri Press.

3

THE THREE-BAY THRESHING BARN

Charles Calkins and Martin Perkins

THE BARN, no matter what type it may be, is the farmer's "bank" on his farm. As it continues to pay dividends by functioning as originally intended in accommodating the particular crop and/or livestock emphasis of a given agricultural system, that particular type of barn will continue to be built and used by successive generations of farmers. Generally speaking, the form of a particular barn will not be altered dramatically unless a fundamental change occurs in how the farmer makes his living within a new and different agricultural economy. Although new environmental conditions encountered by farmers on the move may suggest that the old agricultural system does not fit new surroundings, a farmer still may cling stubbornly to the old way of doing things. Tradition is such a strong motivational factor that a farmer may not even perceive a need for change. In the absence of an overwhelming reason for change, the farmer will abide by the time-honored adage of "If it ain't broke don't fix it." In the mind of many midwestern farmers in the late nineteenth and early twentieth centuries, the barn did not need "fixing."

To a large extent, the situation of prevailing tradition just described applied to grain farming and the accompanying tripartite threshing barn as they both were diffused from the Northeast to the Midwest during the nineteenth century. This barn served farmers well when the emphasis remained on grain, especially wheat. Also economically important were other grains such as oats and barley. The very word "barn" implies grain farming (see chapter 1).

In the United States, the three-bay threshing barn is most commonly referred to as the English barn. Other names associated with it, depending on the part of the country, are the New England, Connecticut, or Yankee barn. Although the name English barn is best known, the most accurate characterization of the structure is indicated by the "three-bay" terminology, which not only announces its basic function, but also is an apt description of its basic architectural form.

Traditionally, this barn was a single-level, rectangular structure divided into three parts or sections, each termed a *bay* (fig. 3.1). Large double doors were always centered on both long sides of the structure. Hand threshing with a grain

Fig. 3.1. Example of a basic, rectangular, single-level, three-bay threshing barn. The Leonard Loomer barn, originally used by a Nova Scotian, has been restored at the Old World Wisconsin Outdoor Museum, near Eagle. The small door to the left is a livestock door. An identical opening is on the opposite end of the bay. See also fig. 3.6. Photo: M. Perkins

flail was done in the central bay, sometimes called the threshing floor or threshing bay. Following threshing, the large doors were opened to create a draft which, during winnowing, would separate the chaff from the heavier grain and carry it away. Flanking the central threshing floor were the other two bays of generally equal dimensions. One was used during the fall or winter to store sheaves of harvested grain awaiting threshing as needed. The other bay was used for storing the threshed grain, commonly in bins, and straw, which was used as feed and bedding for horses and cattle.

Originally and throughout much of its history, the three-bay threshing barn was a single-function structure. Its specific association with grain farming was well established. In western Europe, where this type of barn originated, separate structures on the farmstead often housed the other agricultural operations. No self-respecting farmer would keep animals in his threshing barn. In England, for example, horses were kept in the *stable*, the *byre* or *shippon* held cattle, and pigs found protection in the *sty* (Hart 1975).

41

THE EVOLVING WHEAT ECONOMY OF THE
MIDWEST, 1820-70

Although the threshing barn could handle all types of grain, wheat was the most important crop in terms of overall value to the farmer. Wheat, along with barley for human consumption and oats for animal feed, was introduced quite early to the eastern seaboard.

Beginning about 1800 and continuing to midcentury, increasing numbers of old-stock Americans from New England, New York, and Pennsylvania found their way to the northern parts of Ohio, Indiana, and Illinois and into southern Michigan and Wisconsin. The numerical dominance of native-born northeasterners prompted Schafer (1922-23, 129) to dub this area "Yankee Land." Obviously, this was only part of the larger region that later was identified and mapped by Glassie (1968, 39) as the "North," the extended folk region which was an outgrowth of the New England culture hearth.

In a relatively short time span following settlement, the region also became the nation's breadbasket. Commercial agriculture, in which wheat had a fundamental role, rather quickly followed the pioneering period of settlement. Wheat production increased, especially with the opening of the Erie Canal in 1825, and a flourishing grain trade developed in the Old Northwest Territory (Clark 1966). A growing railroad network beginning in the 1850s enhanced this grain trade. Throughout much of the nineteenth century, wheat dominated the commercial agriculture of the Midwest.

As long as wheat was grown, a continuing need existed for the function provided by the three-bay threshing barn. The barn's diffusion westward went hand-in-hand with the crops it served. Although there were some relatively small modifications in the structure's internal arrangement, the basic one-level, tripartite form was maintained in the diffusion process.

THE THRESHING BARN COMES TO THE MIDWEST

The three-bay barn was first introduced to North America by English and continental European folk (Glassie, 1975). It accompanied many of the earliest settlers, especially to New England (fig. 3.2). The very name *English barn* suggests this connection. The importance of the early introduction is emphasized by Glassie (1975), who maintains that southeastern England is the most direct-antecedent source region for this barn. However, the introduction of this structure also came quite early from other continental sources, especially Germany and France, where in the latter country the term *grange* accurately describes the barn's function (Hart 1975). Later, especially during the nineteenth century, as the barn continued to function well in the New World's developing agricultural economy, other continental Europeans also introduced it. (See chapter 2 for its possible connection to Germans in southern Indiana.)

Following its early introduction, especially into the New England culture hearth, the barn continued to serve farmers in the new setting, even though envi-

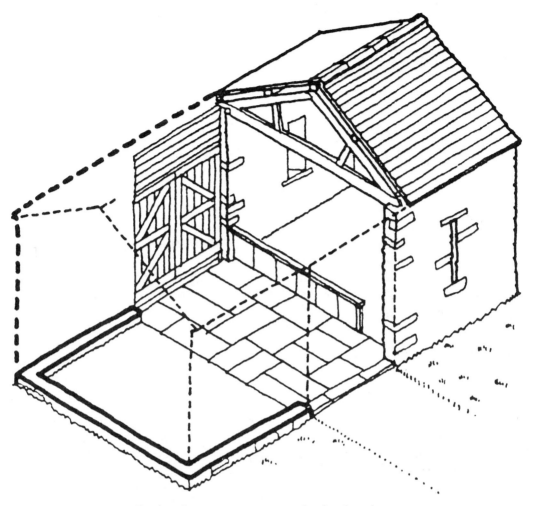

Fig. 3.2. Interior arrangement of a threshing barn.
Source: Brunskill, R. W., 1971.

ronmental conditions were not ideal for wheat production. Kniffen (1965) noted that, in contrast to the diffusion of housing westward from the New England culture hearth, the English barn advanced westward virtually unchanged. Subsequent studies on barns appearing in the last twenty-five years or so confirm and strengthen Kniffen's original observation.

As settlement proceeded across the Old Northwest Territory early in the nineteenth century, the Yankee barn continued its dominance. The earliest occurrence of it may have been in the Western Reserve. In Geauga County, Ohio, as late as 1975, almost one-fourth of all barns were of this type (Coffey 1978). The barns of northwestern Ohio are an extension of the same settlement process (Carlson 1978).

Yankee settlement, the cultivation of wheat, and the threshing barn all continued westward into northern Indiana (Noble 1984; Bauer, Jewel, and Turpin 1975). Bastian (1977) notes that the English barn was "the prevailing traditional barn throughout most of the northern half of the state" (128). From Indiana, a

northerly offshoot of the westward-moving stream of Yankee settlement pene-
trated into southern Michigan. In a general discussion of Michigan barns, Hartman (1976) identified one-story barns, known as the English or Yankee type, as
those dating back to early settlement by New Englanders.

Northern Illinois became the destination for many Yankees, particularly at
the conclusion of the Blackhawk War in 1832 (Larson 1975; Schafer 1922–23).
During the later 1830s, and particularly during the 1840s and 1850s, as wheat became the mainstay of a developing commercial agriculture, English barns became
a conspicuous element in the ensemble of structures characteristic of the evolving
farmstead. An examination of lithographed sketches of northcentral Illinois farms,
contained in illustrated county atlases produced primarily during the 1870s, reveals the three-bay barns to be commonplace, either in original or only slightly
modified form (Swenson 1982) (fig. 3.3).

In Wisconsin, prior to the advent of commercial dairying on a large scale
beginning about 1875, the three-bay barn was the most common form. The structure suited the emphasis on wheat farming engaged in by Yankees and the earliest
arriving immigrant groups, especially Germans. Illustrated atlases for such south-

Fig. 3.3. Three-bay threshing barn in northeastern Illinois
Source: *The Combination Atlas Map of Kane County, Illinois*, 1872, p. 48

ern counties as Rock, Walworth, Dane, Jefferson, and Waukesha are replete with examples of early threshing barns. Field reconnaissance through this section of the state indicates that many of these structures survive, but are being put to quite different uses.

While Yankees were arriving and occupying prairies and oak openings in Wisconsin, large numbers of German immigrants settled in the more heavily forested areas of the eastern lakeshore district. The Germans followed the lead of the Yankees in growing wheat, although the crop was familiar to them from their homeland. They did introduce, however, their own threshing barn, *Scheune*, identical in basic form to that of the Yankees, but built with a different building technology (see pages 73, 74, and 75). Pomeranian Germans, for instance, generally constructed a three-bay barn as the first farm building (Calkins and Perkins 1980). Animals were housed in a separate structure, a forebay stable referred to as a *Stall*, as was the tradition in the homeland. Evidence from German-settled areas in Wisconsin suggests that new threshing barns were being built as late as the 1870s. Other ethnic groups, particularly early arriving Norwegians, built and used the barn, but it appears their form was borrowed from the Yankee model.

DETAILED CHARACTERISTICS OF THE TRIPARTITE FORM

In its purest version, the rectangular, single-level threshing barn existed as a tripartite form. The basic design has been described as a "bilaterally symmetrical whole divided into three units, the symmetrical central one of which differs from the identical units at each side" (Glassie 1974, 182). With large double doors at either end, the central unit or bay acted as a runway. It also furnished the area and environment necessary for the flailing and winnowing of grain. Originally, the side bays provided storage space for both threshed and unthreshed grain. In modified barns where livestock was sheltered in one bay, it became essential to devote some storage space to hay as well. Farmers generally chose an area as close to the livestock as possible. Loft areas above the stalls were considered most practical for this purpose.

Each bay was spatially defined by a system of timbers, each unit of which was referred to as a *bent*. Four bents marked both the outer perimeter and interior divisions of a three-bay barn. The usual distance between bents was sixteen feet, the space needed for properly sheltering a team of horses or oxen. When it was not sixteen feet, it usually was a distance that could be divided evenly into the barn's total length (Noble 1984). Although actual dimensions varied from barn to barn, most structures measured between twenty-four and forty feet in width and forty-eight to sixty feet in length, often in a ratio of 1:2 (Arthur and Witney 1972). Occasionally, the threshing barn was as long as eighty feet (Ennals 1972). However, this longer structure usually included additional bays affixed to one or both ends of the original tripartite form and frequently introduced a second threshing bay. The distance from ground to roof peak was about thirty feet.

FOUNDATIONS

Masonry construction was widely used in the single-level threshing barn's foundation. The most common material employed was fieldstone, abundant in the glacial till deposited in massive quantities throughout the Midwest. Initially considered to be a major obstacle to agriculture, fieldstone soon became regarded as an inexpensive and valuable resource. The annual removal of fieldstones frost-heaved to the surface from cleared cropland provided farmers with a ready supply of a construction material well-suited for fences, foundations, and walls (Perrin 1967).

Barn foundations, constructed of these rounded and unworked fieldstones laid into a bed of mortar, usually extended eighteen inches below the frost line. Builders carefully selected various size stones to assure maximum bonding. Foundation walls rose in a freestanding manner without the benefit of masonry formwork. When completed, the foundation walls measured two to three feet in thickness and usually extended one-and-one-half to two feet above ground level. This solid masonry foundation determined the rectangular building's overall dimensions. In doing so, it provided maximum support and a level base from which to erect the wall, floor, and roof systems.

Some nineteenth-century builders chose to modify the basic foundation. By erecting a series of strategically placed stone piers, the effort and material required for a foundation were substantially reduced. These piers were typically positioned at each corner. Others appeared at locations where load-bearing vertical members joined the sill timber. Like solid foundation walls, piers elevated the barn to an average height of two feet above ground level. This height protected the sill timber and exterior sheathing from coming into contact with the moist ground and most snow cover.

Another variant of the pier foundation allowed farmers building on extremely level ground to use a single, flat-topped boulder, rather than a pier, at each location. The need to locate and transport no less than four mammoth boulders may have discouraged many farmers from using this basic foundation type. Other variations included locally available quarried stone or brick materials.

TIMBER-FRAME CONSTRUCTION

The masonry foundation supported an immense skeletal framework, which characterized timber-frame construction. Generally, farmers furnished from their own farms the large assortment of timbers required to erect their barns. Just as gathered fieldstones became valued by-products of farmstead development, so did felled trees. The thinning and eventual elimination of forest created additional cropland and pasture acreage. The clearing process also produced the necessary materials to develop and expand farmstead buildings.

A farmer's wooded acres usually contained trees of the proper length and species for barn construction. Oak, elm, hemlock, chestnut, and maple were among the species felled and skidded to the barn site. Regional availability and personal preferences resulted in the use of other species as well. The rounded logs received careful evaluation as to length, diameter, and stability.

Larger timbers made excellent sill, plate, or joist members. With axes, these logs were scored and hewn into beams of sufficient size to meet the structural specifications determined by the barn builder. Frequently, the fashioning of larger beams culminated with adz work. This finishing treatment produced a smoother and more perfectly shaped timber; however, it usually failed to remove all hewing scars, leaving behind physical testimony to the barn's age and method of construction (fig. 3.4).

Smaller logs of lesser length and diameter were unsuited for hewing. Some builders chose to leave these lighter-weight pieces in their natural rounded state. However, their portable size also allowed for wagon transport to a nearby sawmill, where they could be processed by water-powered vertical saws into uniformly dimensioned support beams.

Whether the barn timbers were hewn, sawn, or left rounded did not matter; they were uniformly joined together to construct the skeletal framework. Using a system of *mortise* and *tenon* joints, builders produced a network of secure structural connections (see fig. 3.4). With saws or axes, carpenters fashioned tenons or

Fig. 3.4. Scarred hand-hewn timbers joined with a mortise-and-tenon connection and secured with a wooden peg
Photo: M. Perkins

tongue-like extensions into the ends of beams. These wooden protrusions were then carefully fitted into the mortises of adjoining timbers. Craftsmen typically used augers or boring machines to establish the mortise hole's dimensions. They then relied on chisels to remove the excess wood and to more clearly define the mortise hole. The depth of the hole was determined by the size of the connecting timber and its tenon. Those receiving tenons of the largest timbers were cut entirely through the beam. Smaller tenons required mortises of a lesser depth.

Once joined, most mortise and tenon connections were secured with the placement of a wooden peg. Fashioned out of hardwood, the tapered peg was driven through roughly aligned holes drilled into the mortised beam and the tenon. As the peg entered the series of holes, it pulled the tenon firmly into position within the mortise. Builders found it necessary to employ multiple pegs on the joints of larger load-bearing connections, where two or three pegs were not uncommon. However, the joinery of minor braces and smaller timbers was sometimes secured solely by the fit of the engaged mortise and tenon.

The threshing barn's skeletal framework is incorporated into a system of *sill timbers*. Resting directly on the foundation, the sills form the substructure for the floor, wall, and roof networks. In this form, the substructure consists of a frame of two longitudinal and four transverse squared timbers. If additional bays were desired, the longitudinal sill beams were extended and the corresponding number of transverse timbers added. Like the framework's timber components, the sill pieces usually join at each corner with a mortise and tenon connection. Sills used on the longitudinal sides were sometimes spliced together due to the difficulty in locating and transporting single logs of fifty feet or more. The shorter transverse sill timbers were likely to be of one piece.

Once the sill timbers were securely joined, builders notched or mortised floor joists into the base members. Unlike the squared sills, the barn's joists sometimes remained in the round, except for the top side. The flattened top provided the floorboards with a level surface on which to rest loosely or to be nailed. The arrangement of joist systems varies in the single-level threshing barn. Builders installed them to run in either direction. The flooring under the central bay usually received special reinforcement, so that it would not collapse under the heavier weights drawn into the threshing aisle.

A bent was connected to each of the transverse sill timbers. Comprised of preassembled sections of the frame, each bent was carefully raised as a unit into an upright position and anchored into the sill. A variety of bent designs existed for the single-level threshing barn. Yet, most were derivatives of one basic form, consisting of three structural elements, two vertical *posts* and a single horizontal *tie beam*. The latter, also referred to as a *girt*, joined with the posts to create an individual unit of heavy timber construction.

Builders adapted the frame to the farmers' needs by adding various upright, girt, and brace timbers. One typical modification was the addition of a third vertical post. This post provided additional support near the center of the massive girt. The central upright, when incorporated into an interior bent, sometimes functioned as one side of a built-in ladder, offering the farmer access to even the tallest mounds of grain or hay stored in the mows adjacent to the center bay (fig. 3.5).

Fig. 3.5. Ladder incorporated into the central upright of an interior bent
Photo: M. Perkins

Smaller horizontal girts often extended from both sides of the central upright to the bent's endpoints. Positioned into the upright, approximately four feet from the floor, the girts often served as a frame for a short retaining wall, formally separating the center threshing aisle from the adjacent bay.

Another variation to the basic bent was the installation of a network of sawn *braces*. These diagonal pieces reinforced the mortise and tenon joinery which tied the posts into the girt. Once the bent system had been erected, builders capped the exterior posts with the hewn *plate timber*. Like the longitudinal sill member at ground level, the plate was usually spliced together from two or more timbers. The plate secured the upper ends of the outer posts. The uprights were tenoned into the plate as they were to the sill. Smaller longitudinal girts in the plane of the walls were added between the sill and plate for greater stability.

Larger and more elaborately framed single-level threshing barns sometimes included a timber-frame *purlin* system. The purlins supplied the rafters with increased support between the plate timber and the peak. A set of squared uprights or diagonals was tenoned into the upper surface of each bent. These units supplied a base on which the longitudinal purlins rested. Builders using uprights sometimes chose to join the timbers with the addition of a horizontal girt directly below the peak. This, in effect, resulted in a secondary bent being placed atop the primary bent.

The basic three-component form, either with or without an attached timber-frame purlin system, seems to be the design from which most three-bay threshing barns derive their skeletal framework. Adjustments in the number, size, and placement of timbers were regularly made to satisfy varying structural needs or personal preferences of the farmer or builder.

ROOFS

Characteristically, the barn received a gable roof composed of rafters, rough-sawn boards, and wooden shingles. Rafters installed with a medium pitch were fashioned from various available woods (Noble 1974). Unlike the major timbers in the skeleton, the rafters were not hewn square. Some were left rounded with only the upper side hewn so roofing boards could easily be attached to the flat surface. Others were sawn. Sets of rafters were fitted and joined at the peak with either nails or wooden pegs. Ridge poles were rare. The longitudinal plate received the rafter tail. Compatible notchings joined the plate and rafter, which, if not pegged, were nailed together. Roofs with purlin systems supplied additional places where the rafter could be secured. When firmly in place, the rafters furnished the base necessary to support the roof covering.

Wide roof boards, frequently in excess of twelve inches, were laid longitudinally over the rafters and attached with nails. In some cases, the rough-sawn boards' outer edges retained bark. Boards were arranged in rows, usually several inches apart. Rafter placement appears to have been a primary determinant in establishing individual board lengths.

Wooden shingles capped the majority of early single-level threshing barns. Shingles produced from pieces of hardwood were the most favored. Handsplit shingles, although more labor-intensive than the popular machine-made variety, proved to be a less expensive alternative. With little preparatory effort, subsequent wooden-shingle layers could be applied as needed directly on existing roofs. Despite the early popularity of wooden shingles, this ubiquitous material had a tendency to eventually succumb to the weather or modern roofing materials. (The use of slate as a replacement alternative is discussed in chapter 12.) Often times, weather-inflicted damage resulted in modifications to rafter systems and roofing boards as well. Compared to the foundation or the timber-frame skeleton, the roofing fabric generally underwent a greater degree of alteration over the life of the barn.

SIDING

The barn's timber framing was enclosed with an application of boards. Vertically attached boards, some as large as fourteen inches wide, that ran from the sill to the plate were the rule. On the longitudinal sides, boards were nailed into the sill and plate. Secondary girts also served as nailing surfaces between the top and bottom of the board. Because of the additional height on the gable ends, two levels of siding were required. First, board siding covered the area between the sill and the end bent's main girt. A second series of boards extended from the main girt skyward to the roof line or gable peak. A space of approximately one inch between boards allowed air circulation to promote the drying of grain or hay. Where the barn housed animals, especially horses, open spaces were covered by wood battens to reduce drafts. The vertical boards were attached with square-headed, cut nails. Subsequent renailings sometimes integrated round-headed, machine-manufactured nails with the earlier type.

In most areas, vertical boards were favored over other types of siding, especially the narrower horizontal clapboards. The preference possibly may be linked to the inconvenience associated with modifying the frame to receive the clapboarding, or with the cost of clapboards. Horizontally attached clapboards required the addition of vertical nailers. Barn builders incorporated these supplementary pieces between primary horizontal timbers on the lower level. The gable enclosure received the verticals between the main girt and the rafters. Regardless of whether a barn was enclosed with vertical or horizontal boards, the individual farmers made a determination on the exterior finish. Many, especially early on, simply allowed the untreated boards to weather. Others preferred to apply paint, with red and white being among the most popular color choices (see chapter 12).

FENESTRATION

The most prominent feature of the tripartite threshing barn's fenestration is the large set of double doors which provides access to either side of the threshing floor (fig. 3.6). Traditionally hung with hand-forged strap hinges, many of these doors were later modified to be suspended from a track. The doors could be adjusted to regulate the draft needed to carry the winnowed chaff from the threshing floor (Hart 1975).

In its earliest form, the barn rarely had openings other than the two sets of double doors. A row of single-pane transom windows commonly capped these door openings. Cold-weather access could be eased with the placement within one of the double doors of a smaller, human-scale door, allowing the farmer to enter without having to open one or both of the larger double doors, an innovation especially useful in windy weather.

When the threshing barn was modified to provide space for livestock, additional openings appeared. Most common were individual doors cut into one or both longitudinal sides to permit access to one of the flanking bays (fig. 3.1). In some barns, the design of the livestock bay eliminated access to the center aisle. Animal stalls faced the threshing floor and spanned from front to back, usually four feet wide for a single stall and seven feet for a double (Arthur and Witney 1972). This arrangement made at least one door necessary. Where two were used, one was commonly found in the gable end wall. Some farmers also chose to add a

51

Fig. 3.6. Double doors leading to the center bay of the Leonard Loomer barn. Constructed in 1858, Walworth County, Wisconsin. See also fig. 3.1.
Photo: M. Perkins

window opening within the livestock bay. This was usually no larger than a six-pane sash, incorporated into either the bay's gable or longitudinal side.

Other openings for ventilation or light occasionally appeared on the gable. Designs, sometimes called *owl holes* and cut into the sheathing boards immediately below the gable peak, fulfilled decorative and functional needs (Wilhelm 1988). This same area sometimes contained a small window that directed additional light to the threshing floor.

ETHNIC VARIATIONS IN CONSTRUCTION: *FACHWERK*

Timber-frame barns are inextricably linked to barns constructed of other building materials. Although available natural resources proved to be a primary consideration when erecting a barn, cultural preferences dictated architectural

Fig. 3.7. Double-crib log barn built by Norwegian immigrant Johann Sorbergshagen in Vernon County, Wisconsin
Photo: M. Perkins

type as well. This is especially true with *Fachwerk*, or half-timber construction, favored by some midwestern Germans. Like the standard timber frame, *Fachwerk*-hewn members are joined by a system of mortise and tenon connections. But the *Fachwerk* skeleton features heavier timbers joined to create a series of open, square or rectangular panels. It is also distinguished by diagonal timbers bracing each corner. By filling the open, square or rectangular panels with various types of *nogging*, a solid wall was formed. When mud daub was employed as the nogging, wooden staves were inserted vertically into the panels. To secure the pointed staves, builders chiseled a series of holes into the underside of the upper horizontal timber and a groove into the top of the lower horizontal. Rye straw wrapped around the staves acted as a bonding agent for the *daub* that was then used to fill the open panels. German builders also chose brick as a nogging material, although in at least one state it tended to postdate the mud daub infilling (Tishler 1986). In some German threshing barns, the massive *Fachwerk* skeleton never received any nogging. In these instances, the German *Scheune* was enclosed with vertical boards and sometimes battens.

In southern Wisconsin some half-timber barns were covered with thatched roofs. Rye straw bundles were tied to thatching poles which rested on the rafters and ran parallel to the ridge. Although considerably narrower than roof boards, the three-inch thatching poles were attached to the rafters in the same manner. Thatchers applied the bundles from the bottom of the roof to the peak, and overlayed them until a depth of approximately twelve inches was uniformly achieved. Rafters supporting thatched roofs frequently rest upon bolster blocks dovetailed into the plate. These timber blocks support the rafter tails at a uniform height (Pape 1976).

The *Scheune* was associated with northern Germans from the Oder River Valley in Pomerania and Brandenburg. It adhered to the Germanic tradition of separating the threshing barn from the animal shelters. Like the standard, single-level threshing barn, the *Scheune* contained a central threshing area flanked by two bays (Witmer 1983). One bay usually housed a granary for the storage of threshed grain. In some German barns, the granary was framed as an integral part of the structure; in others, it appears to have been incorporated later. In either case, the granary offered valuable space for grain shoveled into bins or stored in bags. The opposite bay supplied storage space for grain bundles that were stacked in the barn until they were threshed. Livestock were excluded from the *Scheune*, sheltered in a separate stable or Stall. The Stall typically shared the Fachwerk characteristics and thatched roof features of the *Scheune* (Calkins and Perkins 1980).

LOG CONSTRUCTION

The presence of the double-crib log barn has been well-documented in the Midwest (Price 1980; Roberts 1984; Hutslar 1986; van Ravenswaay 1977; Jordan 1985). Some examples bear a noticeable resemblance in form and function to the single-level timber-frame threshing barn (see chapter 2). The availability of unlimited timber supplies encouraged many farmers who were isolated from sawmills to use logs when developing their farmsteads. This practical consideration appears to have been a factor in the double-crib log barn's distribution in the Midwest (see fig. 3.7 p. 53).

Typically, one of the log cribs housed livestock. A ceiling above the stable area served as a mow which generally held straw used for bedding. The opposite crib, usually unchinked, was not divided internally, as was a comparable bay in a timber-frame barn used for storing unthreshed grain. It functioned more as a haymow than as a grain storage facility. Walls were unchinked to provide the maximum ventilation needed to properly cure green hay. Unthreshed grain was usually placed above the middle bay in a log overmow for convenient storage (Hutslar 1986). A surface of wooden planks or a simple dirt runway characterized the threshing floor, sometimes referred to as a tramping floor (Roberts 1984).

Another variation occurred when the log units were of unequal size. The smaller crib supplied space for corn storage, and animals were secured in the larger crib (Montell and Morse 1976; Roberts 1984).

MASONRY CONSTRUCTION

To a considerably lesser extent, the single-level, three-bay threshing barn was constructed of masonry material. Whether built of brick or coursed rubble, the barn's form duplicated that of the timber-frame version, with single bays flanking a central drive-through. However, one conspicuous addition was the inclusion of ventilation openings in the exterior walls. In brick walls, the strategic omission of bricks created decorative and functional openings (Arthur and Witney 1972). The best example of this is probably a brick-end barn on Route 3 south of Wooster, Ohio. Rectangular, triangular, and diamond-shaped openings were among the most common patterns. Masons erecting barns of rubble usually incorporated a series of narrow vertical slits into all four exterior walls. These ventilation openings were evenly positioned on both upper- and lower-wall sections to provide a uniform flow of air through the barn (van Ravenswaay 1977). In addition to the ventilation slits, the masonry rubble barn is distinguished by large stone corner quoins securely joining each wall.

GRAIN PROCESSING

Within the single-level threshing barn, the greatest activity occurred in the central bay. Two sets of double doors provided access to the threshing area from either side of the barn. The door openings were large enough to allow a fully loaded wagon, pulled by a team, to enter and exit the central bay. Besides serving as a sheltered location to unload the harvest, the drive-through bay also was the surface upon which the grain crop was threshed or separated (fig. 3.8).

Once the grain sheaves were sufficiently dried, farmers removed them from an adjacent bay and placed them on the threshing floor. Here the separation process began as flails dislodged the grain head from the stalk or stem. Flailers engaged in a rhythmic pounding on the threshing floor until the grain was removed. Straw was raked, bundled, and placed in the adjoining mows.

The process continued as the seed was separated from the chaff by winnowing. With both sets of double doors open, the central bay acted as a wind tunnel when the grain and chaff were tossed into the air in a basket, sheet, scoop, or shovel (Borie 1986). The lighter-weight chaff blew away and the heavier grain dropped to the surface below. This practice was repeated until the grain was generally free of all debris and waste. Farmers then stored clean grain in bags or bins.

Hand flailing generally was done over an extended period. It coincided with the availability of laborers, including the farmer himself, and the continuing need for grain and the straw by-product. The threshing floor often was utilized well into the winter months when the amount of outdoor work lessened (Borie 1986). The constant use of the floor required that it be properly and securely constructed, i.e., sufficiently supported with massive joists running perpendicular to the two-inch thick boards. Frequently, multiple layers of boards helped strengthen the floor so that the surface could absorb the continuous assault of the flails, as well as carry the weight of animals, wagons, and implements.

It was necessary to attach and position the boards as tightly as possible to ensure that loose grain seeds would not become lodged between them during the flailing process (Rikoon 1988). This could be accomplished in several ways, though the builder always began by installing adjoining boards as closely as possible. One method of minimizing grain loss involved nailing a narrow board underneath the flush joints between boards. This method also helped to hold boards together.

Fig. 3.8. Former central threshing aisle in the barn of Vermont native Ira Blood in
Waukesha County, Wisconsin
Photo: M. Perkins

Another joinery technique used a tongue-and-groove connection between boards.
Builders often cut grooves into both sides of every board and then inserted a narrow tongue. This produced a threshing surface of well-fitted joints which, when
individually spiked to the joists, created a permanently tight floor system.

FUNCTIONAL MODIFICATIONS

The most significant functional modification made to the threshing barn involved changing one flanking bay into a stable. In the Midwest, as in the eastern
United States, stalls and mangers were frequently incorporated into the building's
original design (Glassie 1974; Hart 1975). The presence of horses and cattle also
necessitated more hay storage.

The single-level barn adapted easily to other physical modifications. A common solution to overcrowding involved adding an additional bay to either gable
end. A single-level, three-bay barn could easily be lengthened to become a four- or
five-bay structure, providing greater floor area as well as extending valuable
overhead space. If necessary, sheds could be attached to one or both gables by

erecting a hewn framework and enclosing it with vertical boards matching those of the original bays (fig. 3.9).

Another variation involved constructing a full-length lean-to on the rear side of the barn (Pape 1984). The lean-to size was generally determined by the amount of area that could be covered by the extension of the main roof, because most builders maintained the original pitch of the roof.

THE RAISED THREE-BAY BARN

As the midwestern agricultural economy gravitated from grain production to animal raising, a significant change occurred in the threshing barn's basic form. Those farmers who took up dairying after the demise of wheat culture discovered that the single-level barn lacked the necessary space for housing larger numbers of cows. Rarely could a dairy herd of profitable size be effectively squeezed into a modified original bay or a newly added bay on a single-level barn. The raised three-bay barn was adapted to the changing midwestern agricultural economy by farmers providing a basement under the original single level. This additional story allowed the farmer to adjust more easily to the complexities and challenges associated with a more diversified farming operation.

Some farmers decided to move their threshing barns to hillside locations where masons fashioned full basements under the original hewn timber skeleton. The hillside location offered a natural access to the longitudinal side of the upper-level. Elsewhere, on flatlands, some farmers added an earthen ramp leading to the elevated bays. The upper bays continued to function as storage space for hay, grain, and implements. The double doors opposite the hillside, or ramp, and facing the feed lot, usually were eliminated. In the basement, stalls, stanchions, and pens bordered aisles that ran from end to end. Doorways centered on either the gable or longitudinal walls allowed for passage into the basement.

The single-level barn modified to house animals did not differ significantly in function from the newly constructed raised or basement three-bay barn. Farmers opting for a new basement barn tended to construct larger structures than the single-level three-bay barn. Widths of forty to fifty feet and lengths of sixty to one-hundred feet characterized barns built specially for dairying (Ennals 1972). By the mid-1870s, the cost of a large basement barn measuring thirty-eight by ninety-six feet was three to four thousand dollars (Lampard 1963). The raising and conversion costs for the more traditional single-level three-bay barn compared favorably to those of new construction. However, the more expansive new barns easily sheltered as many as thirty milk cows, plus the hay and bedding required to sustain them. Increased crop yields associated with advanced mechanization also had to be considered when weighing the costs and advantages of a larger new barn. (See chapter 6 for an expanded discussion of Dairy Belt barns.)

CONCLUSION

The three-bay threshing barn remained basically unaltered as it diffused westward. So long as wheat and other grains were central in the agricultural

FARM RESIDENCE OF ALVIN PARTRIDGE, MILL GROVE TP., STEUBEN CO., IND.

Fig. 3.9. Example of an expanded threshing barn in northeastern Indiana
Source: *The Atlas of Steuben County, Indiana, 1880, p. 38*

economy of the New England-extended culture region, the barn served an important function. Even when the barn's function was changed by expansion to include the sheltering of animals, the basic form was not altered much. Instead, one of the end bays usually was modified to accommodate livestock.

Throughout much of the period during which the barn was being diffused to the Midwest, the timber-frame building technique was employed in its construction. However, various European ethnic groups who arrived in the latter nineteenth century applied different techniques to the construction of the unaltered three-bay form.

Eventually, dairying replaced wheat in the agricultural economy of much of the area over which the three-bay barn had been diffused. With this change in agriculture, the threshing/storage function which this barn served was no longer primary. In some cases, the barn was raised by placing it over a basement, which would house the animals, especially milk cows. In the process, it became a raised, three-bay, dairy barn. In other instances, the barn remained as it was originally constructed, but serving a totally different function, most commonly as some sort of machinery storage shed. The three-bay threshing barn not only is a reminder of an earlier emphasis on wheat that originally dominated midwestern agriculture, but also represents the early settlement period when timber-frame barns were the dominant structures of the midwestern landscape.

REFERENCES CITED

Arthur, Eric, and Dudley Witney. 1972. *The barn: A vanishing landmark in North America*. New York: New York Graphic Society.

Bastian, Robert W. 1977. Indiana folk architecture: A lower midwestern index. *Pioneer America* 9(2): 115–36.

Bauer, Linda, Doug Jewel, and Jan Turpin, eds. 1975. *Barns and other outbuildings on Indiana farms*. Indianapolis: Indiana Junior Historical Society.

Borie, Beaveau. 1986. *Farming and folk society: Threshing among Pennsylvania Germans*. Ann Arbor: UMI Research Press.

Brunskill, R. W. 1971. Illustrated handbook of vernacular architecture. New York, Universe Books.

Calkins, Charles F., and Martin C. Perkins. 1980. The Pomeranian stable of southeastern Wisconsin. *Concordia Historical Institute Quarterly* 53(3): 121–26.

Carlson, Alvar W. 1978. Designating historic rural areas: A survey of northwestern Ohio barns. *Landscape* 22(3): 29–33.

Clark, John G. 1966. *The grain trade in the old Northwest*. Urbana: Univ. of Illinois Press.

Coffey, Brian. 1978. Nineteenth-century barns of Geauga County, Ohio. *Pioneer America* 10(2): 53–63.

Ennals, Peter. 1972. Nineteenth century barns in southern Ontario. *The Canadian Geographer* 16(3): 256–70.

Glassie, Henry. 1968. *Pattern in the material folk culture of the eastern United States*. Philadelphia: Univ. of Pennsylvania Press.

———. 1974. The variation of concepts within tradition: Barn building in Otsego County, New York. *Geoscience and Man* 5:177–235.

———. 1975. Barns across southern England: A note on transatlantic comparison and architectural meanings. *Pioneer America* 7(1): 9–19.

Hart, John Fraser. 1975. *The look of the land*. Englewood Cliffs, NJ: Prentice Hall.

Hartman, Lee. 1976. Michigan barns, our vanishing landmarks. *Michigan Natural Resources*, 45(2): 17–32.

Hutslar, Donald A. 1986. *The architecture of migration: Log construction in the Ohio Country, 1750–1850*. Athens: Ohio Univ. Press.

Jordan, Terry G. 1985. *American log buildings: An Old World heritage*. Chapel Hill: Univ. of North Carolina Press.

Kniffen, Fred. 1965. Folk housing: Key to diffusion. *Annals of the Association of American Geographers* 55(4): 549–77.

Lampard, Eric E. 1963. *The rise of the dairy industry in Wisconsin.* Madison: State Historical Society of Wisconsin.

Larson, Albert J. 1975. Northern Illinois as New England extended: A preliminary report. *Pioneer America* 7(1): 45–51.

Montell, William L., and Michael L. Morse. 1976. *Kentucky folk architecture.* Lexington: Univ. Press of Kentucky.

Noble, Allen G. 1974. Barns and square silos in northeast Ohio. *Pioneer America* 6(2): 12–21.

————. 1984. *Wood, brick and stone: The North American settlement landscape. Vol. 2, Barns and farm structures.* Amherst: Univ. of Massachusetts Press.

Pape, Alan C. 1976. Harmon Grube threshing barn—Architectural review. Restoration Report, Old World Wisconsin.

————. 1984. Leonard Loomer threshing barn—Preliminary Architectural Review. Restoration Report, Old World Wisconsin.

Perrin, Richard W. E. 1967. *The architecture of Wisconsin.* Madison: State Historical Society of Wisconsin.

Price, H. Wayne. 1980. The double crib log barns of Calhoun County. *Journal of the Illinois State Historical Society* 73(2): 140–60.

Rikoon, J. Sanford. 1988. *Threshing in the Midwest, 1820–1940.* Bloomington: Indiana Univ. Press.

Roberts, Warren. 1984. *Log buildings of southern Indiana.* Bloomington: Trickster Press.

Schafer, Joseph. 1922–23. The Yankee and the Teuton in Wisconsin. *Wisconsin Magazine of History* 6(2): 125–45; 6(3): 261–79; 6(4): 386–402.

Stephens, David. 1982. Dates on the roof. *PAST—Pioneer America Society Transactions* 5:1–8.

Swenson, Russell G. 1982. Illustrations of material culture in nineteenth-century county and state atlases. *PAST—Pioneer America Society Transactions* 5:63–70.

Tishler, William H. 1986. The *Fachwerk* construction in German settlements of Wisconsin. *Winterthur Portfolio* 21(4): 275–92.

van Ravenswaay, Charles. 1977. *The arts and architecture of German settlements in Missouri: A survey of vanishing culture.* Columbia: Univ. of Missouri Press.

Wilhelm, Hubert G. H. 1988. Owl Holes: A settlement residual in southern Ohio. *Ohio Geographers* 16:99–109.

Witmer, Christopher. 1983. The German timber-framed threshing barns of Lebanon Township, Dodge County, Wisconsin. Master's thesis, University of Wisconsin.

4

MIDWESTERN BARNS AND THEIR GERMANIC CONNECTIONS

Hubert G. H. Wilhelm

AMERICANS SHARE certain stereotypical images about the ethnic-economic backgrounds of their fellow citizens' immigrant ancestors. For example, the English are often seen as having been business people and builders of towns, the Irish as coal miners or workers on canals and railroads, and the Germans, farmers. Despite the ethnocentric implications offered by such images, historical evidence supports these general perceptions to a point. The cultural background of the immigrants and the time of their immigration greatly influenced livelihoods and distribution in the New World.

Prior to 1850, most immigrants invested their energies and monies in land, becoming rural and small-town dwellers. Northwest Europeans, especially those from the British Isles and the German lands who arrived during the seventeenth and eighteenth centuries and the first half of the nineteenth century, took advantage of the opening of the western frontier by settling the countryside. After 1850, however, as America rapidly moved into the industrial and urban revolutions, immigrants sought out the booming cities. Eastern and southern Europeans, who arrived in largest numbers during the last quarter of the nineteenth century and the first quarter of the twentieth century, were drawn toward the work and better income offered in the urban centers.

GERMAN MIGRATION TO THE MIDWEST

The single most important German settlement area in America, lying in the glaciated plains country between the Ohio River and the Great Lakes, is representative of the westward thrust out of the Middle Atlantic hearth. A map, drawn from several sources, and based upon membership of typical "German" churches, illustrates the pattern of German settlement in the Midwest (fig. 4.1). Outside Pennsylvania, the greatest concentration of members in these churches is in Ohio and in Indiana, with smaller outlying memberhips in Missouri and Wisconsin.

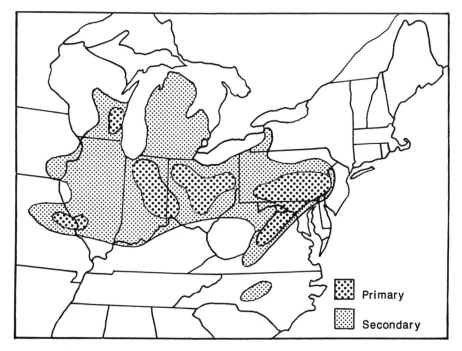

Fig. 4.1. Church membership as a surrogate of German settlement: Distribution of Evangelical United Brethren, Evangelical and Reformed, Church of the Brethren, and Mennonites.
Source: This map was constructed from several maps showing the distribution of German-type denominations. These were published by Wilbur Zelinsky. "An Approach to the Religious Geography of the United States: Patterns of Church Memberships in 1952" in *Annals of the Association of American Geographers*, Vol. 51, no. 2 (1961), pp. 139–93.

A survey of the ethnic origins of Ohio settlers (Wilhelm 1982) showed that in 1850 Germans were by far the most important immigrant group in the state. In fact, many of these Germans were drawn toward Ohio, in typical chain-migration fashion, by the presence of Pennsylvania-Dutch settlers with whom they shared a common language and religion.

By the 1820s, German emigration to America became a veritable avalanche. Between 1850 and 1859, nearly one million persons—that is, more than one-third of all immigrants—came from Germany (Zelinsky 1972). A combination of push forces operating in the "Fatherland," combined with the opening for American settlement beyond the Appalachians, accounts for the large number of Germans.

Devastation and economic ruin had been brought on by the Napoleonic Wars between 1804 and 1812, and severe economic hardship ensued, particularly among small peasants and craftspeople affected by the Prussian-inspired and implemented common customs union or *Zollverein* (1816–34). Additional push forces included the displacement of small landholders during the drive in the 1840s by more powerful owners to consolidate farmland (the Estate Movement), and the political upheavals leading up to and including the unsuccessful revolt against the German monarchy in 1848. Most of these events were especially hard on the rural, village populations, including, of course, large numbers of farmers. Landless folk, who were displaced by the widespread practice of primogeniture or inheritance by the firstborn son and who farmed as renters or worked as day-laborers on farms or as artisans in craft shops, were especially hard hit by the economic problems of the early 1800s. They added significantly to the total emigrant population.

Among the aspirations of these residents of rural German villages and small towns was, first and foremost, the ownership of land in the new country. The realization of their goals was helped through lines of communication between family members or friends in America and Germany and, often, temporary residence with relatives or friends in America. By the 1800s, an important incentive to settle in America was the existence of a government-regulated process of land acquisition, acreage available at a government-set minimum price, according to the United States Land Ordinance of 1785 and later laws. These regulations were first implemented in the public lands of the Northwest Territory, the eventual homeland of the majority of German settlers. Included in this group were new immigrants as well as the excess population from the old Germanic settlement areas in the eastern United States.

GERMANIC FARMING IN THE EIGHTEENTH AND NINETEENTH CENTURIES

The character of German immigration and settlement in America supports the persistent image of the Germans as farmers. They arrived early to benefit from the availability of premier and relatively low-cost farmlands in America's midsection, and they possessed strong agricultural traditions. It is these traditions, shared by others in western Europe, that remain as "food for thought" about the nature of Germanic farming methods. Early writers frequently expounded in flattering language about the Germans and their farms.

Farming practices among different settlement groups were not necessarily better or worse, but simply different. Peoples from the British Isles were influenced by the demise of open field farming and the change to animal grazing in fenced or enclosed pastures. Much of the rural landscape of Britain still is known for its pleasing mosaic of pastures and fields surrounded by hedges and walls. Correspondingly, the agricultural legacy of British farming in America is livestock raising rather than crop farming. Most of our domestic cattle breeds, whether dairy or beef, can be traced to the British Isles. Their names—Guernseys, Jerseys, Herefords, and Angus—evoke memories of the geographical origin of the breeds.

In contrast, agriculture on the continent, especially in the Germanic areas, continued to center on the open fields and common lands, including the ancient three-field rotation. This meant a much greater emphasis on mixed farming. Typical crops included wheat or rye and, depending on location, oats, barley, flax, potatoes, turnips, and beets. There were few animals and these were kept in stables attached to the house, unless pastured on fallow fields or common grounds. In time, increases in rural populations forced the subdivision of field and common areas.

Furthermore, the three-field system of cropping gave way to other rotations, especially after the introduction of clover. These changes increasingly removed animals from the countryside and into shelters. It also heralded the beginning of an agricultural-ecological cycle in which permanently stabled farm animals produced large amounts of dung, which was spread onto the fields. The subsequent increased fertility and productivity, in turn, allowed farmers to add more animals, which, of course, generated more dung, and so on. If one could have asked a traditional German farmer why he had all those crops in his fields, his response would have been, "Because I have all these animals to feed." Conversely, if asked why he had all those animals, his answer would have been, "Because I have all these crops in my fields."

This interrelated agricultural system of people, animals, and crops greatly influenced farmstead form. The unit-farmstead or *housebarn,* which combined all the farm's functions under a single roof, and which remains widespread in the Germanic lands, might be regarded as a logical architectural response. Did the German immigrant-farmer bring that land-use and settlement system to America? Yes and no. The housebarn, for example, survives only as an architectural curiosity in a few locales in the United States (Marshall 1986; Perrin 1961).

Almost from the beginning of German settlement in America, the barn would be separate from the house and part of a loose agglomeration of buildings. Many reasons explain the discontinuance of housebarns, including "geographic abundance, a penchant for individualism, freedom, and a persistent search for privacy and comfort" (Marshall 1986, 67). Also, the German immigrants became known for their eagerness to assimilate. This hastened the demise of a traditional folk structure in favor of those used by the predominant settlement group, the people from the British Isles.

Numerous authors have argued the differences or similarities in farming practices among the various ethnic groups that settled in Pennsylvania. The general conclusion has been that they were not very different. The distinction usually emphasized concerns about the keeping and treatment of animals. For example, one author (Gagliardo 1959), writing about German farming practices in Pennsylvania, states that "the Germans differed from practically all the Pennsylvania farmers . . . in providing shelter for their animals in winter" (197). Kollmorgen (as cited in Wood, 1942, 42) has argued that "the Pennsylvania German farmers did not distinguish themselves so much by the kind of stock they kept as by the care they gave their animals." Another early traveler in Pennsylvania noticed the contrasts in animal husbandry among settlement groups. He observed that, "while the English and Swedes had no stables, the Germans and Dutch preserved the custom of their country, and generally kept their cattle in barns during the winter" (cited by Gagliardo 1959, 197).

Having worked from 1946 to 1954 as a farm manager apprentice on several large and small farms in Germany, I still sometimes cringe when I see cattle standing outside in bitter cold. Indeed, tradition was that the only time the German dairy cows were on the outside was during their infrequent, but recurring sojourn for breeding purposes (this was, of course, before the days of artificial insemination), or when several cows were tethered together and walked back and forth across the dung pile to get exercise and to compact the raw manure. During the warm season, the younger animals did get regular exposure to the small calf-pasture (Jungviehweide) next to the farmstead. There are regions in the German lands, especially in the southern mountains and in the lowlands facing the North Sea, where dairying still takes precedence over crop farming, and where outdoor pasturing remains an integral part of the total land use.

Over large areas, however, agricultural land use survives in close interdependence between crop farming and the stabling of animals. The latter provide the products so essential in the total ecology of this system: dung, meat, hides, wool, milk, and, of course, work. The bond between people and animals is strengthened by keeping dairy cattle. Even by itself, the twice-daily requirement of milking encourages close attachment. All the cows have names and are kept for many years. How could anybody allow fifteen-year-old "Liesel," who had dutifully produced a calf each year and was an excellent 'milker,' to face a harsh winter in the field?

To this day, the tradition of dairy farming remains very strong among American farmers with a Germanic background. The best example may be the Old Order Amish who, often against all odds, continue to practice dairying in the traditional way. In a region best-known for cash-crop production of corn and soybeans, dairying also survives in westcentral Ohio and parts of adjacent Indiana, but particularly in Ohio's Mercer and Auglaize counties. A group of immigrant farmers from northwestern Germany settled in the region in the 1830s and, in more than a century and a half, they have not changed their basic agricultural way of life or system of agriculture.

GERMANIC FARMING IN THE MIDWEST

America's image of the German immigrant as farmer is largely accurate. These settlers came to this country with strong rural-agricultural backgrounds. Also, they emigrated in large numbers at a time when America's choice farmlands were for the taking. They brought with them a system of agricultural land use which differed from that of other settlers, particularly those from the British Isles. Of special significance in that system was the interrelationship between crop farming and animal keeping, a factor that influenced the German's choice of farm structures, especially the barn.

No barn type in the American Midwest, either traditional or of more recent origin, was singularly the result of German settlement influence. There are, however, barns in the region that are "Germanic," including those of Swiss and, perhaps, Dutch origins. Indeed, early German immigrants were a diverse lot of Bavarians, Hessians, Saxons, Palatines, Swabians, Westphalians, and others. Their cultural traits, including their choice of farm buildings, were as different as their ethnic allegiances. Other than language, there were few unifying traits among these immigrants. Even language, because of the great contrast in dialects, was not necessarily an important unifier.

The German settlers, however, did share similarities in farming. The small grains, particularly wheat, were important and, of course, there had to be animals, especially milk cows and hogs. These activities required a sizable barn with sufficient space to store hay and sheaves of grain awaiting threshing, and to accommodate a threshing floor and animal stalls.

Few comprehensive surveys have dealt with America's traditional farm structures. Much of that kind of information is tucked away in obscure archives and publications, including various trade journals. Of course, some field evidence remains, but even that is becoming increasingly scarce. Therefore, we are indebted to those few researchers who have dealt with this question of traditional ethnic influences on form and function of America's rural settlement structures, including barns. An important early source, particularly on Germanic settlers in Pennsylvania, is Dornbusch and Heyl (1965). Other comprehensive studies include those by Kniffen (1965), Fitchen (1968), Glassie (1968), Noble (1984), and Glass (1986). The most authoritative work on the Pennsylvania bank barn, by one of America's fine barn scholars, Robert Ensminger (1992), is just beginning to be appreciated.

THE GRUNDSCHEIER

The earliest barns erected by German settlers in southeastern Pennsylvania were probably of the ground-level type, also known in the Pennsylvania-Dutch vernacular as *Grundscheier* or "Boddem Scheier" (Borie 1986, 17). They were built of log, usually as double cribs, frame or stone, or a combination of these materials. They had a slightly raised threshing floor between the lower-lying animal stalls. Hay and sheaves of grain were stored in the "overhead" or loft areas. In time, these small barns were increased in size by the addition of a second level, which was often cantilevered, thus forming an overhang above the ground level.

The ground-level barn, or *Grundscheier*, by providing shelter for animals, fodder, and subsistence crops, ideally suited German farming practices. Its major functional handicaps included limited stall areas and inconvenient location of overhead mows. The latter meant that hay, sheaves of grain, and straw had to be pitched overhead, hard work under the best of circumstances.

THE STANDARD PENNSYLVANIA BARN

Because of increases in population, the growth of urban centers like Philadelphia and Baltimore, and better overland roads, Pennsylvania's agriculture changed in time from primarily subsistence to commercial. One of the more significant results was that farmers began to keep more livestock. The small ground-level barn, whether of a single story or two, no longer was adequate. It was replaced by a different structure that would become synonymous with Pennsylvania culture and its mixed grain-livestock agriculture.

This new barn eliminated the space problems of the ground-level barn. Hay and sheaves of grain could be unloaded into mows that were at the same level, rather than above the threshing floor or barn driveway. Among the barn's most diagnostic features were a lower story partially dug into the natural slope of the land and an upper level that was accessed from the slope (fig. 4.2) and that extended several feet over the lower or "banked" level (fig. 4.3). Robert Sutcliff, who

Fig. 4.2. The Pennsylvania-German barn was usually "banked," with its lower level built into a slope. In flat terrain, a ramp had to be constructed leading to the threshing floor on the second level. Montgomery County, Ohio.
Sketch: C. Steiner in Wilhelm, 1982

Fig. 4.3. Pennsylvania-German barn in Montgomery County, Ohio, showing the cantilevered forebay extending over the lower livestock level of the barn.
Sketch: C. Steiner in Wilhelm, 1982

traveled through North America between 1804 and 1806, provided one of the earliest descriptions of· this barn. He saw the advantage of the overhanging second story:

> Along the front of the barn, about eight feet from the ground, a wooden stage projects about six feet from the wall, inclosed overhead six or seven feet high, and also at the ends and side, forming a gallery the length of the building; having several communications or doorways out of the barn into it. In the floor of this gallery are several trap doors through which they throw fodder for the cattle into the yard during the winter months. It is obvious that an appendage of this sort must be very useful. (Cited in Yoder 1951, 4)

This structure became the barn of choice among the German settlers and others in Pennsylvania and adjacent Maryland. From there, it moved with the frontier southward, especially through the Shenandoah Valley, and northwestward into southern Ontario, but primarily toward the West, where it would eventually become identified as the "German bank barn" or "Pennsylvania-German barn." Ensminger (1992) has proposed the name "standard Pennsylvania barn" as the best modern designation of the structure.

The actual origins of this barn, however, are Germanic rather than German, located in the mountain cantons of eastern Switzerland. Until quite recently, it was believed that the barn evolved in America. For example, as late as 1968, Glassie noted that "the fully developed Pennsylvania barn seems not to be transplanted from Europe, but rather an American meshing of similar traditions brought from Britain and Central Europe"(62).

Of course, there had always been an implied relationship of the barn with Switzerland. Marion Learned, a professor of Germanic languages and literature at the University of Pennsylvania, was probably the first serious student of this barn type. He related it to Switzerland because of vernacular references in Pennsylvania as "Swisser barn" or "Schweizer Scheier" (Learned 1915, 348). Not until 1980 did two American cultural geographers, working independently, confirm the location and early existence of similar structures among Germanic farmers in eastern Switzerland (Ensminger 1980; Jordan 1980).

Along with the growing importance of commercial farming in Pennsylvania and neighboring states came the increasing size of this standard Pennsylvania barn. The structure became a veritable farmyard castle, with its dimensions eventually exceeding more than one hundred feet in length and sixty or more in width. The earlier log barns gave way to stone, frame, and brick barns. The lower stall level was enclosed by a fence or wall, forming the cattle yard, although this may possibly have been a British contribution to a Germanic structure. Also, a uniquely American function came with the addition of a drive to the lower level, flanked by narrow corn cribs on one or both sides.

Throughout these various changes, the barn's single most characteristic feature, the cantilevered second level, remained. The extension is variously known as a forebay, overhang, overshoot, *vorbau, vorschuss,* or, in Wisconsin, as a porch or shed, and has been a source of considerable controversy for those who have debated its presence based on a variety of specific functions. The survival of the forebay in America was most likely the result of tradition, however. These barns were large, even huge, sturdy, and well maintained, and proof of the productivity of Pennsylvania farms.

DIFFUSION AND FORM CHANGES

The location of the Pennsylvania-German bank barns in Ohio is closely related to Pennsylvania-Dutch and German settlement in the state. In the late 1960s, a series of crosscountry traverses established the southern boundary of the bank barn in Ohio (Wilhelm 1974, 1982). The location of that boundary closely correlates with the distribution of Middle Atlantic settlers in the state by 1850. Robert Ensminger (1980, 1983) has confirmed the presence of bank barns in northern Ohio. The location of these barns coincides perfectly with the thrust of Middle Atlantic settlers across the excellent farm lands of Ohio's drainage divide, also known as the state's "backbone" country.

One of the areas in Ohio where Pennsylvania-German bank barns occur most frequently is in Fairfield County and its neighboring counties of Perry, Hocking, and Pickaway. These counties lie alongside Zane's Trace, Ohio's earliest interior road and the one followed by many settlers from the East on their way into the interior. The location of "German" churches in the area (fig. 4.4) is a cultural residual of both Pennsylvania-Dutch and German settlement.

The expansion of the settlement frontier beyond Ohio and into the prairie lands assured the diffusion of the bank barn. Ensminger (1983) has argued convincingly that the banked forebay barns of Wisconsin were the result of relocation diffusion from the Pennsylvania cultural hearth. However, the presence in Wisconsin of small, ground-level stables with cantilevered second stories is unrelated to the Pennsylvania barn. Instead, this small structure has been traced to Wisconsin immigrants from Pomerania in northern Germany. The structure, therefore, was identified by Calkins and Perkins (1980) as a "Pomeranian stable" (fig. 4.5).

According to Ensminger (1992), who has extensively studied the distribution and diffusion of the German bank barn, this structure spread from its source area in southeastern Pennsylvania northward into southern Ontario, and southward along the Great Valley migration axis into Tennessee. It can be found westward as far as Iowa and Nebraska, with adjacent outliers in Missouri and, of course, Wisconsin. After Pennsylvania, Ohio is the state with the largest number of bank barns. They are less apparent in their traditional forebay form in Indiana and Illinois. One observer pointed out, "Forebay barns . . . are infrequent in rural Indiana. They stand isolated or in small, widely scattered clusters, north and south of the old National Road" (Bastian 1977, 131).

Changes in barn technology and in popular perceptions eventually brought an end to the building of Pennsylvania-German bank barns. Some of the changes included enclosure of the area under the forebay because the interior stall areas were rearranged (i.e., for longitudinal alignment of cow stanchions), the addition

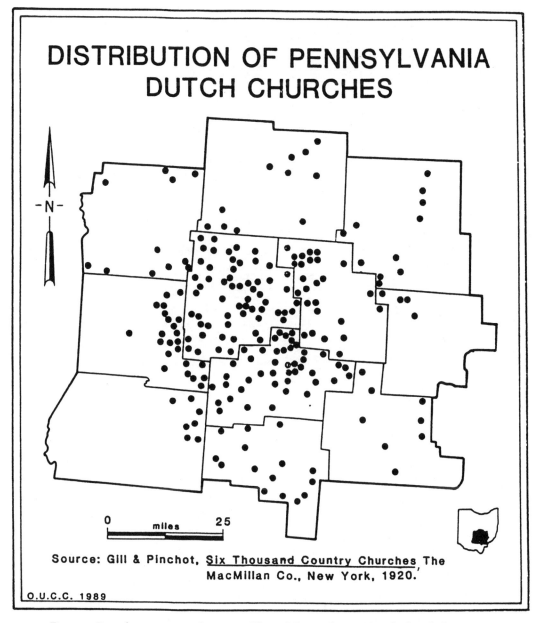

Fig. 4.4. Distribution in southeastern Ohio of Pennsylvania-Dutch church denominations
Source: Hubert Wilhelm. *The Barn Builders, Pennsylvania Settlers in Ohio: A Study Guide.* Athens, Ohio, Cutler Printing, 1989, p. 21.

of more window space, and the disappearance of the cattle yard. Much of the barn-based activity—for example, automatic manure removal, unloading of hay and sheaves of grain, and the supply of ensilage from a silo—shifted to the gable end of the barn. Furthermore, banking was increasingly viewed as a problem because the barn's lower level tended to be dark and damp, and, thus, perceived as

Fig. 4.5. "Pomeranian stable" located in the outdoor museum, Old World Wisconsin, near Milwaukee
Photo: H. Wilhelm

unsanitary. Of course, these problems were less serious in the plains areas where the levelness of the land discouraged banking. Here, instead, earthen ramps provided access to the second level. In time, even the ramps disappeared as fodder and grain crops were increasingly lifted, blown, or conveyed into the barn. As a result, the central barn drive returned to ground level, where it had been in the earliest of Pennsylvania barns.

In some parts of the Midwest, especially in central and western Ohio and in adjacent Indiana, two-level hay and livestock barns often acquired a small, secondary roof projecting over the first story. This pent-roof provided protection for stall areas usually on one gable side or, less often, on the front or long axis of the barn (fig. 4.6). In Ohio, these barns are typical in areas of earlier bank barns and Pennsylvania Dutch and German immigrant settlement. As a form element, the pent-roof is reminiscent of the forebay or overhang on the old bank barns. It may represent the survival of an architectural feature with both traditional and functional values for its builders. These pent-roof barns, because of their distribution, should be recognized as a Germanic barn form in the midwestern landscape (Wilhelm 1976, 1983). Chapter 1 of this book provides other information and raises additional questions about other gable pent-roof barns.

Fig. 4.6. Typical barn of northern Madison County, Ohio.
Photo and Sketch: H. Wilhelm

ANOTHER GERMANIC BARN

Quite unrelated, at least in form, to the various barns described so far, is another ground-level barn common throughout the Midwest. It occurs most often in the western prairie states where it became known as a horse barn or feeder barn. Its diagnostic features are gable entrances, huge roof, and large haydoor with overhanging hayhood. In recent years, the name "three-portal barn" has been applied to this structure (Noble 1984, 11).

The development of the three-portal barn has been linked with Appalachian folk structures, especially the transverse crib barn (Kniffen 1965) (fig. 4.7). The latter has a central drive, parallel to the roof ridge, and next to the drive are corn cribs and stalls. There is an overhead hayloft underneath a large roof. This barn probably had its origin in the log-building practices of the Upland South. Because log-building techniques diffused from the Swedish-Swiss-German settlement core of southeastern Pennsylvania and the Delaware Valley into the southern Appalachians, the transverse crib barn and its midwestern offspring, the three-portal barn, may be circuitously related to Germanic settlement influences.

A more direct geographic path to the midwestern three-portal barn may relate to Dutch settlement in the Hudson Valley and early immigrants in western Ohio and neighboring Indiana from the German province of Lower Saxony (Nied-

Fig. 4.7. Early log transverse crib barn located in Vinton County, Ohio. Sketch: C. Steiner in Wilhelm, 1982.

ersachsen). Whether Dutch, Frisian, or Lower Saxon, these low-country folk lived in a housebarn variously known as the "Lower Saxon hall house" (Niedersaechsisches Hallenhaus) or "Lower German house" (Niederdeutsches Haus). This housebarn is built around a large kitchen and threshing floor (Halle). A central drive extends from the threshing floor (Tenne) and lies parallel with the roof ridge. Cow stanchions and horse boxes face toward the central drive. There is a large, steeply pitching roof over the lower part, where hay, sheaves of grain, and straw are stored.

In America, where only the barn portion of the "hall house" survived, it became known as the "New World Dutch Barn" (Fitchen 1968). I have located a single example of this kind of barn in Mercer County in western Ohio (Wilhelm 1981). This county and adjacent ones in Ohio and in Indiana were settled by immigrant farmers from Lower Saxony in northwestern Germany. The barn has a central drive flanked by animal stalls (fig. 4.8). It resembles those of the Hudson Valley, even down to the framing details, which included the "Dutch" tenon or mortise with the mortise cut entirely through the post to allow the tenon to project through to the opposite side of the post, where it was secured with a peg (fig. 4.9). Noble (1984), who recognizes a similar barn type prevalent in Iowa, suggests that it "may be derived from a north German barn" (60).

The diffusion path of the midwestern three-portal barn remains unclear.

Fig. 4.8. Possible Dutch barn in Mercer County, Ohio.
Photo: H. Wilhelm

Fig. 4.9. Detail of interior framing of barn shown in fig. 4-8. Note the extension of the tenon through the mortise, a framing characteristic typical of the low-land areas of the Netherlands and northwestern Germany.

Nevertheless, whether its origins are among the Appalachian crib barns or with those introduced by the Dutch and Lower Saxon settlers, the linkage to Germanic settlement influences appears likely. Additional study is needed to more clearly establish the antecedents and diffusion path of the barn type.

CONCLUSION

The barn has always occupied a special niche in America's collective psyche, possibly because it stood for freedom, individualism, success, and pride. These perceptions are perhaps best represented by the Pennsylvania-German bank barns. Their size, red-painted siding, and overhanging second story were symbolic of the mixed grain-livestock agriculture that spread from Pennsylvania into the heartland of the country. Because many of the barn's builders came from "Dutch" culture, the barn's recognition as "German" was perhaps to be expected.

During the eighteenth and nineteenth centuries, German emigrants entered America in large numbers. The majority of them came to Pennsylvania, where they experienced the development of an agricultural system that relied on raising a variety of small grains, especially wheat, and keeping large numbers of livestock. The German settlers were culturally preadapted to this system and, in fact, became its principal progenitors in the new country.

They built ground-level barns in which animals could be stabled, and hay, grain, and straw stored. The importance which the German farmer attached to the sheltering of his animals influenced the adoption of the banked, two-level barn. The barn offered expanded space for livestock on the first level and a threshing floor and storage space on the upper level. People often referred to it as Swisser or Schweizer barn, but its origins in eastern Switzerland were not substantiated until 1980.

It became the barn of choice among Pennsylvania farmers. German immigrants, especially, identified with this structure, and the barn became known as the Pennsylvania-German bank barn. Remaining a popular farmyard building until the early twentieth century, the bank barn moved westward to Missouri, Nebraska, and Wisconsin, although in much reduced numbers (see chapter 8).

However, changes in technology and personal preference eventually altered the appearance of this structure. The overhang or forebay, the barn's most diagnostic feature, disappeared, as did the practice of banking the structure. But traditions are difficult to erase. So, in the old Pennsylvania-German settlement areas, where banked, forebay barns had been prominent, pent roofs were added to new barns. They are a reminder of the persistence of a traditional form, the second-story overhang.

Finally, the three-portal barn may represent traditional Germanic influence on American barn forms. A definitive link has yet to be established, but the barn's evolutionary relationship to earlier Appalachian crib barns is reasonable, and such a relationship would tie it to Germanic log-building techniques (see chapter 2). In addition, there is the possible link with the New World Dutch barn of the Hudson Valley and similar structures among settlers from Lower Saxony (Niedersachsen) in Ohio and Indiana.

In retrospect, German settlers in America did not leave a uniquely "German" barn on this landscape. Their traditional housebarn did not survive in great numbers in America. Instead, they adopted a "Germanic" type of barn because it suited their way of practicing agriculture and, at the same time, was the landscape manifestation of their status as farmers. Whether the three-portal barn, so common in the Midwest, is related to the Low German house (Niederdeutsche Haus) remains a riddle, waiting to be solved, in America's landscape.

REFERENCES CITED

Bastian, Robert W. 1977. Indiana folk architecture: A lower midwestern index. *Pioneer America* 9(2): 115–42.

Borie, Beauveau, IV. 1986. *Farming and folk society: Threshing among the Pennsylvania Germans.* Ann Arbor: UMI Research Press.

Calkins, Charles F., and Martin C. Perkins. 1980. The Pomeranian stable of southeastern Wisconsin. *Concordia Historical Institute Quarterly* 53(Fall): 121–25.

Dornbusch, Charles H., and J. K. Heyl. 1956. *Pennsylvania German barns.* Vol. 31. Allentown: Pennsylvania German Folklore Society.

Ensminger, Robert F. 1980–81. A search for the origin of the Pennsylvania barn. *Pennsylvania Folklife* 30(2): 50–71.

_____. 1982. A comparative study of Pennsylvania and Wisconsin forebay barns. *Pennsylvania Folklife* 32(3): 98–114.

_____. 1992. *The Pennsylvania barn.* Baltimore: Johns Hopkins Univ. Press.

Fitchen, John. 1968. *The New World Dutch barn.* Syracuse: Syracuse Univ. Press.

Gagliardo, John G. 1959. Germans and agriculture in Pennsylvania. *Pennsylvania Magazine of History and Biography* 83:192–218.

Glass, Joseph W. 1986. *The Pennsylvania culture region: A view from the barn.* Ann Arbor: UMI Research Press.

Glassie, Henry. 1968. *Pattern in the material folk culture of the eastern United States.* Philadelphia: Univ. of Pennsylvania Press.

Jordan, Terry G. 1980. Alpine, Alemannic, and American log architecture. *Annals of the Association of American Geographers* 70(2): 154–80.

Kniffen, Fred B. 1965. Folk housing: Key to diffusion. *Annals of the Association of American Geographers* 55(December): 549–77.

Learned, M. D. 1915. The German barn in America. *University of Pennsylvania Lectures Delivered by Members of the Faculty in the Free Public Lecture Course, 1913–1914,* 338–49. Philadelphia: Univ. of Pennsylvania Press.

Marshall, Howard Wight. 1986. The Pelster housebarn: Endurance of Germanic architecture on the midwestern frontier. *Material Culture* 18(2): 65–104.

Noble, Allen G. 1984. *Wood, brick, and stone: the North American settlement landscape.* Vol. 2, *Barns and Farm Structures.* Amherst: Univ. of Massachusetts Press.

Perrin, Richard W. D. 1961. German timber farmhouses in Wisconsin: terminal examples of a thousand year building tradition. *Wisconsin Magazine of History* 44(Spring): 199–202.

Ridlen, Susanne S. 1972. Bank barns in Cass County, Indiana. *Pioneer America* 4(2): 25–43.

Stephens, David. 1990. Ohio's agricultural regions. In *The Changing Heartland: A Geography of Ohio*, edited by Leonard Peaceful. Needham Heights, MA: Ginn Press.

Wilhelm, Hubert G. H. 1974. The Pennsylvania-Dutch barn in southeastern Ohio. *Geoscience and Man* 5:155–62.

———. 1976. Amish-Mennonite barns in Madison County, Ohio: The persistence of traditional form elements. *Ohio Geographers: Recent Research Themes* 4:1–8.

———. 1981. A Lower Saxon settlement region in Western Ohio. *PAST: Pioneer America Society Transactions* 4:1–10.

———. 1982. *The origin and distribution of settlement groups: Ohio 1850.* Athens, OH: Cutler Printing.

———. 1983. Tobacco barns and pent roofs in Western Ohio. *PAST—Pioneer America Society Transactions* 6:19–26.

———. 1989. Double overhang barns in southeastern Ohio. *PAST—Pioneer America Society Transactions* 12:29–36.

Wood, Ralph, ed., 1942. *The Pennsylvania Germans.* Princeton, NJ: Princeton University Press.

Yoder, Don, ed. 1951. Description of Dutch barn. *Pennsylvania Dutchman* 2:17 Lancaster: Pennsylvania Dutch Folklore Center, 1, 4.

Zelinsky, Wilbur. 1961. An approach to the religious geography of the United States: Patterns of church membership. *Annals of the Association of American Geographers* 51(2): 139–93.

———. 1972. *The cultural geography of the United States.* Englewood Cliffs, NJ: Prentice Hall.

5

AFFORDABLE BARNS FOR THE MIDWEST: BEGINNINGS

Lowell J. Soike

BARNS OF THE prairie states share a history of their own, largely apart from that of their eastern neighbors. From Ohio westward through Iowa, signs of the earlier origins and thinking that shaped the predominant character and look of barns gradually fade. By the time farmers and builders were putting up barns in any numbers on the prairies, barn-building was in the throes of change. New agricultural practices, path-breaking inventions, changing construction methods, and altered availability of building materials brought about new generations of barn design. Whereas eastern states dominated the main ideas of barn-building until the Civil War, thereafter the midwestern states became the center of barn-building developments. Together, the barns of the prairie states represent a legacy of change that shaped the barn-building era.

To date, geographers and folklorists have contributed most to our understanding of barns. From their works come valuable observations on the forms of barns and their relative distributions across the various regions of the country. By examining the diverse concentrations as expressions of ethnic and cultural settlement patterns, these researchers have offered useful insights into the particular spread of barns. With the older eastern barn forms perceived by most researchers as having spawned the kind of barns elsewhere, midwestern barns have attracted less attention, their age and character treated as derivative and less visibly tied to ethnic and folk barn-building traditions.

This chapter follows a different idea: that the thinking, technologies and materials, agricultural practices, and market economy current at the time of barn construction largely shaped the kind of midwestern barn erected. Older building patterns existed among some farmers who wanted to have what they had known back East, but faith in the older ways did not thrive in midwestern states, where farmers faced new circumstances during different agricultural times. These influences, albeit of ethnic subregional variety, prompted the building of more suitable barns and dissolved building patterns that fit an agricultural economy of an earlier day. As industrial and technical forces promoted standardization in various ways, so did their experimental evolution bring about great variety in the process.

Specifically, the history of the nineteenth-century midwestern barn departed from that of its eastern cousins when differing agricultural circumstances called forth, and prairie farmers took advantage of, the hay carrier and fork, the hay barn, and plank and balloon-frame construction. In the twentieth century, the economical midwestern barn achieved perfection through light-truss framing and its crown of clear span lofts enclosed by a laminated curved-arch gothic roof, the production of pre-cut barns, promotion of experimental types, and the widespread adoption of specialized dairy barns and the litter carrier.

LOOKING EASTWARD

"A barn is the real headquarters of the farm" wrote the Reverend Henry Ward Beecher in 1869. "The dwelling-house represents the people; the barn, the work" (*Hearth and Home* 1869, 165). This sentiment, shared by those of Beecher's Hudson Valley class and wealth, also expressed the dream for a good barn held by ordinary farmers in this timbered region.

In the West of that time (today, the midwestern states), barns that typically appeared early on the farms of large landowners rarely showed up elsewhere. By the 1850s, however, eastern parts of the settled Midwest were outgrowing their pioneer beginnings, and increasing numbers of prospering farmers were thinking about replacing their rude facilities with a better house and, perhaps, a barn. When they did, those whose farming resembled eastern agricultural areas naturally looked back there for their models.

They found that opinions differed about barns. The would-be barn-builder in search of a plan first had to decide whether he wanted to concentrate functions under the single roof of a large barn or, instead, put up a small barn and then add sheds and other buildings as needed. The customary practice had been "to build small barns, to add others on three sides of a yard, perhaps of several yards, and to construct sheds, pigpens, corn houses, and such minor structures as might seem desirable, "letting the open area shelter stock from severe winter winds, and allowing manure to be continuously piled up in the center until spring (Halsted 1881).

Such an arrangement was falling into disfavor by the 1860s, however, as farmers understood that the "small crowded village" of buildings presented them with an inconvenient hodgepodge of uses and an expensive problem of maintenance (*American Agriculturalist* 1867c, 286; Halsted 1881; *Illustrated Annual Register of Rural Affairs* 1878, 1881; Thomas 1862; *Iowa Homestead* 1869). The warm memories of past generations might lead the farmer to keep the house in good repair, said one "large barn" farmer, but "no such claims to consideration can save the inconvenient old barns and sheds" (*Iowa Homestead* 1869, 73). The scattering of buildings around the farm also was criticized because it required traveling in the winter from one to the other to dispense the crops and to otherwise attend the animals (Halsted 1881).

The 1860s farmer faced less uncertainty when it came to concentrating or dispersing buildings for farm operations. An up-to-date builder of "a modern

American barn" knows that "one good building takes the place of a score of others of all ages" that had been "as diverse in character as ingeniously inconvenient" (*Iowa Homestead* 1869, 73). Another writer of more philosophic bent echoed the thought.

> Later experience, corroborated by reason, indicates the superiority of a single large building. There is more economy in the materials for walls; more in the construction of roofs—a most expensive portion of farm structures; and a saving in the amount of labor, in feeding, thrashing, and transferring straw and grain, when all are placed more compactly together. (Thomas 1862, 127)

That being the case, who knew most about this and where were the prime examples to be found of such ample barns?

A farm editor wrote in 1867:

> This is better understood in Pennsylvania than in any other part of the country, and the barn that bears the name of the State is, in many respects, a model. It contemplates the shelter of all stock, and the storage of all crops raised upon the farm; and if it also provided shelter for manure, it would, with abundant light and free ventilation, meet every want. (*American Agriculturalist* 1867e, 402)

Pennsylvanian barns had gained decades before midwestern farmers even thought of barns in general, let alone ones of large size. They were "commented upon by travellers from Europe as well as from every section of our country," declared a farm editor in 1847, for in showing the agricultural "perfection" in Pennsylvania, "nothing more forcibly attracts the stranger's eye on entering within the bounds of that state." Even though the farmer's "dwelling be an unpretending character, the means for housing his crops and sheltering his flocks, are on an ample scale" (*American Agriculturalist* 1847, 24–26). More than three decades later, another editor agreed that "Southeastern Pennsylvania is remarkable for its large and excellent farm barns, many of them of stone, and three stories high" (*Illustrated Annual Register of Rural Affairs* 1878, 252–53).

These big monarchs of the East satisfied many, but not all. By the late 1850s, some detractors thought them out of touch with the times, since new barns were showing more attention to "economy of space and warmth" for wintering animals. "I have recently visited some of the best barns in this vicinity," noted one observer, "and find them as different from the big timbered, high beamed, cold barns of 30 years ago, as chalk is from cheese" (Bagg 1858, 76).

Nevertheless, if people generally had much that was good to say about the big-roofed, "concentrated function" barn, they had little to admire in the older, humble 3-bay barn, later to be dubbed the English barn. To ambitious farmers, the old 3-bay barn seemed a visible confession of backwardness. Those who adopted it after the mid-1860s in the Midwestern states were swimming against the current of popularity, where it stood as a ridiculed example of out-of-date barns, too small to satisfy increasing storage requirements and too cramped to provide serviceable shelter for any but a few animals.

Although "a barn of some kind is found upon every farm" in "thrifty New England," a writer complained in 1867 that their small size and no basement made them obsolete, whereby "a large part of the hay and corn fodder is stored in stacks, and the open yard is still often met with as the only receptacle for manure" (*American Agriculturalist* 1867e, 402). Surely these old barns must be improved, inveighed another. "The 30x40-foot barn is an 'institution' known from one end of the country to the other, almost certainly throughout the older Northern States. They are unsightly, inconvenient, and poorly adapted to any use but that of storing hay and straw. Those of the usual style, with a wide bay, a narrow barn-floor, and a still narrower row of stables, are poor, inconvenient barns" (*American Agriculturalist* 1866, 215). The New York writer instead advocated taking these "old fashioned" affairs with their "hay mow at one end, stables and granary with loft over them, at the other, and barn floor between" and converting them to modern requirements. He had modernized his own barn by raising it up, adding twenty feet to its length for stabling, thus having a basement of the building thirty-by-sixty feet, and grading a wagon-way up to the great doors for hauling in hay. Adding basement room beneath such barns would prove a common way of continuing the traditional English barn in use (see also Thomas 1856).

Although installing a basement helped keep in use the farmer's English barn, those who decided to build a new barn found mixed opinion on the subject of basements. Whether to build one's barn with a basement sparked vigorous discussion during the middle of the century. According to published eastern opinion, the majority favored a barn basement, while a strong minority contested its wisdom. Debate boiled down to a few arguments.

"The best farms," said one, "invariably were those that had the barn cellars. These are the stomachs of the farms, indispensable in the North, and soon to be so on the new farms of the West." Such words, penned by a farm editor who had just traveled through Connecticut and Massachusetts during 1867, equated the possession of manure cellars with first-class barns and declared the mark of sound-thinking farmers (*American Agriculturalist* 1867d, 316). This was the "farmer's Bank," argued its proponents, the vault where "very large quantities of excellent manure may be made with a minimum amount of labor." Ten years earlier, the idea of housing manure in barn cellars was frowned upon, but "now such a cavity is considered of the utmost importance. Once, liquid manure was considered less valuable than solid. Now, the reverse is the case" (*American Agriculturalist* 1868c, 255–56; Bagg 1858, 76). The obvious daily advantage of being able to drop the manure from the stable above was matched with the long-term benefit of helping improve one's farm. "Above all things kept in a barn cellar, keep the greatest capital of a farmer, in the shape of a large pile of manure, which if judiciously applied, liquid as well as solid to your land, you will soon have the satisfaction of saying that 'my land don't depreciate, it is growing better every year'" (*Iowa Homestead* 1868, 186).

Opponents saw more harm than good to keeping manure in cellars and kept up a running fight on the issue. Argued one, "The gases and fumes of the manure will spoil all the hay and grain in the barn" (*Iowa Homestead* 1868, 186). Others went further, alleging that such manure heaps would harm the animals as well. Wintering cattle and hogs in the cellar is bad, one observer claimed, because the air becomes "foul and close" and "hurtful" to the cattle, he added "least of all do we approve of making barn cellars the place for manufacturing and storing manure. It may economize the dung-heap, but it harms the domestic animals and the hay and grain above." Instead, he recommended making the cattle shed distinct from the main barn and confining the barn cellar to "storing turnips, carrots, potatoes, pumpkins and the like food for stock" (*American Agriculturalist* 1858, 360).

Numerous articles favoring basements for barns appeared in agricultural journals from the mid-1850s to the 1870s, but they became less frequent after the 1860s, especially in the western Midwest. There, the misgivings of skeptics persisted. A common complaint connected cattle diseases to barn-fed cattle. "While large barns, with basements, are convenient and comfortable, many have long doubted their financial policy. The basement is generally dark and through long use becomes foul, in many instances inducing disease in the stock and in more cases impairing digestion and destroying profits" (*Western Stock Journal and Farmer* 1879a, 69).

By the 1860s, when hay harvesting advances and increased emphasis on animal husbandry made such barns seem obsolete, the small English barn, even when equipped with a basement, attracted few eastern admirers. To the western farmer with no barns in his area, however, even the lowly English barn seemed a luxury.

CUTTING THE KNOT

"The barns of the West," sneered the editor of the *American Agriculturalist* in 1868, "have hitherto not been models either of architectural style or practical utility, which could be held up for imitation" (1868d, 326). This sting of eastern criticism initially prompted western farm editors to wax apologetic: "It is apparent to every person traveling through the West that there is a great want of barns and other out-houses on the farms" (*Northwestern Farmer and Horticultural Journal* 1859, 17). These two comments revealed strains of sectional opinion. To prideful easterners the absence of barns in the prairie states stood as a metaphor for western inferiority. To many westerners, after a period of expressing defensive-minded regrets, the subject became a metaphor for eastern ignorance.

All recognized the fact that, during the initial years of western settlement,

> the farmer in the clearing, or upon the prairie, has everything pressing upon him at once, and must meet his most imperious wants first. He must have shelter for his family, and food for himself and stock. The log-house and barn upon the most limited scale will answer for a while. (*American Agriculturalist* 1867e, 402)

As time passed and few barns materialized, however, impatience surfaced in the agricultural press. A Dubuque, Iowa, farm editor lamented how only "a few . . . have put in practice the Eastern custom of having barn-room sufficient to shelter their stock from the cold storms of autumn and winter. Well, farmers," he decried:

> You who have no barns for your cattle . . . just examine your stock in the spring after one of our hard winters, and then, while their gaunt frames, rough hair, sunken eyes and shivering limbs are fresh upon your memory, go to the farm of your neighbor, who has a good barn for the protection of his stock, and compare the condition of his, plump, sleek and satisfied as they are, with the condition of your own. (*Northwestern Farmer and Horticultural Journal* 1859, 17–18)

Nevertheless, the relative absence of barns persisted on farms of the Midwest, especially in its western half. The eastern desire for barn shelter seemed unrealistic to many. Answering claims for the benefits of barns made by someone signed "Connecticut," an "Iowa Farmer" wrote: "Now I do not uphold slow torture or any kind of torture for the dumb brutes, but it does not follow because they are not in warm stables that they are uncomfortable." Indeed, he continued, the February 1868 report of the livestock market of New York showed "nearly one half of the cattle were from Illinois, numbering 2,052, while only 97 were from Connecticut." Since "I do not suppose one half of these Illinois steers were ever inside a stable," but rather left the state "fine, fat, sleek fellows, and did not look as though they were suffering slow torture," one can rightly conclude that "few of the men that have fed these steers are at present in much danger of going to the poor house" (*American Agriculturalist* 1867a, 129).

Others, even if they agreed on the need for barns, thought large ones an expensive luxury. Instead of building a costly barn which "adds but little to the selling value of the farm" and "looks larger in the eyes of the assessor than those of the buyer," a thrifty farmer prescribed the building of "simple, plain barns, cheaply constructed." Under this scheme, "broad and dense timber belts around the yards, plain, substantial barns for hay and grain, and plenty of sheds, answer the necessities for cattle" (*Western Stock Journal and Farmer* 1879b, 91).

Midwestern farmers, especially those west of Indiana, relied mainly on hay sheds and hay barracks as their "half-way house to the barn" until well into the 1880s. Contemporary observers and farm journal reports overwhelmingly testified to farmers' continued reliance on such sheds and shelters (Whitaker 1975; Hopkins 1928; Bogue 1968; *American Agriculturalist* 1868a; *Western Stock Journal and Farmer* 1881). Conversely, farmers in the eastern Midwest, long influenced by what the older states deemed acceptable, wintered cattle outside only at the risk of feeling "the cuts of satire and the lash of open reprobation" from neighbors who preferred barns (*American Agriculturalist* 1868a, 15).

Many readers of the *Ohio Farmer* no doubt enjoyed and agreed with the sarcastic description of Iowa having "remarkably little house accommodation for cattle" except for what "they may find around a hay stack, or in that elegant erection designated an 'Iowa barn'—a building of some fame in the Far West, and costing just about as much as the turf hen house of the Highlands of Scotland!" (100). "Drive two opposite rows of posts into the ground . . . , lay a network of sticks across the tops of these, cover that with a liberal coating of straw, held down by sticks, and you will have an Iowa barn in all the glory of its architectural grandeur!" (1877, 100). Earlier, in the 1840s and 1850s, the "Iowa barn" had been known as the Illinois "sucker barn" (Bogue 1968, 69).

In Illinois and Iowa, ridicule made few farmers abandon their straw sheds and hay barracks. Necessity dictated something less than barns, notwithstanding easterners' scornful claims that westerners' appeals to their pocketbook were "heard above the lowings of the shivering herd" (*American Agriculturalist* 1868a, 15–16).

Due to an "absence of wood, water and stone, materials so essential for comfort, for building, fuel and fencing," barns were too expensive for most settlers in the prairie states, especially until railroads opened markets and access to products. Barns were "rarely seen on the prairies," where, for decades after settlement, timberland remained costlier than more productive prairie land (*Cultivator* 1857, 275–76; Bogue 1968, 53). Equally important, when the farmer pondered whether his scarce capital would be more profitable if invested in more cattle rather than buildings, expensive buildings usually took second place (Hopkins 1928). Thus, "to the majority of farmers," wrote an Iowa farm editor in 1880, "expensive barns . . . are matters they have to defer, or refer to their richer neighbor" (*Western Stock Journal and Farmer* 1880, 2). Of course, as the editor acknowledged,

> thousands of farmers in the West the past winter, as they dug their half rotten hay out of stacks, covered with ice and snow, wished they had barns. But a barn that will hold fifty or a hundred tons of hay costs a good deal of money, and many of them will have to wait many years before they will be able to build barns. To these farmers I would suggest hay barracks. (*Western Stock Journal and Farmer* 1881, 50)

Surrounded by these makeshift and add-on barns, it did not take long for a prairie state farm editor to realize that things were not what Easterners had come to regard as acceptable and necessary. The *Prairie Farmer*'s editor could see this trend by 1866.

> The fact is we have given too little attention to the planning of cheap farm buildings on the prairie, and too many have waited for the "big barn" through long years, when by a little exertion and a little planning they could have made their cattle and horses more comfortable and kept their farm implements from serious damage by the elements (281–82)

Eastern farmers moving West often made the same mistake. "There has been a large amount of money wasted in the West on barns," declared the editor of the *Iowa Homestead* (1890), for, unwittingly, "farmers bring with them from the Eastern states ideas adapted to that locality. They construct large and expensive buildings with heavy lumber, and often a stone basement, forgetting that the conditions of farming are very widely different in the East and West" (1). Ultimately, as we shall see, these and other circumstances brought forth different solutions to the problem of farm shelter.

BREAKING FREE

Major changes were in the offing, changes that midwesterners inaugurated and from which they most benefitted (Case and Myers 1934; Holmes 1929; Lloyd, Falconer and Thorne 1918; Soike 1989). Between mid-century and the Civil War, horse-drawn rakes, replacing six to ten men with hand rakes, came into general use, except among poor farmers working subsistence farms and in the rocky parts of New England. This increased the amount of hay that could be harvested, enabling more livestock to be winterfed. It also prompted the development of better hay-moving equipment, for hay needed to be put in a barn or stacked while in optimum condition lest it be soaked by rainstorms. After horses delivered a loaded wagon of hay to the stack or barn, relays of men with pitchforks usually moved the hay into its storage place (Schlebecker 1975).

The hot, sweaty, hard work and frustration of filling the loft of a traditionally built, heavy-timber barn made many a farmer wish for something better. "If you have ever pitched hay over the main girt in a barn," observed a man in 1861, you know it is a "great inconvenience" until "the hay in the bay is up to it." Moreover, having "to pitch hay as high as one can reach, only to see it fall again to the same level, seems to be outrageous, if one may judge by the amount of grumbling—saying nothing of the too frequent profanity heard on such occasions." Because of this, he knew several barn owners who had "cut out the middle part of the main girt," an act which he feared weakened the frame "just where it needs most strength" (*Northwestern Farmer and Horticultural Journal* 1861, 209).

The introduction of the horse hay fork in the 1860s set the stage for a transformation from barn "thinking" to prolific barn building in the Midwest. People soon sensed possibilities in what was then variously called the "horse fork," "horse pitchfork," or "hay elevator" for unloading hay from the wagon to stacks, sheds, or buildings. This work-saving device greatly reduced the many hard hours of pitching hay by hand, whether shifting, loading, or unloading it, and the agricultural press gave it increasing attention. Descriptions and discussion multiplied while manufacturers advertised its special features.

The adoption of horse hay forks began to change work routines. Numerous models appeared during the early 1860s. By 1867, three distinct varieties were in use: single forks with wood handles, grappling forks which grasped their load between two sets of tines, and harpoons which were thrust down into the top of the hay and then, when opened, exposed barbs for holding the hay as it was pulled upward. No matter the type, the fork was usually attached by rope to a pulley mounted on a cross piece in the center of the loft. After lifting and dragging the hay up to this pulley, the farmer then jerked on a hand rope to release it. As the forkfuls dropped in the middle of the mow, one or more men used hand pitchforks to roll hay down the mound into the barn corners (*American Agriculturalist* 1868b, 18).

While the horse hay fork eased the farmer's work of filling the mow, the major advancement was yet to come. William Louden, a 26-year-old inventor living in Fairfield, Iowa, had a knack for seeing "human need unrecognized by those on whom it bore," and realized what would make the horse hay-fork complete: a horizontal hay carrier. Soon after obtaining a patent for his hay carrier in 1867, he was looking for sales agents and advertising in the *Prairie Farmer*. "It elevates the hay perpendicularly any height, then conveys it horizontally to the back of the longest mow and returns the Fork back to the load without a single effort of the Pitcher" (*Prairie Farmer* 1867, 431; *Agricultural Engineering* 1921; Giese 1946).

The superiority of the hay carrier with its wooden track fixed to the roof rafters (fig. 5.1) led to the quick replacement of the old horse hay-fork just as the gasoline tractor later would end the brief day of its bulky steam-powered predecessor. Horse hay fork brands soon disappeared from advertisements, replaced by manufacturers' versions of Louden's hay carrier, such as Hinman, Hicks, or Kirkpatrick's horizontal carriers. Several advantages over the former rope- and pulley-operated horse forks attracted farm clients. The editor of the *Prairie Farmer* (1872) noted some good points of the Louden hay carrier. Two advantages touted were:

> It raises the hay *perpendicularly* from the load, thus requiring no boards to slide up on, never catching under nor dragging against beams. . . . "It carries the hay clear of all obstructions to the end of the longest mow, or stack and *holds it suspended* so that it may be readily swung to either side and dropped in any place wanted, thus saving all rehandling whatever." (129)

What Louden's invention meant for the barn's future soon became apparent. One farm editor observed that there would be "less necessity for the three-story barns" built into sloping ground to enable a loaded wagon to gain entrance to the upper story; "the horse-fork will lift its load to any ordinary required height," as a horizontal carrier runs the load "to any desired distance" (*Illustrated Annual Register of Rural Affairs* 1870, 61). With the new device, reported another, "it is less necessary than formerly to build low barns" and "wider bays may be stored with hay without the labor of side-pitching by hand" (*Illustrated Annual Register of Rural Affairs* 1881, 64–65). An Iowa journalist put it less elegantly: "There is no excuse for wasting material in squatty barns" and "the hay carrier that should be in every barn can as well receive the hay from the end of the barn" (*Western Stock Journal and Farmer* 1881, 50). Additionally, "in these days of steam, and all kinds of machinery, there is no difficulty in using long narrow [dairy] buildings, for, with the hay fork and the hay carrier, the forage can be readily stored in the longest barn and dropped wherever it is desired" (Halsted 1881, 63). Thinking more grandly, the *American Agriculturalist*'s editor perceived how "a change has been made in the construction of barns" which now requires them "to be free from obstructions overhead, so that the movable fork can have freedom to act in any part of the barn." Those who design or build barns, instructed the editor, must realize that modern barns are "to be high rather than spacious," thus saving on roof cost, "and to be so arranged that there should be no crossbeams to interfere with the run of the hay fork with its load from end to end" (1879, 182).

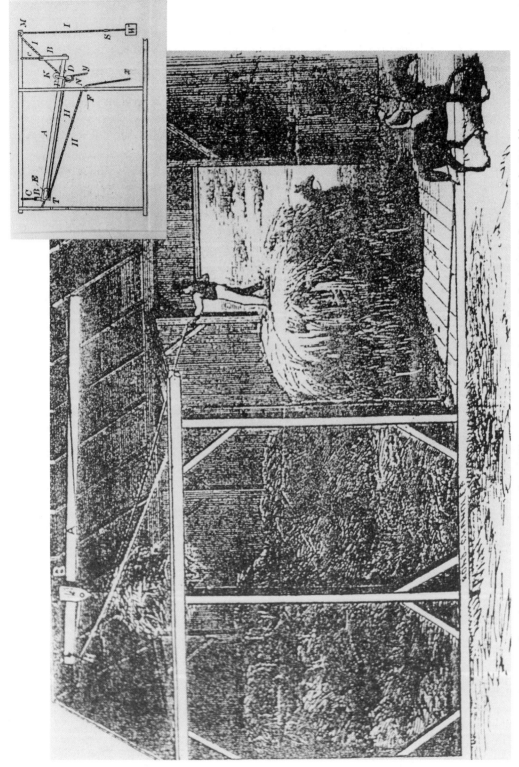

Fig. 5.1. William Louden's hay carrier at work in a barn. Inset at upper right shows Louden's 1867 drawing submitted for patent. Source: *Prairie Farmer*, April 27, 1872

Louden's hay carrier encouraged farmers to think about building higher barns, longer barns, barns free of driveways for loading and unloading by hand, barns free of crossbeams, and barns with a hay door for outside access to the loft, especially at the gable end (fig. 5.2). The design of older eastern barns had been circumscribed by their own history, a past where heights and widths were suited to hand-pitching methods. This limited the size of storage bays and the practical height and length of working areas. Farmers had responded accordingly, building low and comparatively short barns, except on larger farms, where available hired hands made possible two- or three-story barns. Whether because of inconvenience or old farming habits, fewer people in the older farming areas would consequently upgrade their barns with hay carriers (Robertson 1939). As progressive farmers in the older eastern states struggled to accommodate the hay carrier to their low, big-beamed barns, the midwesterners, most of whom had yet to build a barn, knew few such constraints.

GETTING OUT THE WORD

As these new developments entered discussions in the agricultural press and attracted reader interest, they helped buoy farm construction trends during prosperous times of farm building and improvement. In a comparison of fre-

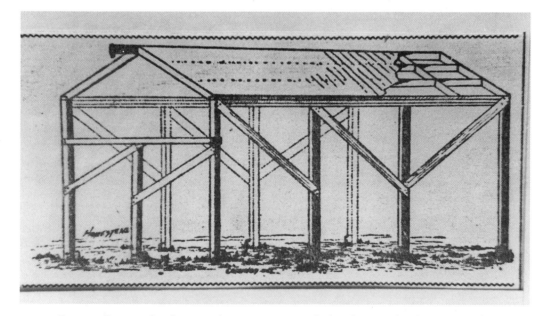

Fig. 5.2. Framing for the central storage section of a hay barn at the cheapest end of the economic scale. To this frame, measuring forty-by-twenty-six and twenty feet high to the plates, the farmer would then attach sheds on three sides to feed cattle and to shelter manure. Upright support posts were either eight-by-eight inch timbers spiked to posts set in the ground (as done here) or full-length telegraph poles. Such a so-called pole barn for cattle feeders would hold thirty-five to forty tons of hay. Source: *Iowa Homestead*, May 31, 1889

quency of articles on farm buildings published between 1865 and 1905 in two leading midwestern farm papers, the *Ohio Farmer* and the *Iowa Homestead*, certain trends
are evident (Chasse 1981; Hussman 1983). Barns and farm buildings drew increasing space in these expanding farm journals, with more than one-half of the
total coverage on barns during this forty-year period appearing during the final
ten years. Barns attracted somewhat greater interest in the *Ohio Farmer*, averaging
29 percent of its total farm-buildings articles. The *Iowa Homestead* devoted 25 percent of its articles on farm buildings to barns, a percentage that perhaps represented lesser western interest. Throughout this period, the *Ohio Farmer* printed
articles on both barns and farm buildings more frequently with an annual average
of nine articles on barns and twenty-two items on other farm buildings. By comparison, only four articles on barns and eleven on farm buildings were published
in the *Iowa Homestead*.

These two journals not only printed news about farm buildings, but also became leaders in the major nineteenth-century innovations in barn building. The
Iowa Homestead led in bringing the midwestern hay barn into popularity during
the 1880s and 1890s, while the *Ohio Farmer*, beginning in 1894 and continuing for
the next dozen years, popularized plank-frame construction embodied in Joseph
Wing's "joist frame" and, more importantly, in the light-timber construction ideas
of Ohio builder John Shawver.

AN AFFORDABLE BARN

On the prairies of Illinois and Iowa, where expensive, big timber-frame
barns were out of the question, and where farmers yearned to move beyond hay
sheds to an economical barn for sheltering stock and hay, the "hay barn," later also
called a cattle feeder barn, took form (fig. 5.3). Though eventually destined to be a
common barn in prairie states, it was not so in the early 1880s.

Changes came as beef production in Illinois and Iowa soared during the last
two decades of the nineteenth century. The two states developed into the regional
center for prime beef (fat cattle) production with the maturation of feeding practices. While farmers who had rougher land—fit more for pasture than growing
crops—commonly raised their cattle from birth to finished beef, those with more
tillable corn acreage increasingly bought young cattle that had been raised on the
western range. These feeder cattle were then fattened on surplus corn, alfalfa,
and feed supplements, and sold to the rail-connected beef-processing industry in
Chicago. Aided by the refrigerator boxcar, a growing dressed beef trade was carried on with other urban centers. This major change placed the western half of
the Midwest in an advantageous "position between the range country and the
consuming sections of the East" to finish cattle for market (Hopkins 1928, 41;
Whitaker 1975). While this led many Iowa and Illinois farmers to put what money
they had into buying more cattle rather than buildings, the growing investment
and profits also stimulated a desire for better buildings to bring their crop of hay
and cattle through the harsh winter in better condition. Hay sheds had helped in
this regard earlier, but much hay nevertheless went to waste from dust and mold.

Fig. 5.3. W. B. Seeley, a Lee County, Iowa, cattle feeder, shows his 1893 hay barn, the kind that became so popular among farmers across the western Midwest. In the background is another such barn that dated to 1891.
Source: Chicago *Breeder's Gazette*, December 7, 1898

In the *Iowa Homestead*, the number of articles about inexpensive hay barns grew after the mid-1880s. With the main criterion being to find an economical or "cheap" barn to replace hay sheds and financially out-of-reach eastern-type buildings, prairie farmers began hearing about what might work. One message was to forget about basements, notwithstanding their possible good points. A hay barn may not even need "a stone foundation," wrote the *Iowa Homestead*'s editor in 1885. "Telegraph poles set in the ground and the side boarded down four feet from the top around, with a good roof, will answer" at the cheapest end of the scale (1885a, 4). In fact, said another, "some of our largest cattle men in this region" build such barns, depending on "the price of stone for foundation, the price of lumber, the presence or absence of timber protection as well as the peculiar kind of stock kept on the farm" (1885b, 4). A portent came from a barn built on one of the largest farms in Marshall County, Iowa. The farmer placed his hay in the middle, alongside which, it was reported, the "posts supporting the [gable] roof are about twenty feet high" and "the track for the hay fork runs the entire length, depositing the hay at any point desired." Then he built on one side "stalls for twenty horses," while on the other side "twenty-five cows are stanchioned," and, at one end, "large bins for oats, ground feed, etc." (*Iowa Homestead* 1885c, 1). It is by the use of such hay barns and other labor saving devices, foresaw one writer, that "the Iowa farmer is to attain supremacy in the beef markets of the world" (1885a, 4).

A second message to prairie farmers was that "a great deal of useless lumber is put into barns." They read that "the fashion of timbered countries prevails too much, that of building barns with immense sills, posts, beams, girders, braces and so forth, costing heavily, and often very unhandy." The inexpensive way to get the needed shelter was to build a hay barn that would "shed over your hay in the center and shed the sides for stock" (*Iowa Homestead* 1889a, 8).

By May 1889, the editor of the *Iowa Homestead* saw "an awakening among farmers this spring to the economical importance of hay barns," and, within two months, he could see that the barns had aroused "a very deep interest" (1889b, 3; 1889c, 6). This hailed the major campaign to promote the building of hay barns. After having built such a barn at one of the *Homestead* farms in 1887, the publisher then described and illustrated it in the issue of May 31, 1889. By repeating the article again and again in issues over the next several years, along with publicizing the variations of other barns, the influential farm paper helped make the hay barn a widespread feature of farmsteads in the prairie states.

Light timbers would suffice, advised the paper: for upright posts six-by-sixes, twenty feet long; two-by-sixes, twelve and fourteen feet long, doubled and laid flat on the uprights; for rafters, two-by-sixes, sixteen feet long; for girts to nail the roof onto, two-by-fours, fourteen and twelve feet long; for braces, two-by-sixes, eighteen feet long. Posts in this barn were set in the ground to the depth of three feet, but, if the builder's "pride runs to a stylish barn," farmers could "have rock for a foundation wall" (*Iowa Homestead* 1889a, 8; 1889b).

A full front-page spread on "Barn Building" filled a spring 1890 issue. The rationale for hay barns, argued the editor, rested on the premise that a barn needed to suit the farmer's line of farming, and older eastern barns offered little for western farms.

> The original idea of these large barns was to provide a place where all the grain could be kept in shelter and threshed out on the broad threshing floors by old-fashioned machines in any weather, and at the same time the straw kept at its best estate. The introduction of improved threshers and separators has rendered these unnecessary. The small comparative value of straw, and the cheapness and abundance of hay in the West renders it entirely unprofitable to construct large and expensive barns for the protection of so cheap a product. Neither will it pay to build a large and expensive barn for the protection of cheap cattle from the storms of winter. Protection is needed . . . but it is not necessary to have a building with foundation and timbers massive enough for a grain elevator.

An economical kind of barn such as the *Iowa Homestead* had "frequently described, with shedding attached, and costing in all about $200, will protect hay and stock as well as a barn costing $1,000, and is in every way more convenient" (1890, 1).

A principal advantage of this barn lay in the weight of the hay resting on the ground, which made large timbers unnecessary. "With no burden to support and nothing but lateral pressure to sustain, the timbers in it may be very light and the only great expense is the roof" (*Iowa Homestead* 1892, 8).

From these beginnings, the hay barn rose in popularity to become one of the most frequently built barns. A special "Hay Barn" supplement to the *Iowa Home-*

stead in 1899 lauded the growing interest and varieties of barns then being built to accommodate different sizes and purposes of farms, the numbers of animals to be fed, and the financial means of each farmer. By 1917, one factory provider of such buildings identified the general-purpose cattle feeder barn (fig. 5.4) as one "so often met with in the corn and blue grass states of the Central West." In fact, the manufacturer added, "this barn is often called the typical Iowa barn, and is to be counted by thousands on farms of that State" (Gordon-Van Tine 1917, 40).

The adoption of the hay carrier and the introduction of the hay barn thus were the two leading innovations of midwestern barn development during the nineteenth century. They changed the character of barns and set the stage for what was yet to come, namely, fundamental change to the framing of barns. Here, Ohio became the center of activity.

A New Era

The many innovations between the 1860s and 1940s put barn ownership increasingly within the reach of prairie states' farmers. Affordable barns helped democratize the farmscape, making them a predictable and expected feature on every holding, whether large or small, wealthy or not. Ohio builders saw this potential, reckoning their plank-frame barns (discussed in chapter 8) to be "among the prominent inventions of the present generation" for farmers of moderate means. They were barns to satisfy "the struggling young farmer who needs a barn and wants to build at no unnecessary expense" (Shawver 1896, 104; Hickox 1902a). Meanwhile, on the western prairies of the Middle West, the development of economical feeder-cattle practices encouraged hay barns. They proved a great boon to farmers, and soon outnumbered the few transplanted big Pennsylvania or Ohio types. After the turn of the century, talk faded about the great want of barns in the Midwest. Now nearly everyone had or was about to have a barn, and that marked a great step forward.

Through all this, and up until two-story barns stopped being built, the methods and forms of their construction never did achieve exact standardization. With the coming of standard-sized lumber framing, for example, past traditions of solid frame construction receded, faster in the prairie areas where desires for affordable barns could now be met, and slower in heavily timbered parts of the Northeast where the older square timber-framing techniques were still used in new small building construction until the 1930s (Office of Education 1956, 8). Moreover, even when barn builders began adopting standardized dimension lumber, they rarely built barns the same. The reverse in fact was true; local builders experimented, applying their knowledge and experience to the new light-frame possibilities, just as they had worked to accommodate their construction techniques to the hay-carrier's potential.

Gordon-Van Tine Barn No. 439. For Materials Furnishe
for this Barn, read Class B Specifications on page 19.

Fig. 5.4. By 1915 precut materials for cattle feeder barns were available for shipment by Gordon-Van Tine Company, Davenport, Iowa. These barns also went by the name of hay, pole, feeder, and beef cattle barns.
Source: Gordon-Van Tine *Farm Buildings* Catalog, 1921

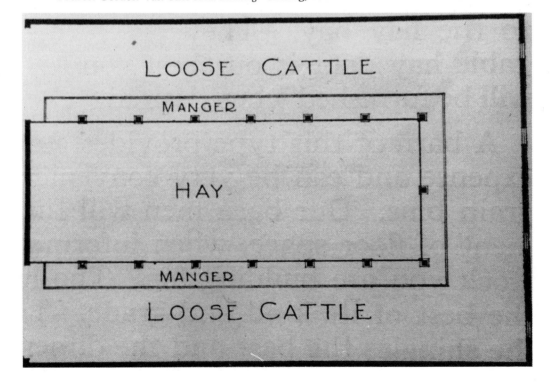

REFERENCES CITED

Agricultural Engineering. 1921. William Louden. 2(April): 89.

American Agriculturalist. 1847. A Pennsylvania barn. 6(January): 24–26.

————. 1858. Hints on farm buildings. 17(December): 360

————. 1866. Improving old barns. 25(June): 215.

————. 1867a. Slow torture at the stack. 26(April): 129; and follow-up reaction in 26(May): 169.

————. 1867c. The barn of Mr. David Lyman. 16(August): 286–87.

————. 1867d. Barn cellars. 26(September): 316.

————. 1867e. More barn-room wanted. 26(November): 402.

————. 1868a. Wintering stock on the prairies. 27(January): 15–16.

————. 1868b. Dispense with the "big beam" in Barns. 27(January): 18.

————. 1868c. Barn cellars free from posts. 27(July): 255–56.

————. 1868d. Barn building at the West. 27(September): 326.

————. 1879. Barn without crossbeams. 38(May): 182.

Bagg, J. N. 1858. Farm buildings. *The Cultivator* 6(3): 76.

Bogue, Allan G. 1968. *From prairie to corn belt: farming on the Illinois and Iowa prairies in the nineteenth century.* Chicago: Quadrangle Paperback Books.

Case, H. C. M., and K. H. Myers. 1934. Types of farming in Illinois. University of Illinois Agricultural Experiment Station Bulletin No. 403, (Urbana), 97–226.

Chasse, Ronald S. 1981. Unpublished bibliographic research of all farm-building entries contained in available issues of the *Iowa Homestead* from 1862 to 1909, compiled in 3x5-inch card files and located at the State Historical Society of Iowa, Historic Preservation Bureau, Des Moines. (Years for which issues were unavailable included 1874 and 1878–79.)

The Cultivator. 1857. Notes about the West-III. 5(3): 275–76.

————. 1858. J. N. Bagg. Farm buildings. 6(3): 76.

Giese, Henry. 1946. Trends in farm structures. In *A century of farming in Iowa, 1846–1946,* 250–61. Ames: Iowa State College Press.

Gordon-Van Tine Company. 1917. *Farm buildings.* Davenport: Gordon-Van Tine.

Halsted, Bryon D., ed. 1881, reprint 1977. *Barns, sheds and outbuildings.* Stephen Greene Press.

Hearth and Home. 1869, reprinted from letter by Henry Ward Beecher. Plan of a barn up the Hudson. 1(March 6): 165.

Hickox, C. H. 1902a. Improved barn building. *Ohio Farmer* 101(February 6): 184.

Holmes, C. L. 1929. Types of farming in Iowa. Iowa Agricultural Experiment Station Bulletin 256, (Ames), 119–66.

Hopkins, John A., Jr. 1928. *Economic history of the production of beef cattle in Iowa.* Iowa City: State Historical Society of Iowa.

Hussman, Matt. 1983. Unpublished bibliographic research of all farm building entries contained in available issues of the *Ohio Farmer* from 1859 to 1906, compiled in 3x5-inch card files and located at the State Historical Society of Iowa, Historic Preservation Bureau, Des Moines. (Years for which issues were unavailable included 1858, 1860–64, 1878, 1884, and 1887–92.)

Illustrated Annual Register of Rural Affairs. 1878. Construction of barns. 24(Albany, NY: Luther Tucker & Son): 229–53.

———. 1881. Farm buildings—country improvements. (Albany, NY: Luther Tucker & Son): 61–67.

Iowa Homestead. 1868. Building barns—advantage of barn cellars. 13(June 17): 186.

———. 1869. David Lyman's barn—Middlefield, Conn. 14(March 12): 73, identified as quotation from Agriculture Report, U.S. Department of Agriculture.

———. 1885a "Hay Barns," 30(April 10): 4

———. 1885b. Barns. 30(April 17): 4.

———. 1885c. A Marshall Co. barn. 30(May 8): 1.

———. 1889a. Farm barns. 34(February 8): 8.

———. 1889b. Hay barns. 34(May 31): 3.

———. 1889c. Hay barns. 34(July 5): 6.

———. 1890. Barn buildings. 35(May 9): 1.

———. 1892. The economy of hay barns. 37(June 10): 8.

———. 1899. Hay barns and their construction—A special supplement issue. 44(May 4): 1–10.

Lloyd, W. A., J. I. Falconer, and C. E. Thorne, 1918. The Agriculture of Ohio. Ohio Agricultural Experiment Station Bulletin 326, (Wooster), 1–428.

Northwestern Farmer and Horticulture Journal. 1859. Farmer's out houses. 4(January): 17–18.

———. 1861. Barn girts and storing hay. 6(June): 209.

Office of Education, U.S. Dept. of Health, Education and Welfare. 1956. *Light Frame Construction,* Washington: Government Printing Office Vocational Division Bulletin No. 145 (Reprint of 1931 edition).

Ohio Farmer. 1877. 52(August 18): 100.

Prairie Farmer. 1866. Our friend Toby and his barn. 18(November 3): 281–82.

———. 1867. Advertisement for Louden's horse fork attachment. 19(June 29): 431.

———. 1872. The Louden hay carrier. 43(April 27): 129.

Robertson, Lynn. 1939. *Farm buildings in relation to farm management in Indiana.* Purdue Univ. Agricultural Experiment Station, Bulletin 435 (Lafayette).

Schlebecker, John T. 1975. *Whereby we thrive: A history of American farming, 1607–1972.* Ames: Iowa State Univ. Press.

Shawver, John L. 1896. The plank barn frame: The "Shawver" frame. *Ohio Farmer* 89(February 6): 104.

Soike, Lowell J. 1989. Viewing Iowa's farmsteads. In *Take this exit: Rediscovering the Iowa landscape,* edited by Robert F. Sayre, 153–72. Ames: Iowa State Univ. Press.

Thomas, J. J. 1862. Farm buildings. In *Illustrated annual register of rural affairs*, 125–44. Albany, NY: Luther Tucker & Son.

———. 1856. Side-hill barn in the usual form. In *Illustrated annual register of rural affairs*, 184–85. Albany, NY: Luther Tucker & Son.

———. 1870. Farm buildings. In *Illustrated annual register of rural affairs*, 61–65. Albany, NY: Luther Tucker & Son.

Western Stock Journal and Farmer (Cedar Rapids/Iowa City, Iowa). 1879a. Barns. 9(April): 69.

———. 1879b. Farm talks: Jones and I. 9(May): 91.

———. 1880. In a stable. 10(December): 2.

———. 1881. Hay barracks. 11(May): 50–51.

Whitaker, James W. 1975. *Feedlot empire: Beef cattle feeding in Illinois and Iowa, 1840-1900*. Ames: Iowa State Univ. Press.

6

DAIRYING AND DAIRY BARNS IN THE NORTHERN MIDWEST

Ingolf Vogeler

DAIRYING IN THE northern Midwest is a major source of farm income. It also creates a distinctive landscape. The relative importance of midwestern dairy farms is best illustrated by a cartogram, which depicts the size of each state according to the number of dairy farms (fig. 6.1). The cartogram demonstrates the national importance of Wisconsin, Minnesota, and Michigan. Dairy farms leave their imprint on the cultural landscape because such farms include various kinds

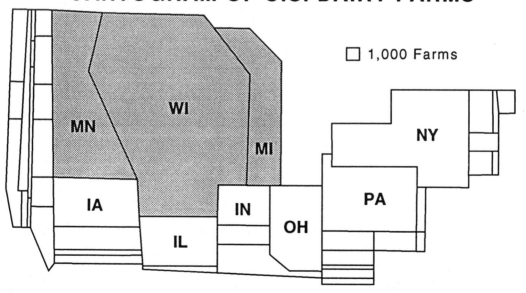

Fig. 6.1. Cartogram of U.S. dairy farms. In the cartogram, the size of the state is related to the total number of farms.

of land uses, buildings, and cattle, all of which help to define and identify the landscape. The number of dairy farms, rather than the number of cows or rate of milk production, is the best measure to demarcate the dairy landscape (fig. 6.2).

Dairy farmsteads have a distinctive regional character which has been studied by many scholars, including several prominent geographers such as Glenn T. Trewartha, Clyde F. Kohn, Fraser Hart, and Loyal Durand. Dairying requires greater investments in buildings than does cash grain farming. Large barns with attached milk houses for cooling and storing milk and tall silos supplying green fodder are the salient features of this cultural landscape. Dairy barns are ubiquitous along the highways in the northern Midwest, where their presence helps make the rural landscape interesting and attractive to travelers. To aesthetically inclined travelers, a red barn in a wintry scene, or a set of white barns against the greens of summer, is a beautiful sight. While visitors from outside the region may value these buildings only for their beauty, barns are foremost practical structures reflecting the traditional rural values of hard work, cooperation, and love of the land.

The feeling for dairy barns has been captured by Rippley (1977), and although he wrote only of Minnesota, much of what he wrote applies equally well to most of the Midwest. "One of the aesthetically pleasing features on the rural Minnesota landscape is the variety of barns. Barns eventually came to dominate the horizon of the American dairy belt. The great dairy barns of the northern, winter-plagued U.S. states are, in a manner of speaking, the New World's cathedrals" (5). However, he pointed out, "The big American barn . . . is a fading phenomenon on the Minnesota horizon. Ignored, forgotten, no longer constructed, Minnesota's majestic dairy barns are gradually shrinking back to the earth" (Rippley 1977, 1).

Huge barns remain characteristic of the northern Midwest, nevertheless. In the South, small outbuildings and simple shelters are adequate for domestic animals, and in the western plains, range cattle are protected near stacks or in open-ended sheds. Even in the heart of the corn-soybean belt, large barns are not the necessity they are in Minnesota, Wisconsin, Michigan, and the rest of the dairy belt.

> Giant-sized barns have enabled farmers to mock the short growing season because they could store up enough feed for the nine-month siege of barren cold. Surely the merciless weather more than any other factor has stocked the Minnesota horizons with beautiful and regal barns (Rippley 1977, 4).

All farm outbuildings perform specific functions and often have distinctive forms. These functions and forms have evolved as the American farm economy has evolved. When U.S. agriculture was industrializing, farm magazines, farm building companies, and government agencies were promoting more efficient ways of doing things, including dairying. As the Midwest became the center for dairy farming, this region produced a host of publications dealing with dairy barn design, construction, equipment, and practices. Although the number of dairy

100

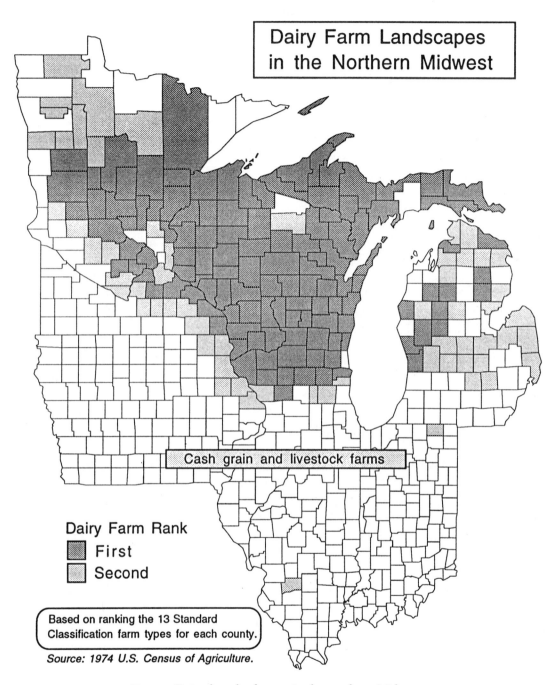

Fig. 6.2. Dairy farm landscapes in the northern Midwest

farms has declined dramatically, especially since the 1950s, and newer dairy technologies have emerged, earlier patterns are still very much present in the cultural landscape.

BARN BUILDING MATERIALS

As dairy farming spread into the northern Midwest during the late nineteenth century, most of the pioneer structures, which were often log, were replaced by new dairy barns, and older buildings were used for other activities, especially to house young stock, horses, and, later, tractors and mechanized equipment. Increasingly large dairy herds and more stringent sanitary requirements often meant that updating of older facilities was impractical. New barns were predominantly board-sided, plank-frame structures. Usually, boards were nailed side-by-side; or less often, vertical boards were overlapped, in a method known as board and batten, to better protect the interior of barns from rain, snow, and wind.

The earliest barn basements were constructed of locally available building materials, usually either fieldstone or quarried stone. In the later nineteenth century, some barn walls were even built of bricks, and, less commonly, of "stovewood" (Tishler 1979). Such construction is also sometimes termed "cordwood" or "stackwood." Northern Wisconsin, especially the Door peninsula, contains the largest number of such structures (Tishler 1982). Stove-length pieces of oak or cedar were laid on their side in mortar, similar to laying bricks. In the early 1900s, tile blocks became popular for some barn basements, silos, and even, sometimes, for barn walls.

In southern Minnesota, fieldstone was less common than limestone for foundations and barn walls; in Wisconsin, the former was more common. Irish immigrants in southern Minnesota around Cannon Falls built many limestone-walled barns (Rippley 1977). By the 1910s, homemade concrete was being used. In many parts of the glaciated Midwest, sand and gravel are readily available, and in the past, were used to mix concrete directly on farms (White and Griffith 1916). By the 1920s, barn basements were being built out of concrete or tile blocks. For example, a dairy barn in Springfield, Minnesota was constructed in 1926 with tile bricks from the A. C. Ochs Brick and Tile Company (Wells 1976). Barns with similar foundations dot the landscape of the dairy belt.

PLANS AND CONSTRUCTION

One important early influence on modern barn designs in the dairy belt was the Department of Agricultural Engineering, University of Wisconsin, Madison, which published five detailed drawings and a list of materials necessary for various kinds of dairy barns (White and Griffith 1916, 29–32). Three were *general purpose* barns, the fourth was a *dairy* barn, and the last a *pioneer* barn. Barn sizes varied from one that was thirty-six-by-eighty-four-feet long, used to house twenty-two head of cattle and six horses, and containing a calf pen, a bull pen, and two box stalls; to a thirty-six-by-eighty-six-foot long barn with a silo off to the side; to a thirty-four-by-fifty-six-foot barn designed for an 80–120 acre farm with four horses and fourteen head of cattle.

Although the horses have gone and the number of cows has increased, the layout of dairy barns dating from these decades reflects the basic construction and floor plans seen in dairy-belt areas today (fig. 6.3). One plan, explicitly identified as a dairy barn, called for a separate hay and feed shed attached to a one-story, forty-four-cow-capacity barn, but this design was never very popular.

The James Manufacturing Company of Fort Atkinson, Wisconsin, was

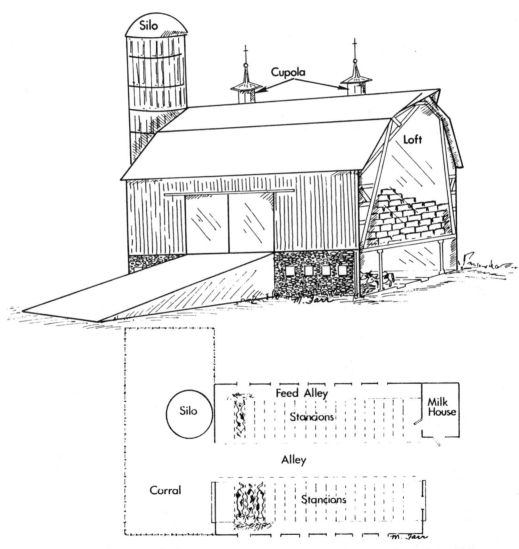

Fig. 6.3. Cut-away dairy barn and floor plan. Raised or basement barns are ideally suited for dairying. Hay from the upper stories is lowered through chutes to the cows below. The adjacent silo(s) provides the silage for winter feeding to maintain high milk production. Milk is collected via plastic pipes and stored in the milk house, which is attached at one end of the barn.

formed in 1906, and by 1914 claimed to be "the largest exclusive barn equipment manufacturer in the world" (*The James Way* 1918, 304). *The James Way* book demonstrated how to build and equip practical, up-to-date dairy barns in the late 1910s (12), and included numerous photographs of impressive looking barns from across the United States. At the back of the book, a partial list of users of James equipment is given. The longest lists in the Midwest, in order of length, are from Michigan, Iowa, Minnesota, Ohio, and Wisconsin. *The James Way* is a good source for barn construction techniques. It suggests several important factors which affect the appearance of dairy barns and the cultural landscape of this farm type: site, size, windows, framing, and roof details.

Barns should be at least two hundred feet from farmhouses and located so that prevailing winds do not carry barn odors toward the house. Usually a location at one side and somewhat to the rear of the house is best. Driveways to the barn should not be close to the house and preferably should be screened from the house by lawn and trees (White and Griffith 1916).

Because "sunlight is the best of all disinfectants," the long sides of barns should be aligned in a south-north direction to permit the maximum amount of sunlight to reach the interior of barns (White and Griffith 1916, 15). In the northern latitudes this orientation is particularly important to maximize the low-angle of the sun in the winter months. Also, barns oriented north and south are generally cooler in the summer, as the prevailing winds from the south and southwest create a draft through the structure.

"South windows are always excellent, but, unless numerous, do not admit as much light on all parts of the barn as when placed on both east and west sides" (*Farm Buildings* 1919, 31). Several technical sources agree that the amount of lighting required in barns is four square feet of window glass for each animal, or one square foot of glass for twenty square feet of floor space. The long dimensions of all windows in barns should be vertical, not horizontal, to allow light to penetrate interiors to the maximum depth (*Farm Buildings* 1919, 31). Warm basements can be assured by building into a hillside. In addition, barnyards should have natural drainage to permit water to run away from structures.

Burnett (1913) argued that dairy barns with two rows of stanchions for cows should be about thirty-six feet wide. Barns were built as wide as forty-two feet, but such buildings made for cold stables in the winter and because of their large area wasted time when chores were done (Burnett 1913). The story-and-a-half barn provided adequate storage space, particularly for baled hay, but the full, two-story barn gave far greater storage capacity in proportion to cost. White and Griffith (1916) showed several typical barn sizes: forty-two-by-thirty-six-foot gable-roofed barns, sixty-by-forty-foot gambrel barns, and one hundred-by-forty or fifty-foot gothic barns. These dimensions resulted in the rectangular buildings still so characteristic of dairy areas.

Several minor design features characterize traditional barns throughout the dairy belt. In the late nineteenth century, cupolas were commonly used as decoration on Italianate houses, sheds, and barns, although only a few northern midwestern dairy barns have cupolas, which are more characteristic of older barns in the

East. Dormers were used to provide light and ventilation to the hayloft as well as to improve the appearance of barns. Midwestern dairy barns commonly have sets of lightning rods along the ridge pole, but these frequently are not maintained. "Many godly farmers believed that lightning was God's will" (Sloane 1967, 88) and so refused to use lightning rods. Some scientists argued that the heat of fresh hay attracted electricity and that a good ventilator would repel lightning. Therefore, farmers who refused "heathen" lightning rods often accepted the cupola ventilators.

Roof Types

Barns with gable roofs, the simplest to build, are normally the oldest. However, by the beginning of the twentieth century, when dairying became a midwestern specialty, gambrel-roofed barns had become the standard (see chapter 8). The advantage of the gambrel over the gable roof is increased hay storage area without increased height. Ideally, the height of the gambrel roof should be equal to half the width of the building.

The types of roofs on dairy barns reflect the changing need for more storage space and, therefore, also frequently identify the age of the buildings. The type of barn roof determines square feet of loft profile: one-third gable provides 216 square feet; half-pitch gable, 324; and gambrel-roof, 490 (fig. 6.4). Three barns, each eighty feet long and thirty-six feet wide, with these three roof profiles, will contain for hay storage: 17,280, 25,920, and 39,200 cubic feet, respectively. At 512 cubic feet of hay per ton, the barn capacity measured in tons of hay ranges from 33.7, to 50.5 and 70.6, respectively (*Farm Buildings* 1919, 23–24). Despite these figures, gable roofs were still being built until 1916 in Minnesota; gothic-roofed barns until 1929; and gambrel roofs thereafter (Wells 1976).

Perfected in the 1920s, round-roofed, gothic-roofed, or rainbow-roofed barns had even more loft space and, therefore, were very suitable for livestock, or dairy, farming. Farmers could store more hay in round-roofed and pointed gothic-roofed barns than in gambrel-roofed ones. The gothic roof design, with its pointed top, and the rainbow roof, with its flatter top, were promoted by agricultural experiment stations. Local lumberyards provided preassembled rafters for these roofs shapes which were most popular in the late 1910s and 1920s. As freestanding structures in the dairy belt, these barns are heavily concentrated in western Wisconsin and in the Upper Peninsula of Michigan, where they were erected when this last-settled part of the upper Great Lakes was replacing frontier-stage structures (Noble 1984). Throughout the dairy region, round-roof barns were more often additions to older gable- or gambrel-roofed barns.

Since the 1950s, low-height, gable-roofed, pole structures have become the dominant type of barns built. These buildings consist of a rectangular set of poles sunk into holes excavated in the ground. The siding consists of metal sheets hung on the poles. Although in the nineteenth and early twentieth centuries, barns were built to last for several generations, pole barns are not expected to last more than forty to fifty years.

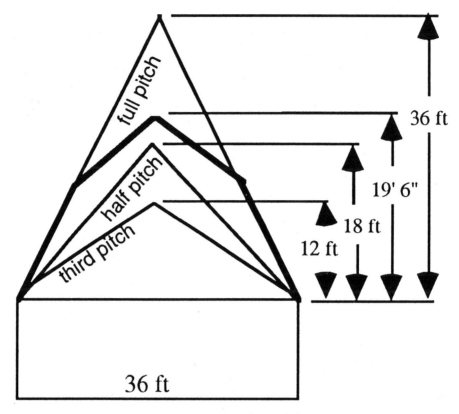

Fig. 6.4. Barn roof pitches and shapes

BARN TYPES AND THEIR DISTRIBUTIONS

In his study of the distribution and diffusion of barns in northeastern North America, Noble (1984) included Wisconsin and Michigan, but not Minnesota. For these two states—and, by extension, also for Minnesota—only five barn types, representing 25 to 100 percent of all barns per county, are important in the northern midwestern dairy region. Although English and German barn types occur only in a few places within the dairy region, raised or basement and Wisconsin barn types are distributed throughout. Round roof barns are scattered thinly across the entire region.

The design for English, or three-bay, barns was brought to the northern Midwest by settlers from New England and New York. This barn type is discussed more fully in chapter 3. Noble (1984) argues that, in the dairy regions, single-function English barns are no longer common because they did not allow for the dual function of animal shelter and grain storage and processing.

The basic German barns are considered in chapter 4. County agents report that only the northwestern corner of Wisconsin has this type of barn and that none are found in Michigan (Noble 1984), but other studies indicate that eastern and central Wisconsin also have forebay barns (Ensminger 1992).

Only two barn types, raised or basement and Wisconsin, compete for primacy in the Great Lakes region. Raised or basement barns are an elaborated form of the simpler, three-bay English barn, and, therefore, are more suited to dairy operations. Hence, these barns are common over large areas of both Wisconsin and Michigan (Noble 1984). Adding a straw shed over a basement further expanded not only the hay storage capacities of the structure, but also the herd capacity.

In the last quarter of the nineteenth century, the Agricultural Experiment Station at the University of Wisconsin, Madison, was promoting an improved barn design, one better suited for the growing dairy industry of the state (fig. 6.5). "Wisconsin dairy barns are normally only about 35 feet wide and often 100 feet long" (Noble 1984, 46). The longer versions result in noticeably rectangular shapes. These barns characteristically have rows of windows along the basement walls. Not only is much more light admitted, making milking, feeding, and manure removal easier for farmers, but the greater sunlight also promotes more hygienic conditions. In Wisconsin and the northeastern portion of Michigan,

> More county agents reported more occurrences of this barn than of any other except the raised three-bay, which may well confirm the effectiveness of this barn for dairy farming. In many counties of Wisconsin, between half and three-quarters of all barns are of this type. (Noble 1984, 61)

Fig. 6.5. Plank-frame dairy barn with additions in Emerald Township, Wisconsin. To the original gambrel-roofed barn a gothic-shaped barn and a pole barn have been added. In addition, the three silos reflect the evolving designs, materials, and heights of silos. The two short ones are made of poured concrete and cement blocks, and the newest and largest one is in the back.
Photo: I. Vogeler

Pole barns, which were developed in the eastern Midwest, are the newest types of barns in the dairy region. As a recent innovation, pole barns are associated with prosperous agricultural areas where farmers can borrow enough capital to build new buildings. Originally, dairy farms usually were not very representative of such prosperous areas. Pole barns are built today in the dairy region because they are cheaper to construct and maintain, and easier to use, than the multistory barns built only several decades ago. Most of Michigan, except the Upper Peninsula, has a large number of these one-story structures, but as a percentage of all barns, pole barns are not important in the heart of the northern midwestern dairy region of central Wisconsin and Minnesota (see also chapter 11 for additional material on pole barns).

SILOS: KINDS AND MATERIALS

Silos are a conspicuous and central feature of dairy farms. As the center of dairy farming shifted from New England and New York to the northern Midwest, so did the concentration of silos. By 1880, silos had appeared in Wisconsin; by 1882, in Michigan; and by 1884, in Minnesota (Noble 1984). By 1924, Wisconsin had more silos (100,060) than any other state. New York and Michigan only had 53,300 and 49,000, respectively (Noble 1984).

Wisconsin has been a pioneer in the design of silos. The first stone silos apparently were built in Michigan and in Wisconsin (Sloane 1967). In 1880, L. W. Weeks built an above-ground silo in Oconomowoc, and Arthur McGrevch had what was claimed as the world's largest silo built in 1898 at Lake Mills. It was sixty-four feet in diameter and sixty feet high, and held as much corn as could be raised on two hundred acres of land. By the late 1880s, circular cement silos were being built in Wisconsin (Noble 1984).

Initially, square and rectangular silos were built inside barns. Round wooden silos constructed above ground and attached to barns became popular after the 1890s. With silage, farmers could keep larger herds of dairy cows during the winter, and the cost was lower than with dry feed. Nevertheless, many arguments were made against this new storage technology and silage: cows would lose their teeth, calving would be difficult, and silage would burn out cows' stomachs and affect the quality of milk. Some even claimed silage made cows drunk, an argument which appealed to many temperance-oriented farmers. As late as 1908, a few creameries still refused to accept milk from farmers who fed their cows silage (Vogeler 1978,132).

Few square wooden silos are left, but the many round silos, which were perfected in the 1890s, come in many heights, widths, and materials. During the 1910s, round wooden-stave silos were replaced by masonry, poured-concrete, and cement-stave silos. Farm building-design handbooks recommended that silos be placed at the end of the "feeding alley," or the end of barns (Wooley 1946), and this is where most dairy silos are indeed found. Alternatively, silos were placed on the long side of barns.

By the late 1940s a new kind of silo appeared, the blue-and-white, thermos-like Harvestores. They were constructed of fiberglass bonded to sheets of metal, and perfected in Wisconsin. A glass-coated steel beer vat, erected on Swiss Tom Farms near Beloit in 1945, served as the prototype. The Harvestores were first exhibited at the 1948 Wisconsin State Fair, because shortages of steel during World War II had delayed their wide utilization. The glass-coated surface prevented silage from freezing and rust from forming, and because the container was air-tight, silage could not spoil. Augers, derived from coal-mining equipment, were used to bore the silage out at the bottom of the silo, a great change from earlier top-unloaded silos. A large plastic bag at the top of the structure allowed changes in gas pressure to be equalized and to take up the space vacated by removed silage.

Today, these distinctive blue silos are found throughout the Midwest dairy region, especially in Wisconsin, Minnesota, and the southern half of Michigan, where large dairy operations justify their high cost. Indeed, Harvestores are good indicators of high-value farming areas and high farm indebtedness, because the initial investment is about twice as much as for similar-sized cement silos. The dairy farmsteads of the southern part of the Midwest dairy region are the biggest and most prosperous, frequently characterized by two or more Harvestores. In the northern parts of the region, dairy farmsteads reflect the harsher physical and economic conditions of farming; hence Harvestores are generally absent. Nevertheless, every dairy farm has one or more silos, and many have three or four, although they may be of different ages, heights, and building materials (see fig. 6.5 page 107).

MILK HOUSES

Milk houses attached to dairy barns are another distinctive and important element of the dairy landscape. Originally, primitive spring houses provided the cleansing and cooling needed for dairying. Later, empty milk cans were washed in an interior "wash house" and the milk also was stored there temporarily.

No dairy barns in New York state had exterior milk houses in 1881, as documented by contemporary photographs (Halsted 1983). By 1915, at least one source, *Agricultural Drawing and the Design of Farm Structures*, indicated no milk houses were being built (French and Ives 1915). However, about this time, farm books began to promote separate milk storage facilities.

> A milk room should be located near, but preferably not inside the dairy farm. The entrance of the milk room, it is often urged, should be gained from the barn only after going entirely out of the stable. Milk, of course, is easily contaminated by odors. This room could be conveniently located underneath the barn bridge or near the entrance to the barn. (White and Griffith 1916, 23)

When milk was stored and transported in milk cans, milk rooms were inside barns. However, after 1945, separate milk houses for washing equipment and storing milk were used widely, dictated by various state laws designed to ensure an uncontaminated milk supply. After World War II, separate milk houses and bulk storage containers became common. Large-scale dairy farmers have shifted since the 1960s to labor-saving, automated pole-barn, milking parlors, with pipelines to bulk storage tanks.

MAP SYMBOLS AND FIELD EVIDENCE:
BARN SHAPES AND FUNCTIONS

The distinctive narrow-width Wisconsin-type barns have a strongly rectangular plan. As farmers increased their dairy herds, these barns could easily be enlarged, usually by further elongating the structures.

If the distinctive rectangular form of dairy barns can be identified on topographic maps, such maps might be useful in identifying the extent of dairying at the time of the map's issue. To that end, topographic maps at a scale of 1:24,000 were selected from across counties with concentrations of seven thousand or more dairy cows per county—in Minnesota (eight maps), Wisconsin (twenty-four maps), and Michigan (seven maps). The number of dairy cows per county in these three states and the location of the topographic traverses are shown on figure 6.6.

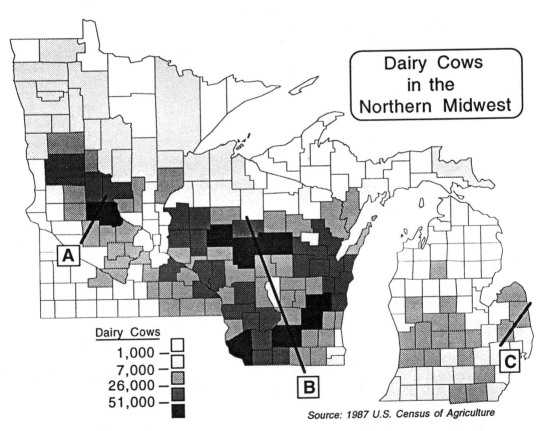

Dairy Cows
in the
Northern Midwest

Dairy Cows
1,000 —
7,000 —
26,000 —
51,000 —

Source: 1987 U.S. Census of Agriculture

Fig. 6.6. Dairy cows in the northern Midwest are highly concentrated in only a few counties in Wisconsin and Minnesota. Michigan has noticeable fewer cows. Topographic maps were selected from three traverses through the highest dairy cow counties in each of the three states.

110

The number of rectangular and square outbuildings, shown as white shapes associated with houses, black squares, were counted for each one-mile by six-mile strip on each map (fig. 6.7). Eight strips one-mile wide and six-miles long were examined on each of the thirty-nine maps. By dividing the number of buildings in each strip by six, the number of buildings per square mile could be estimated.

Wisconsin proved to have the highest density of rectangular barns per square mile with 8.3. Michigan has 6.5, and Minnesota only 3.8. Total density of all barns (i.e., both rectangular and square) per square mile reflects the same rank order, but gives less difference between the three states: 13.7 in Wisconsin, 12.5 in Michigan, and 10.5 in Minnesota.

The distribution and relationship between rectangular and square barns were examined in these three traverses. Rectangular buildings seem to be largely found in counties with large numbers of dairy cows (fig. 6.8). Overall, the frequency of square barns varies independently of rectangular barns in each traverse. The number of rectangular barns decreases markedly as the amount of land in forests, bogs, ponds, and lakes increases, yet square barns continue to be common (see fig. 6.9 p. 113). For example, in the low dairy cow counties of Juneau and Adams in Wisconsin's sand plains, rectangular barns almost completely disappear, yet square barns are common, albeit fewer than in the more productive areas to the north and south (see fig. 6.10 p. 114). An analysis of 298 buildings taken from these traverses shows that the correlation between square and rectangular buildings is very low.

The relationship between dairy cows and rectangular-plan buildings on maps was tested by correlating the number of dairy cows, in each county through

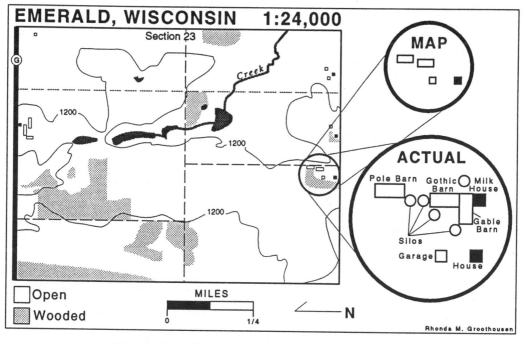

Fig. 6.7. Dairy farmstead: Map symbols and actual layout

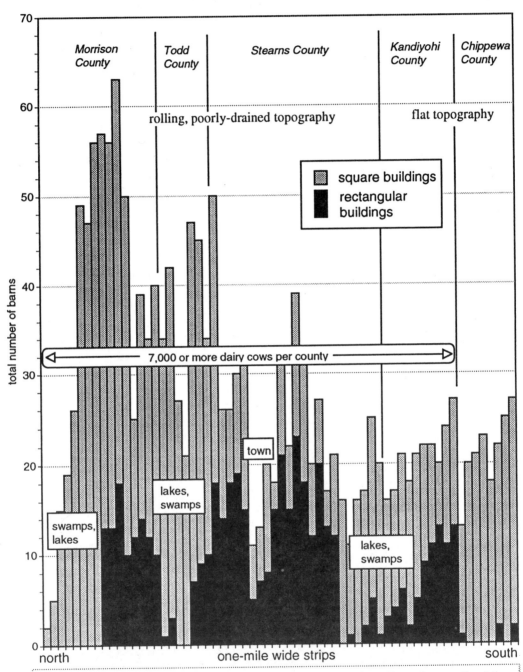

Fig. 6.8. Barn shapes on farmsteads across Minnesota's dairy region

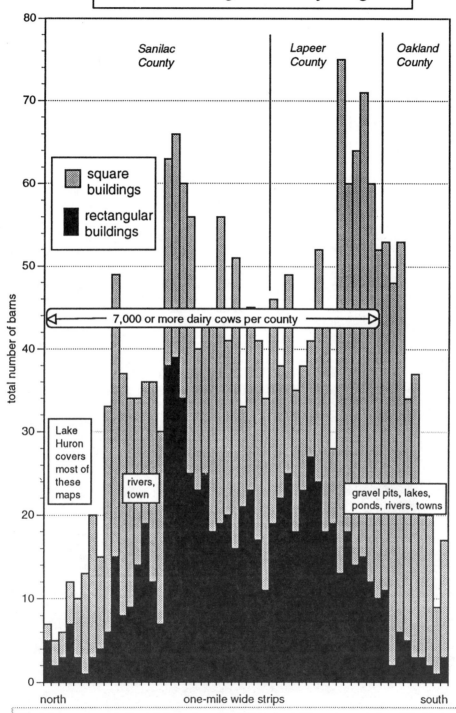

Fig. 6.9. Barn shapes on farmsteads across Michigan's dairy region

Barn Shapes on Farmsteads
Across Wisconsin's Dairy Region

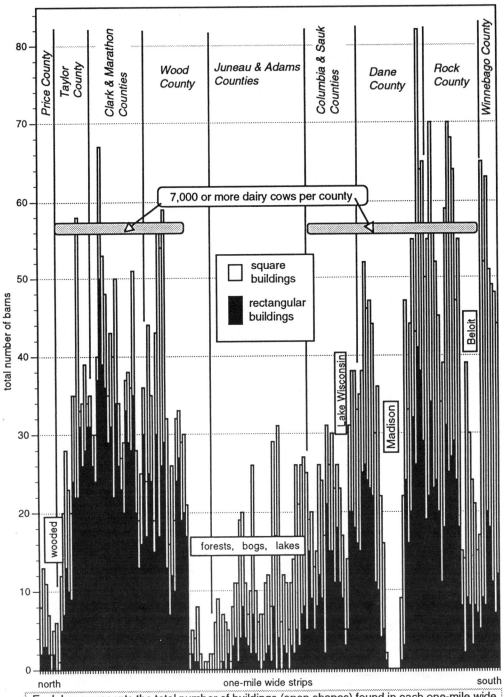

Fig. 6.10. Barn shapes on farmsteads across Wisconsin's dairy region

which the map traverses passed, with the number of rectangular and square buildings. All dairy cows in a county were correlated with only a sample of barns in each county. Although the number of counties in this study is probably too small for one to have a great deal of confidence in the statistical analysis, the trends and significance levels of the correlation coefficients do confirm the topographic data and subsequent field checks. The correlation between rectangular barns and dairy cows in Wisconsin is strong and statistically significant, whereas the relationship with square barns is very weak and not statistically significant (fig. 6.11).

The Minnesota data show similar results: a significant, highly correlated relationship between dairy cows and rectangular-plan barns, and the reverse for square buildings. The Michigan data show no statistically significant results. Although the function of buildings cannot be determined by their shape on maps, rectangular-plan buildings in counties with large numbers of milk cows invariably are dairy barns. Associating rectangular buildings in these rural areas with dairy farms is, then, a very conservative technique of identifying and counting dairy barns.

The best way of testing whether a direct relationship between rectangular barns and dairy cows exists would be to randomly select several counties in high- and low-dairy cow areas in each of the three dairy states and to count all the structures on all the maps. This would be extremely time-consuming. For example, although thirty-nine topographic sheets were examined for these traverses, this many sheets would have to be examined for one county (Marathon) in Wisconsin alone!

In order to provide some ground truth, forty-two farmsteads were randomly selected on the Emerald and Jewett topographic sheets (1:24,000) in St. Croix County, Wisconsin, to test the relationship between the shape of rural buildings on maps and the ground. Few barns are exactly square, i.e., have dimensions of 1:1. Field work indicates that barns shown as squares on the maps varied in ratios from 1:1.5 to 1:3.5, and that barns shown as rectangles had ratios of 1:4.0

Figure 6.11
Dairy Cows and Barn Shapes in Selected Counties

	Minnesota	Wisconsin	Michigan
counties	5	11	3
average cows/county	12,091	33,838	12,091
average rectangular barns/county	95	210	243
average square barns/county	255	205	428
average total barns/county	350	415	671
Pearson correlation			
cows and rectangular barns	.8946	.6223	.9619
significance level	.040	.041	.176
cows and square barns	.4769	.0089	.8968
significance level	.427	.979	.292

or greater. Rectangular barns originally were either larger structures or, more commonly, smaller barns that have had several additions. The rectangular-plan barns generally indicated: (1) larger and more prosperous individual operations, and (2) when clustered together, more productive farming areas.

In the Midwest dairy regions, several other types of farm buildings are rectangular and, therefore, might appear as rectangular shapes on topographic maps. But, each is slightly different from dairy barns. Tobacco sheds, as they are called in Wisconsin and Minnesota, are narrower and often shorter (see chapter 7), and poultry sheds are longer than dairy barns. A sample of broiler houses and tobacco barns in Wisconsin were located on topographic maps. The owners of the farmsteads were identified from platbooks, and they were asked over the telephone to verify the actual uses of these buildings. Although tobacco sheds are easily identified in the field, they are not distinctive on topographic maps; the differences in dimensions are not sufficiently large enough to show up on the maps. Broiler houses, on the other hand, are clearly differentiated on maps; they are noticeably longer than rectangular dairy barns.

Because the topographic maps used for the traverses were published from the mid-1970s through the 1980s, the structures still standing are not always the same as shown on the maps. Some old barns are gone, but some new pole barns have been erected. The map evidence and the barn count on the ground shows that, in the sample area and throughout the Midwest dairy region, dairy farming was once much more important than it is today. The number of barns actively used for dairying is certainly fewer. Government agricultural statistics, of course, confirm this as well.

Despite their decline in number, dairy barns are memorials to past agricultural practices and indicate not only the spatial extent of dairy farming in the Midwest, but also its former intensity. The diffusion of dairy farming into the Midwest and its intensification transformed the landscape. Each transformation added an historical layer to the existing dairy landscape. Commercial dairying diffused from east to west through the Midwest, from Michigan to Wisconsin, and finally to Minnesota. Because Wisconsin and Minnesota continue to be the most important dairy states in the Midwest, the developments in these two states are more or less typical of the entire region and are discussed in detail below.

DAIRYING IN WISCONSIN

Wisconsin was the third frontier area to shift from wheat to dairying after 1880 (see chapter 3). Many Yankee pioneer settlers in Wisconsin were eager for easy profits in the new wheat areas of the Dakotas during the 1870s and 1880s. They sold their Wisconsin farms to the newly arriving Germans, Scandinavians, and Bohemians, who had no choice but to work "hard and persistently, the long year through" to make a living. To the new immigrants, milking cows twice a day, feeding and tending cows, delivering milk to the factory, and working in the fields were all in a day's work, and no greater hardship than they had left behind in Europe.

Commercial dairying was a regular business among some farmers as early as 1860. These early dairy farmers were widely scattered in southeastern and southern counties of Wisconsin. Kenosha, Racine, Milwaukee, Walworth, and Green counties were the largest per capita producers of butter. Most farmers kept only a few cows for their own use. Intensive dairying developed rapidly from the 1860s to the 1890s.

Four major influences account for this transformation: (1) New York dairy farmers settled in Wisconsin; (2) research and extension work by the College of Agriculture encouraged dairying; (3) foreign-born immigrants participated in the practical application of dairy knowledge; and (4) the short growing season discouraged reliance on grain crops. New Yorkers who came to Wisconsin in large numbers during the 1830s to the 1850s brought with them knowledge of, and skill in, scientific and commercial dairying. Prior to Wisconsin's rise to prominence in dairying, New York was exemplary for good breeding approaches and well-run dairy operations. Transplanted New Yorkers frequently headed local movements to build cheese factories and to organize breeder associations and other kinds of dairy improvement societies in Wisconsin.

The College of Agriculture at the University of Wisconsin, Madison, encouraged dairying and, beginning in 1887, provided short courses and winter classes to dairy farmers. Research at the college resulted in the Babcock milk tester, bacteriological tests for detecting diseases, and practical methods of pasteurizing milk. The college also held farmers' institutes throughout the state, the earliest in 1886, at which scientists and farmers shared experience and knowledge.

During the 1870s, several developments helped strengthen the cheese industry in Wisconsin. In 1871, refrigerator railroad cars became available to deliver cheese shipments to East Coast markets. At the 1876 Centennial Exposition in Philadelphia, Wisconsin cheese and butter rated second, bested only by New York's. By 1920, pure breed dairy cattle accounted for 1.5, 4.2, and 3.7 percent of all Minnesota's, Wisconsin's, and Michigan's dairy cattle (Pirtle 1926). Minnesota clearly developed later as a dairy state than the other two states did.

Every cultural landscape has its focal points. The Midwest dairy region has the dairy shrine. In the Hoard Historical Museum in Fort Atkinson, the history of the Wisconsin dairy industry is displayed, including W. D. Hoard's office and memorabilia, and the archives of the *Hoard's Dairyman* are housed. Hoard was an early promoter of silage and silos and of scientific breeding of dairy cows. His scientific ideas about dairy farming appeared in his magazine, *Hoard's Dairyman*. He was also active in the Wisconsin Dairymen's Association (founded in 1872 and continued until 1955), serving as president between 1891 and 1893 (Osman 1985).

DAIRYING IN MINNESOTA

Stearns County, the largest and most important dairy county in Minnesota, exemplifies the development of dairying in the state and in the northern dairy region in general. Brinkman (1988) identifies three major transformational stages that occurred in this county and elsewhere: (1) a subsistence stage up to the

117

1890s, (2) a mechanized stage from 1900 to 1945, and (3) a consolidation stage since World War II. During the first two stages, both barn and house designs changed considerably and left their imprint on the landscape.

In the first stage, small herds were typically milked outside. Only a few, small, general-purpose barns were built. Fred Peterson (cited in Brinkman 1988) points out that pioneer farms had several primitive structures grouped around farm barns, that either sheltered cattle or protected livestock feed. These structures were small and simple and used log construction methods familiar to most German and Scandinavian immigrants. After 1865, when milled lumber became available, balloon-frame construction was commonly used for buildings.

With the increasing affordability of machines, steam-powered equipment began to be used in in the second stage of commercial dairying. Pasture and fodder acreage were converted into cropland, so that more feed could be raised to assure year-round milk production. Shortly after the turn of the century, cream separators and milking machines were introduced.

The mechanization of milk production changed farm architectural forms, and this is nowhere more apparent than in Stearns County. Large, specialized dairy barns with silos appeared in the landscape in large numbers. Silos revolutionized the dairy industry by providing prolonged storage without spoilage for corn, grass, and legumes. By 1922, twelve-hundred silos had been built in Stearns County alone. During the 1920s, the Farm Bureau and county extension agents in Stearns County promoted new, efficient dairy barn designs (Brinkman 1988). Plans for barns and silos also were published by the federal government and commercial lumberyards.

PHYSICAL LANDSCAPE

The physical geography of the northern Midwest is well suited to dairy farming. The northern Midwest dairy region is characterized by a glaciated topography of rolling hills with poorly drained swamps, bogs, lakes, and rivers, and with acidic and thin soils. Only ten thousand years ago, mile-high glaciers covered this part of the continent, leaving the topography undulating or rolling with morainic deposits: outwash plains, kettle and terminal moraines, and glacial erratics. The poorly drained, often stony soils can best be used for hay and pastures—necessary ingredients for dairy farming. Farmers have left much of this land forested, and use the steeper slopes with stony and thin soils only for pasture. In 1982 the percentage of hay and pasture acreage of cleared farmland in the heart of the dairy region in Minnesota and Wisconsin ranged from 33 to 67 percent (Hart 1991).

Midwestern dairy farmers, especially in Wisconsin, less in Minnesota, and least in Michigan, produce larger quantities of milk than the New England dairy region, but rely less on milk for their overall income (Hart 1991). Specialty crops such as tobacco, canning vegetables, fruits, cash crops, and livestock production are important sources of family farm income on most dairy farms in the Midwest. As the growing season decreases northward from 150 to 110 days, the concentration of dairy cows increases (see map in Hart 1991, 164). Field work on dairy farms also is adjusted to the seasons and daily weather conditions (fig. 6.12).

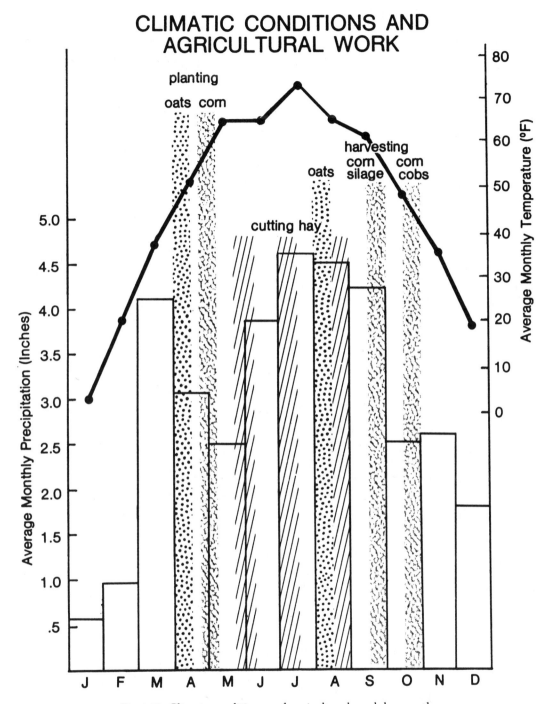

Fig 6.12. Climate conditions and agricultural work by month

Midwestern dairy farmers, in contrast to those of New England, grow almost all the feed required for their cattle. This is achieved by using a corn-oats-hay rotation system. Corn is cut while still green for silage or allowed to mature and used as grain. Oats are grown mainly as a nursery crop for hay and used as supplemental feed for cows, especially during the winter months.

In the past, milk production was much higher during the summer months and relatively low in the winter months. During the 1930s, freshening cows during the fall became common and, thus, winter milking production increased. However, state milk production per cow still varies substantially between seasons. Cows produce less milk during the fall and winter, when cattle depend on silage. In March, cows are calving and milk production jumps, peaking in May when summer pastures are available.

SETTLEMENT PATTERNS

In the past, milk usually had to be picked up once a day from dairy farms, regardless of weather conditions. Therefore, rural roads in the midwestern dairy regions have hard or improved surfaces and are very well maintained to this day. Even secondary section roads are paved.

The relatively small size of dairy farms results in a high density of rural population, which is true even today as fewer dairy farms operate larger acreages. The nonfarm rural population has increased, with families occupying farm houses and using out-buildings for recreational or part-time farm purposes while they work in urban areas. The high density of rural settlement in dairy regions is still very noticeable on topographic maps. A dense pattern of central places—e.g., hamlets, villages, and towns—dots the landscape. Until the 1960s these smaller places invariably had a creamery for turning milk into butter and cheese. Most of these are now abandoned or have been converted to other uses. Across the dairy region, they remain, nevertheless, some of the largest structures in small towns and are historical markers of a prosperous past, when the countryside was filled with numerous small-scale family farms.

A high density of fences is characteristic of the dairy region, where small-sized farms and fields require a great deal of fencing. Formerly, cows were sent out to pasture after each milking, but today most dairy farmers feed their cows in or near the barns. Occasionally, a dairy herd can still be seen in the fields, but this is rapidly becoming a photo opportunity. Still, wire fences remain, especially around pastures and wood lots, since it takes more effort than it is worth to remove them. Actively used pastures frequently are enclosed only by nearly invisible two- or three-strand electric wires attached to metal posts. They are effective barriers for cows, but they do not add much to the visual landscape.

CONCLUSION: IN APPRECIATION OF BARNS

Barns, like our friends, are often taken for granted until they are gone. Now that the labor-intensive wooden hay barns of an earlier agricultural era are being replaced by steel buildings, we are beginning to appreciate the old ones. Our interest is aroused by biking or hiking in rural areas, visiting working farm and ethnic museums such as Old World Wisconsin, buying a painting or photo of barns, using barn boards for paneling living rooms, or eating at country restaurants. T-shirts and coffee mugs with black-and-white cow and cheese-head themes are popular in truck stops and boutiques alike throughout Wisconsin and Minnesota. Both locals and travelers enjoy the "Down Home Dairyland" radio show on Wisconsin PBS stations.

As the number of dairy farms decreases, many barns are being used for alternative purposes. In suburban areas and along major highways, large dairy barns are being converted into restaurants, furniture stores, garden centers, and other facilities. These converted barns, and barns with murals, no doubt are more noticed by travelers and shoppers than the thousands of plain dairy barns throughout the countryside, a tendency that reminds us that barns are so common in the northern Midwest as to go largely unnoticed. This dormant resource awaits our appreciation.

ACKNOWLEDGMENTS

Rhonda Groothousen drew the farmstead diagrams. Elizabeth Manor counted the farm structures on the topographic maps. Both are undergraduate geography majors at the University of Wisconsin-Eau Claire. William Laatsch provided the initial bibliography.

REFERENCES CITED

Arthur, Eric, and Dudley Witney. 1972. *The barn: A vanishing landmark in North America*. Toronto: McClelland and Stewart.

Bastian, Robert. 1975. Southeastern Pennsylvania and central Wisconsin barns: Examples of independent parallel development? *The Professional Geographer*, 27(2): 200–204.

Brinkman, Marilyn, 1988. *Bringing home the cows: Family dairy farming in Stearns County, 1853–1986*. St. Cloud, MN: Stearns County Historical Society.

Burnett, Edward. 1913. *Modern farm buildings*. New York: McBride, Nast.

Clark, James I. 1956. *Wisconsin agriculture*. Madison: State Historical Society of Wisconsin.

Dairy plant directory. 1978. Madison: Wisconsin Department of Agriculture, Trade and Consumer Protection.

Durand, Loyal, Jr. 1949. Dairy barns of southeastern Wisconsin. *Economic Geography* 19(January): 37–44.

_____. 1949. The American dairy region. *Journal of Geography* 48:1–20.

_____. 1952. The migration of cheese manufacture in the United States. *Annals of the Association of American Geographers*. 42(4): 263–82.

Ensminger, Robert F. 1983. A comparative study of Pennsylvania and Wisconsin forebay barns. *Pennsylvania Folklore* 32(3): 98–114.

_____. 1992. *The Pennsylvania barn: Its origin, evolution and distribution in North America*. Baltimore: Johns Hopkins Univ. Press.

Farm buildings. 1919. Chicago: Breeder's Gazette.

Fish, N. S. 1925. The history of the silo in Wisconsin. *Wisconsin Magazine of History* 8(Winter): 160–70.

French, Thomas E., and Frederick W. Ives. 1915. *Agricultural drawing and the design of farm structures*. New York: McGraw-Hill.

Halsted, Byron D., ed. 1983 (originally published 1881). *Barns, sheds, and outbuildings: Placement, design, and construction*. Brattleboro, VT: Stephen Green Press.

Hammond, Jerome W. 1989. *The Minnesota dairy farm sector*. St. Paul: Minnesota Agricultural Experiment Station, Univ. of Minnesota.

Hart, John Fraser. 1911. *The land that feeds us*. New York: W. W. Horton.

Higbee, Edward. 1958. The economic geography of dairy farming. In *American Agriculture*, 257–84. New York: John Wiley.

Kohn, C. F. 1951. The use of aerial photographs in the geographic analysis of rural settlements. *Photogrammetric Engineering* 17:759–71.

Lewis, Philip H., Jr. 1982. *Future development imperatives for Circle City*. Madison, WI: Environmental Awareness Center.

Lewthwaite, Gordon R. 1964. Wisconsin cheese and farm type: A locational hypothesis. *Economic Geography* 40:95–112.

Logan, Ben T. 1975. *The land remembers*. New York: Viking Press.

Mather, Cotton, John Fraser Hart, and Hildegard Binder Johnson. 1975. *Upper Coulee Country*. Prescott, AZ: Trimbelle Press.

McNall, P. E., H. O. Anderson, A. R. Albert, and R. W. Abbott. 1952. *Farming in the central sandy area of Wisconsin*. Univ. of Wisconsin, Agricultural Experiment Station, Bulletin 497 (Madison).

Noble, Allen G. 1984. *Wood, brick, and stone: The North American settlement landscape*. Vol. 2, *Barns and Farm Structures*. Amherst: Univ. of Massachusetts Press.

O'Neil, Paul. 1973. How now world's greatest cow? *Atlantic Monthly* (September): 47–51.

Osman, Loren H. 1985. *W. D. Hoard: A man for his time*. Fort Atkinson, WI: W. D. Hoard & Sons.

Peterson, Fred. 1988. Dairy farm architecture in Stearns County. In *Bringing home the cows: Family dairy farming in Stearns County, 1853–1986*, edited by Marilyn Brinkman, 47–51. St. Cloud: Stearns County Historical Society.

Pirtle, T. R. 1926. *History of the Dairy Industry*. Chicago: Mojonnier Bros.

Raitz, Karl, and Cotton Mather. 1971. Norwegians and tobacco in western Wisconsin, *Annals of the Association of American Geographers*. 61(4): 684–96.

Rippley, LaVern. 1977. The American barn. *Golden Nugget* (May 18, June 1, July 6): 1–5.

Schafer, Joseph. 1922. *A history of agriculture of Wisconsin*. Madison: State Historical Society of Wisconsin.

Schuler, Stanley. 1984. *American barns*. Exton: Schiffer Publishing.

Sloane, Eric. 1967. *An age of barns*. New York: Funk & Wagnall.

Soike, Lowell J. 1983. *Without right angles: The round barns of Iowa*. Des Moines: Iowa Historical Department, Office of Historic Preservation.

The James way. 1918. Fort Atkinson, WI: The James Manufacturing Company.

Tishler, William H. 1979. Stovewood architecture. *Landscape*. 23(3): 28–31.

———. 1982. Stovewood construction in the upper Midwest and Canada: A regional vernacular architectural tradition. In *Perspectives in vernacular architecture*, edited by Camille Wells, 125–36. Annapolis: Vernacular Architecture Forum.

Trewartha, Glenn T. 1948. Some regional characteristics of American farmsteads. *Annals of the Association of American Geographers*. 38(3): 166–225.

———. 1926. The Green County, Wisconsin, foreign cheese industry. *Economic Geography* 2:292–308.

Vogeler, Ingolf. 1978. *Wisconsin*. Boulder, CO: Westview Press.

Wells, Wilson L. 1976. *Barns in the U.S.A.* San Diego, CA: Acme Printing.

Whitbeck, R. H. 1913. Economic aspects of the glaciation of Wisconsin. *Annals of the Association of American Geographers* 3(1): 62–87.

White, Frank M., and Clyde I. Griffith. 1916. *Barns for Wisconsin dairy farms*. Madison: Agricultural Experiment Station of the University of Wisconsin, Bulletin 266 (Madison).

Wisconsin agricultural statistics. 1983. Madison: Wisconsin Agricultural Reporting Service.

Wisconsin dairy facts. 1983. Madison: Wisconsin Agricultural Reporting Service.

Wooley, John C. 1946. *Farm buildings.* New York: McGraw-Hill.

7

TOBACCO BARNS AND SHEDS

Karl Raitz

TOBACCO DIFFERS FROM other crops grown in the Middle West in three important ways. First, American farmers have never produced the crop in quantity for subsistence, as they have grains and livestock. Rather, tobacco has remained a commercial cash crop since first produced and exported by John Rolfe in Virginia's Jamestown Colony after the turn of the seventeenth century (Gage 1937). In part, this has meant that farmers have been attracted by the potential profits of growing tobacco. It also has meant, however, that successful tobacco farmers were motivated to practice careful crop husbandry and, because the crop could not be marketed until cured, to pay careful attention to appropriate harvest and curing techniques. To do that required the right kind of barn (Hart and Mather 1961).

Second, unlike corn or most other grains, tobacco varieties are sufficiently different that husbandry techniques vary substantially from one type to another. This is especially evident in the curing process where flue-cured, air-cured, and fire-cured varieties must be accommodated by different barn configurations. The latter two tobacco types, air- and fire-cured, are found in the Midwest. Third, although tobacco responds differently to varying soil conditions—light sandy soils, for example, often producing a superior burn and taste—the crop has diffused to its present production regions, not so much because growers were seeking compatible or superior soils, but simply because farmers who knew tobacco culture carried it along as they moved on the nineteenth-century frontier (Whitaker 1939). Therefore, in considering the structures built to accommodate tobacco, one must keep in mind that tobacco barn forms are as much a product of the diffusion of ideas carried by migrating farmers as a pragmatic solution to the problem of properly housing and curing the crop.

Tobacco is like several Middle West crops in that, since the 1930s, production has been strictly controlled by a federal government allotment program (Rowe 1935). One important result of the United States Department of Agriculture's Agricultural Adjustment Act (AAA) was to restrict future production to a certain percentage of the 1933 acreage. Allotment program enforcement became the responsibility of the Agricultural Stabilization and Conservation Service (ASCS). Since 1936, planting restrictions have contained or "institutionalized" tobacco production within those areas in active production (Raitz 1971). Further diffusion of the crop to other areas has not taken place. Thus, the 1990's tobacco-production pattern is a result of decisions and choices farmers made more than sixty years ago.

Many burley tobacco farmers in Indiana, Ohio, and Kentucky have actively maintained their allotments, effecting little change in the producing areas since the 1930s. The cigar-tobacco growing areas in western Ohio, south and northwestern Wisconsin, and central Minnesota, have declined steadily, so that production is a fraction of what it was when the allotment system was established. Moreover, the manner in which farmers discontinue tobacco production does not seem to be random. Farmers farthest from the core growing areas, where tobacco auction markets, warehousing, and processing facilities are concentrated, tend to discontinue the crop at a faster rate than those near the center. The effect is that of a retreat toward a regional core. In old producing areas tobacco barns now stand abandoned or have been converted to other uses such as hay or machinery storage. To place the tobacco barn into its appropriate regional context, it is important to understand where different tobacco varieties are grown and how they came to be there.

THE BURLEY TOBACCO REGION

The strains of *Nicotiana tabacum* brought west from Virginia into Kentucky during the eighteenth century included a variety called *burley*, named for the plantations of Lord Burleigh where it may have first been grown (Axton 1975). Prohibitive overland transportation costs of boxes or hogsheads to East Coast markets encouraged Kentucky tobacco growers to seek a cheap water route to New Orleans. By 1803, U.S. navigation along the lower Mississippi had been secured, and tobacco production in Kentucky increased substantially. Production became concentrated within a short distance of navigable streams. Several Ohio River tributaries flow northwest across Kentucky: the Licking, Kentucky, Salt, Green, and Cumberland rivers. The government inspection and storage warehouses built along these streams served as export points for downriver shipments (Whitaker 1929). Because growers preferred the convenience of farming close by these shipping points, Kentucky's tobacco production by the 1850s was clustered along the Ohio River and its major western tributaries. Production in southern Ohio and Indiana also was proximate to the Ohio River. Some nineteenth-century Kentucky farmers migrated West, and many moved to central Missouri's Little Dixie region carrying tobacco with them. By 1860, Missouri production, centered in Chariton County, had spread to all but two of the state's counties (William Noble, pers. comm., July 13, 1991). Most of this early tobacco was heavy, dark, and oily, and was air or fire cured for export to European markets.

In 1864, a farmer in Brown County, in southern Ohio along the Ohio River, discovered light-textured plants among his seedlings. When cured, the mature leaves had a light tan or golden color and a pleasant taste. The strain, apparently sprung from mutated burley seeds, won premiums at the 1867 St. Louis Fair and

126

sold for five times the usual dark-tobacco price. Other Ohio Valley farmers began planting the new strain, now known as *white burley*. When air cured, the plant proved well adapted to a variety of products preferred by American consumers: sweet plug chewing tobacco, cigarettes, and pipe tobaccos (Whitaker 1929; Gage 1933). Today, burley tobacco is widely distributed across Kentucky's central Bluegrass Region, several eastern mountain counties, and the southcentral Pennyroyal. Production continues in southern Ohio and southeastern Indiana (Noble 1977) (Fig. 7.1).

Burley is grown also in Missouri, concentrated in Platte County, north of Kansas City. This outlier was established in the late 1890s when William Raleigh Hull migrated to the fertile, loess-covered Missouri River bluffs near Weston from the Mt. Olivet area of Robertson County, Kentucky. Other Hull family members followed, and the first burley was shipped by river to Louisville, Kentucky warehouses. Farmers established tobacco warehouses and an auction sales system in Weston by 1911 (Hull 1991).

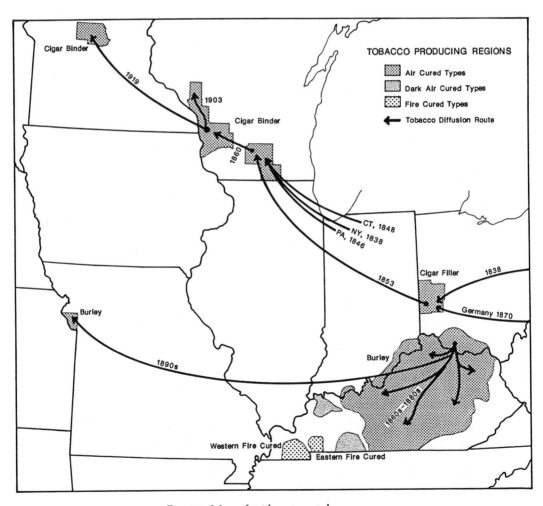

Fig. 7.1. Map of midwestern tobacco areas

The old dark tobaccos are still grown in western Kentucky. Some strains, such as *one sucker* and *Green River*, are air cured; others are fire cured. Production today is relatively small and is used in a variety of chewing and smoking products, much of it destined for export.

THE CIGAR TOBACCO REGION

The route taken by cigar tobaccos into the Midwest followed the general movement of eastern migrants moving to open lands on the expanding frontier. In the early 1800s, farmers on the limestone soils of southeastern Pennsylvania, centered on Lancaster County, grew broad- and narrow-leaf Havanna tobacco strains. At that time cigars were one of the most popular tobacco products (the blended cigarette did not appear until much later), Pennsylvania manufacturers used three different tobacco types to make cigars, and Pennsylvania growers produced the filler tobaccos. Filler tobacco formed the core, a binder tobacco leaf held the filler together, and a high quality wrapper leaf provided the outside cover.

A farmer from the Maryland-Pennsylvania producing district introduced the broadleaf tobacco strain into the Connecticut River Valley in 1833 (Garner 1951, 36). When grown on light silty soils, this tobacco produced a high-quality wrapper leaf, and production spread rapidly among the Yankee farmers in the valley (Raitz 1973). In 1838, only five years after the popular broadleaf tobacco had been introduced into Connecticut, Thomas Pomeroy, of Suffield, migrated to Ohio's Miami Valley and began farming and raising tobacco in Montgomery County near Miamisburg (Smith 1964). By the 1850s, production had spread from the Pomeroy neighborhood into surrounding counties. Within twenty years, additional Havanna strains had been introduced and southwestern Ohio had become an important cigar-filler-tobacco producing area.

The first settlers in southwestern Ohio were probably Yankees and other migrants from the northeast and mid-Atlantic states (Hudson 1984). By mid-nineteenth century, these early migrants were joined by German sectarians, who had traveled to the area by way of the National Road and the Ohio and Miami rivers. Although no documents have been found that reveal how the Germans became tobacco growers, it is quite likely that they worked as laborers or tenants on Yankee tobacco farms and so learned cigar tobacco culture from the first residents. For the German Lutheran, German Baptist, and Old Order Brethren migrants, tobacco was a cash crop that provided the income needed to purchase farm land for the family's sons. Within two generations the Germans had become closely associated with cigar-tobacco production in Ohio (Raitz 1973).

A fall in demand for cigar tobaccos after the Civil War corresponded with an increase in the demand for lighter-smoking tobacco products, especially blended cigarettes made from white burley and flue-cured Carolina tobaccos. Ohio cigar-tobacco production fell steadily, and by the mid-1960s, tobacco acreage was only about 5 percent of the 1910–19 average. Nevertheless, the link between tobacco and Germans remained. Even in the early 1970s, almost 78 percent of Ohio growers were still German or had mixed-German parentage (Raitz 1973).

A second major cigar-tobacco producing district was established in Wisconsin in the mid-1800s. Migrants from Connecticut, New York, and Pennsylvania introduced the crop in a small way in the 1830s and 1840s. But, in 1853, Ralph and Orrin Pomeroy, members of the same family that had introduced Connecticut tobacco into Ohio's Miami Valley fifteen years earlier, moved to Madison, Wisconsin. On a prairie farm southwest of the city, they raised a Connecticut variety that yielded about one ton per acre and sold for 3.5 cents per pound. Although other southern Wisconsin farmers had grown small amounts of tobacco earlier, the Ohio migrants are credited with its successful commercial-scale cultivation (Raitz 1970).

Tobacco production in southern Wisconsin soon passed to Norwegian immigrants through work relationships with established growers, much as it had among the Germans who settled in southwestern Ohio (Bufton, Hintzman, and Goodell 1951). By the time Norwegians began arriving in substantial numbers in the 1840s, the cheapest middlewestern frontier lands were in Wisconsin. Since most immigrants were poor to begin with and had spent what little they had for transAtlantic passage, they began farming as day laborers or renters. American farmers grew tobacco adjacent to Norwegian settlements in Dane and Rock counties south of Madison. By working as "sharemen" on tobacco farms, Norwegians mastered proper tobacco-husbandry techniques and then produced a crop on their own rented farms. The Norwegians, who taught other new arrivals, soon displaced the American farmers as primary tobacco producers (Raitz 1973).

By the 1850s the southern settlements around Madison had become too expensive for Norwegian newcomers. Consequently, after a year or two, many moved on to another Norwegian settlement around Viroqua in Vernon County, more than 100 miles to the northwest where land was cheaper. Norwegians carried tobacco from Dane County into these northwestern Wisconsin settlements. Certainly other ethnic groups, Germans and Irish in particular, learned how to grow tobacco and contributed to the region's production, but the Norwegians continued to dominate Wisconsin production. By the late 1960s, almost 70 percent of the Wisconsin growers still raising the crop were Norwegian (Raitz and Mather 1971).

In 1919, a Norwegian from southern Wisconsin carried tobacco some 260 miles north and west to Benton County in central Minnesota. Because Minnesota had no tobacco market, the crop had to be hauled to the Wisconsin tobacco market in Vernon County. This proved a major difficulty, so he introduced the crop to German Catholic immigrant farmers in adjoining Stearns County west of St. Cloud. The Germans proved receptive to a profitable cash crop that required very little land. By 1929, 135 German Catholics were raising tobacco in Stearns County and had formed a local grower's marketing association (Raitz 1970). Production remained exclusively within the German community. After World War II, production declined steadily, and by the early 1970s only fifteen Minnesota farmers were raising the crop (Voegler and Dockendorff 1978).

Unlike wheat, oats, and corn, subsistence crops that were ubiquitous with nineteenth-century frontier settlement, tobacco was grown successfully only where introduced to people who were willing to learn its culture and to commit labor and other resources to its production. Consequently, tobacco barns can be found only in those areas.

129

Growing Tobacco

The details of tobacco production vary with the variety being produced, but air-cured and fire-cured tobaccos have a number of production techniques in common. During the winter months, the farmer makes plans for the approaching season by selecting the field and testing soil samples, and purchasing seed and fertilizer. A century ago, before the development of modern agricultural chemicals and fertilizers, tobacco fields had to be rotated on a regular basis to retard disease and to provide sufficient natural fertility for the nutrient-demanding tobacco plant. Today, liberal chemical applications and disease-resistant plant strains make it possible to use the same field over several years. Often the tobacco barn is built beside the field for convenience in hanging the harvested crop.

As the spring planting season approaches, a seedbed is tilled and sterilized. Since tobacco seeds are tiny, more than four hundred thousand per ounce, and susceptible to a host of diseases and insect pests, they are not planted directly into the field, but are cultured first in long, narrow seedbeds. Once planted, the beds are covered with thin white muslin to protect against cold and disease or insect contamination (Bufton, Hintzman, and Goodell 1951). When the seedlings are about six inches tall and have two or three leaves, they are pulled from the bed and transplanted into the field. The transplanter or "setter" is a simple one- or two-row cart with seats and a fifty-five-gallon water drum that is pulled by a tractor. Two people sit on a one-row machine and place seedlings into a fingered wheel, which sets each plants into the dirt at a standard depth and spacing. Each plant receives a small amount of water to ensure the transplant will "take."

After planting, the field must be regularly weeded and sprayed for insects. When the plants are four-to-five-feet high, usually in July, they form a terminal flower head that must be broken off to force the plant to redirect its energy into leaf development. Removing the flower, however, often encourages new leaves or suckers to form and, since suckers do not mature and ripen properly and they divert nutrients from the rest of the plant, they also must be removed by hand. About ninety days after transplanting, the plants begin to ripen. Burley now turns a light yellow, and preparation for harvest and curing begins.

Fire- and air-cured tobaccos, both raised in the Middle West, are harvested by cutting the entire stalk at the plant base and impaling the stalk on a four-and-one-half-foot hardwood stick. Five or six stalks are hung on each stick. The curing process reduces moisture, since a tobacco plant contains 75 to 90 percent moisture at harvest, and it also initiates chemical changes in the leaf, so that particular characteristics in demand by tobacco manufacturers are achieved. Although fire- and air-cured tobaccos share many production characteristics, the curing process differs in each region. Therefore curing barns are more or less distinctive from region to region (Hunt and Brooks 1937; Hart and Mather 1961).

The Role of the Tobacco Barn

Tobacco barn shape is determined by its framing, which in turn is decided by the type and amount of tobacco to be cured. Internal barn framing is relatively consistent for both fire- and air-cured tobaccos, the major difference being the distance separating the horizontal frame members that support the tobacco sticks (Oldum 1905; Garner 1951; Hart and Mather 1961) (fig. 7.2a). The barn frame is a series of timbers or "bents" spaced about twelve feet apart (fig. 7.2b). Farmers usually refer to the twelve- to sixteen-foot space between frames as a bent, so the term refers both to the wood-frame sections and the spaces between these frames (McMurtrey 1961; Eastwood 1989). Horizontal or vertical plank siding covers the

Bent Frame

Three alley Burley barn, Platte County, Missouri. Gable entry doors. Vertical 8" by 8" posts stand on concrete piers.

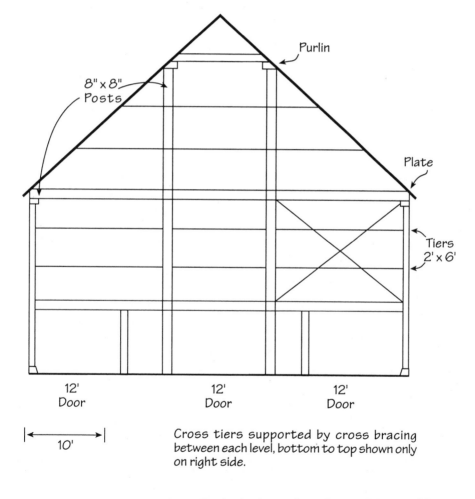

Cross tiers supported by cross bracing between each level, bottom to top shown only on right side.

Fig. 7.2a. Bent frame of a three-alley burley barn, Platte County, Missouri. Note gable entry doors, vertical eight-by-eight-inch posts on concrete piers, and cross tiers supported by cross bracing between each level, bottom to top (shown only on the right side). (See fig. 7.6 for additional description.)

131

Bent Frame

Switzerland County, Indiana Burley Tobacco barn based on English-style side entry. Tier boards not shown but run across frame at five foot spacing.

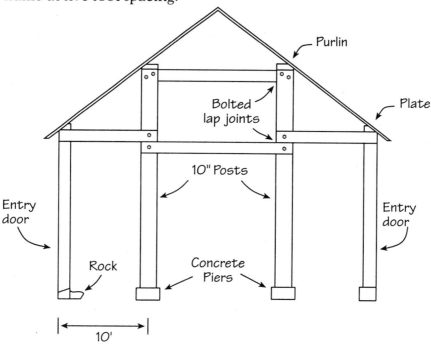

Fig. 7.2b. Vertical posts set on rocks or new concrete piers. Hewn posts joined with simple lap joints and bolts. The two center posts are not continuous to the roof, but run to plate level and are butted to upper posts. Cross bracing and tier two-by-sixes not shown.

entire barn frame, and a roof of simple rafters covered in plank and shingles or galvanized steel (often referred to as "tin") sheets completes the barn.

Horizontal crossbeams that make up each bent are spaced vertically according to the length of the tobacco stalk. The dark tobaccos may grow only to four feet, whereas burley may reach five and one-half feet in height or more. Therefore, crossbeams in the fire-curing barn may be less than five feet apart. Because many farmers use four-and-one-half-foot long tobacco sticks, the horizontal tier poles that support the curing tobacco are laid at about four-foot intervals across the beams (Fergus and Hammonds 1942) (fig. 7.3). To support the great weight of green tobacco and to resist heavy winds, hardwood, especially oak, is the preferred framing material (McMurtrey 1961), although other woods such as pine or cottonwood also are used where plentiful.

Air-cured tobacco barns have some type of ventilation doors that are opened or closed to control the humidity in the barn and the rate of leaf moisture loss. Some barns have large swinging or sliding doors, large enough for wagons, spaced

Fig. 7.3. Six men, on the tier poles of a Fayette County, Kentucky, burley barn, lift tobacco sticks over their heads. In the larger barns, the tiers may be six high, although only three are shown here. Labor shortage during harvest prompted some farmers to build smaller barns requiring fewer workers. The arrangement of bent frame, bracing, and tier poles is much the same in other air-cured barns.
Photo: James Rebmann

every fifteen to twenty feet along the sides. Others have tall narrow doors, no more than two feet wide but extending from near the sill at the bottom to the plate just below the eaves. Metal or wooden vents, one for each bent, may be placed along the ridge line (fig. 7.4) in some barns. Barns may be painted (Eastwood 1989; Duncan 1991), although many are old and any initial paint coat has long since weathered away. Others, especially the fire-curing barns, are sheathed in tar paper.

Fig. 7.4. Burley barn (bluegrass style), Switzerland County, Indiana. The full-length roof vent and horizontal sidewall vent doors suggest that this Indiana barn was built following a plan recommended by the Kentucky Agricultural Extension Service in the 1930s. The roof vent is opened and closed as weather conditions change. Rarely encountered additions include rain gutters, downspouts, and lightning rods. The shed provides additional curing space.

FIRE-CURED TOBACCO

Perhaps the oldest tobacco-curing methods are utilized in the western Kentucky fire-cured area, centering on Murray in Caldwell County. Dark tobacco, closely related to that first grown in tidewater Virginia in the 1600s, is grown here for export and manufacture into snuff and plug products. When the dark tobacco is full of "gum" and takes on a slight yellowish cast, the plant is ready to be cut. Using a tobacco hatchet or tobacco knife, a farmer will cut the stalk just above ground level. Five or six stalks are then impaled on a tobacco stick and hung, leaves down, on a scaffold or wagon to wilt. When properly wilted, the stalks are hauled to the barn to be hung.

Fire-curing barns are relatively small, sixteen to thirty feet wide, by twenty-four to forty-eight feet long, and twelve to nineteen feet up to the plate. Some barns are almost square in plan. Until about 1880, most barns were simple log pens (Killebrew and Myrick 1909). These are rare today. Modern barns usually are frame, sided with sawn lumber, and built tight enough to contain heat and smoke. Most barns have hinged or sliding doors on both gable ends, although the doors may not be wide enough to admit wagons (fig. 7.5).

Fig. 7.5. This tall, fire-curing barn stands in a grove of oaks in eastern Calloway County, Kentucky, a quarter mile from the farmstead. The stack of seasoned sawmill scraps in the foreground provides firewood, with sawdust used to control the burn and the barn temperature. Bents in this barn have four tiers, each about four-and-one-half-feet high. The narrow door suggests that tobacco is hand-carried into the barn.

The favored location for the fire-curing barn is in a low place in or near a grove of trees. The trees shelter the barn from cold fall winds and allow better internal temperature control. The farmer stacks hardwood lumber scraps and sawdust near the barn for use during the cure. Though termed "fire cure," the process is more one of heavy smoking. After the tobacco plants have hung long enough to yellow, the building is sealed, and several low hardwood fires are built along the length of the barn's dirt floor. A moist heat and smoke are produced by

135

controlling the intensity of burn with damp sawdust. Barn temperature rarely exceeds 100 degrees Fahrenheit. The leaf turns from yellow to light brown as it cures. After a week or more of firing, the fires are put out for a day or more to allow the leaf stems to turn black. Then the fires are started again and the leaf is cured dry to a brown color (Williams and Brabant 1934).

Once the tobacco has properly cured, it is taken down from the barn when it is "in order" or "in case," meaning that it is damp enough to handle without breaking. It is then stored in a pile or "bulk" and covered by a tarp for up to a month before stripping and grading. Most growers strip fire-cured tobacco by simply standing in the barn door, using natural sunlight to judge the quality of each leaf as it is stripped from the stalk. Small stripping sheds can be built as part of the tobacco barn or they may be free standing several feet away. Leaves are sorted by quality and tied into "hands" of six leaves each. The hands are laid in neat piles to await the trip to the auction market (Williams and Brabant 1934).

AIR-CURED TOBACCOS

In addition to dark fire-cured tobacco varieties, western Kentucky also produces dark air-cured and burley tobaccos. Both are cured under natural weather conditions, using only the side and roof top vents to control barn temperature and humidity levels, and both may be cured in the same barn. Many farmers in western Kentucky, however, grow two or three tobacco types, requiring two kinds of barns, one fire-cured, the other air-cured.

Burley tobacco cures best if the relative humidity can be held at about 65 to 70 percent. If humidity is too high the tobacco may turn dark and even begin to decay with a condition known as "pole sweat" or "house burn" (Garner 1951). Very low humidity, on the other hand, slows the curing process and may even stop necessary chemical transformations in the leaf. Since temperature, humidity, and time of day are usually closely interrelated, the air-cured-tobacco barn ventilators, which often occupy one-fourth to one-third of the barn's sidewalls, are used to carefully regulate barn conditions (Duncan and Walton 1991). On warm, bright days when the humidity drops, the ventilator doors are opened. In the evening, when the temperature drops and the humidity moves above 80 percent, the doors are closed. To capitalize on prevailing wind direction, many farmers have built their air cure barns on a hill or ridge crest, with one side facing the prevailing breezes to encourage air flow through the vents (Oldum 1905) (fig. 7.6). High winds during the fall curing season, however, have prompted some farmers to nail their vent doors shut to prevent damage to hanging tobacco.

Dark air-cured-tobacco barns and burley barns are similar in appearance, although the bluegrass burley barn tends to be bigger. This is in part because the burley tobacco plant is larger, requiring more cubic space, but also because burley allotments tend to be larger, requiring more overall curing room (fig. 7.7). Although the burley barn varies substantially in form from one section of the burley belt to another, it is the quintessential American tobacco barn. At twenty-eight to forty feet wide and sixty to three hundred feet long, it is often the largest building on a Kentucky bluegrass farm. Vertical sideboards extend from sill to plate, a dis-

Fig. 7.6. Burley tobacco barn, Platte County, Missouri. Burley tobacco in western Missouri is air cured in large barns that closely resemble the burley barns of central Kentucky. This three-alley barn is about thirty-four-feet wide, eighty-feet long, and twenty-four-feet to the plate. The bents are framed with eight-by-eight-inch vertical posts and two-by-six-inch tiers and cross braces. Midway along the south side is a lean-to stripping shed. Most such barns here are constructed of cottonwood or other cheap wood.

tance of sixteen to twenty-four feet. Most barns have simple gable roofs, the ridge standing thirty-two feet or more above the ground (Steed 1947; Montell and Morse 1976). A wide sliding or hinged door in each end allows wagons access to a central alley, or alleys, since some barns have two or three. A stripping room is often directly attached to the side of the barn for convenience (Hart and Mather, 1961). This shed-like appendage usually has an old iron stove that not only keeps the room warm on November days, but by keeping a tub of water hot enough to encourage evaporation, also helps keep the humidity high and the tobacco pliable enough to handle without shredding.

After the leaves are stripped from the stalks and graded, the leaves are bound together in small bales for storage until the auction markets open sometime after Thanksgiving. The stalks are piled near the barn or, because they are high in residual potash, may be spread out on a field where their nutrients leach into the soil over winter. Meanwhile, the barns may serve other functions. Some shelter feeder cattle during the winter, others are used as garages or machine sheds.

Where this burley barn form originated is not clear. Near Paris, the county seat of Bourbon County, Kentucky, a barn of this configuration was built in the 1890s and is the earliest known structure. Since the 1920s, the university agricul-

Fig. 7.7. Pennyroyal burley and dark air-cured tobacco barn. In Todd County, Kentucky, one-sucker dark tobacco is air cured in the same barns as burley. Air circulation through this two-alley barn is provided by one-inch spacing between the exterior siding planks and a continuous gable ventilator. The construction date is unknown, but predates 1950.
Sketch: M. Margaret Geib

tural extension offices in each tobacco-producing state have helped standardize barn forms through published reports and bulletins that summarize research on barn function, and plans for building barns that will produce predictable curing results (Montell and Morse 1976). Present barn design is likely the product of adopting the simplicity of the old English, side-entry, three-bay barn, to the practical needs of proper internal tobacco placement during the cure, access to the interior by tobacco wagons, and a ventilator system to control the rate of cure (Arthur and Witney 1972; Rawson 1979). Throughout the burley-producing region, barn design varies only in superficial ways. The southern Ohio burley barn is essentially the same as the bluegrass barn (fig. 7.8). In Switzerland County, Indiana, some tobacco barns resemble those in Kentucky, whereas others are based on the English, side-entry barn (compare figs. 7.4 p. 134 and 7.9).

AIR-CURED CIGAR-TOBACCO BARNS IN OHIO

The Ohio cigar-tobacco barn, or "shed" as it is usually termed, does not resemble the large burley barn, even though both are built as air-curing structures. The classic cigar-tobacco barn is as distinctive as the fire cured barn. Found in Montgomery and Darke counties northwest of Germantown, it looks like a simple, elongated machine shed with large outside-mounted sliding doors along both sides, giving access to interior cross driveways (compare Wilhelm 1983) (fig. 7.10).

Fig. 7.8. Burley barn, Brown County, Ohio. This single-alley, three-bent barn is relatively small. About thirty-feet wide and forty-five-feet long, the bent frames are positioned on concrete piles. Purlins on either side of the gable carry the rafters. A single-board vent door is inserted below the gable ridge.

The likely source for this barn form is the old Connecticut tobacco barn, itself a simple variation of the English side-entry barn (Billings 1875). The old Connecticut barn was rectangular, about twenty-four feet wide and thirty-six feet long. Wide sill-to-plate doors opened a quarter of the side to air flow. One gable end was fully open below the plate-level tie beam.

The Connecticut farmer who brought cigar tobacco to the Miami Valley in the 1830s probably erected a barn very much like the ones he knew in Connecticut. Tobacco farmers have long had an aversion to experimenting with new—and, to them, unproven—production techniques, including barn design. The crop is so labor intensive, and requires such substantial investment in fertilizer, that crop or cure failure can have a catastrophic effect on the year's income. This explains why barn form tends to change so slowly. If traditional barns had not produced successfully cured leaf, then barn form could be expected to vary, perhaps radically, from one farm or neighborhood to the next. Instead, barn form closely follows exchange-labor networks in which the best carpenter led a crew of neighbors in building a barn for a farmer who had decided to raise a tobacco crop. The barn they built was one that everyone knew would work properly. Innovation and experiment held no appeal for the nineteenth-century farmer who suspected that an unproven barn design could lead to an improper cure (Raitz 1970).

Today, the tobacco barns of the Miami Valley resemble several old Connecti-

139

Fig. 7.9. Burley barn (English side-entry type), Switzerland County, Indiana. Perhaps influenced by the English-style stock barns in southern Indiana, this barn has sliding doors on each side. The barn is thirty-five-feet wide and about thirty-eight-feet long. The bent frames are ten-by-ten-inch hewn posts originally set on flat rocks, but now on concrete piles. Ventilation is provided by the large side doors.

Fig. 7.10. Cigar-tobacco barn, Montgomery County, Ohio. Standing in a nineteenth-century German settlement, this English-type, side-entry barn appears relict, but has solid interior frame construction and is currently used to store vehicles. Though the barn has no roof vents, the doors on each side were opened as needed during the tobacco cure. The lean-to functioned as a stripping room.

icut barns spliced together. The Ohio barn is long, some of them over one hundred feet. Distance from ground to plate may be fifteen to eighteen feet, and the roof is a simple low-angle gable. Along each side, outside-mounted sliding doors, ten or more feet wide, provide access to tobacco wagons and air flow. Some barns may have as many as ten such doors on each side (Oldum 1905). Tobacco is stripped either in attached rooms, as with the burley barn, or in rooms set inside the barn.

AIR-CURED CIGAR-TOBACCO BARNS IN WISCONSIN

Wisconsin tobacco barns have several features in common with other air-cured barns. They most closely resemble burley barns in size, ratio of width to length, a gable-end door that gives access to a central alley down the length of the barn, and vertical side-wall ventilator doors. Some Wisconsin barns have stripping sheds attached. In detail, however, the barns vary substantially from the southern producing area near Madison to the northwestern area near Viroqua. Subtle variation also is apparent from one neighborhood to the next, and these variations can be used to trace the movement of farmers and tobacco across the state half a century or more ago (Raitz 1975).

Since cigar tobaccos were introduced into Wisconsin during the 1830s, 1840s, and 1850s from Connecticut, New York, Pennsylvania, and Ohio, it should not be surprising that different barn types also would have been introduced. The prevailing barn form in the southern Wisconsin tobacco district is much like that of the Pennsylvania air-cured barn (Long 1972) (fig. 7.11). Rectangular in plan, often twenty-nine feet wide and about twelve-to-fourteen feet to the plate, it has an alleyway door in each gable end, and tall, narrow, ventilator doors down each side.

From about 1900 to the 1920s, many Dane County farmers substantially increased their tobacco acreage. By 1920, some were raising fifteen acres, or more. Such an increase necessitated either a larger barn or additional barns. A popular solution was to build a large barn, well over one hundred feet in length. To decrease the wind stress on such a structure, some carpenters built them in an "L" shape. Other differences relate to farm location relative to soil types. When the first settlers from the East arrived, the vegetation of south central Wisconsin consisted of mixed hardwood forest and prairie or oak openings (Martin 1965). The glacially-smoothed hills north and east of Madison were largely forested. Farms here tended to be smaller and not as productive as those on the large prairies that were settled later, often by Norwegian immigrants. Tobacco barns on forest soils in rolling country tended to be smaller; those on prairie soils substantially larger.

Barns in the northwestern tobacco area around Viroqua, Vernon County, show subtle variations not found in the southern district. Some barns have gambrel roofs, although most have simple gable rooflines. The gambrel roofs are often indicative of a newer barn, sometimes a replacement for an original structure which may have collapsed in a strong summer storm. Many northwestern Wisconsin barns have a set of vertical ventilator doors in the gable end, between the top of the end door and the gable comb. Some barns have three doors in this position, others four (fig. 7.12). As Norwegian tobacco farmers migrated to outlying settlements in northern counties, they took with them this barn type, complete

Fig. 7.11. Cigar-tobacco barn, southern Wisconsin. This eight-bent barn stands in southeastern Dane County in the nineteenth-century Norwegian settlement on the Koshkonong Prairie. The eight-foot tall, sliding, gable-end door will accommodate a low tractor and trailer loaded with tobacco. A central alley extends the length of the barn and vertical ventilator doors on each side provide air circulation during the cure. An identical barn can be seen a few feet to the right.

with gable end ventilator doors, thus barns in Trempealeau and Polk counties are replicas of those in Vernon County, 140 miles to the south. The only L-shaped barns are in a Norwegian outlier settlement near Otter Creek in Dunn County. Here, in 1906, a migrant from Dane County built a large L-shaped barn of the same plan and shape as the large barns on the prairies, 250 miles to the south (Raitz 1975).

Tobacco production in Wisconsin has fluctuated substantially since the end of World War II. In 1968, the state's farmers grew the crop on approximately 7,700 acres. By 1987, acreage had fallen to 4,400, and production was consolidated by a small number of growers who leased allotments to raise seventy acres or more. As farmers discontinue production, often because of the lack of labor availability during transplanting and harvest, tobacco barns are put to other uses. Some are modified for use as machine sheds. Others shelter the large round hay and straw bales so common on today's dairy farms. (The round bale is also the product of rural labor shortage. The small rectangular bale required a crew of four or five to load it onto wagons and to put it up in a barn. The invention of the oversized round bale allowed a single tractor operator using a hydraulic lift to move bales from field to farm yard for feeding or storage.)

Fig. 7.12. Cigar-tobacco barn, northwestern Wisconsin. The original tobacco barn on this farm blew down, in part because of a lack of internal bracing, and was replaced by this gambrel-roofed building in the early 1950s. The barn stands south of Westby in Vernon County near the heart of a nineteenth-century Norwegian settlement on Coon Prairie. Tobacco is no longer produced on this farm (the field in the foreground belongs to a neighbor), and the farmer has converted the barn to machinery storage. To accommodate taller equipment, he recut the door openings on each end to the plate and hung new steel doors. He also cut the cross ties and braces out of each bent frame to the same height to allow clearance along the length of the barn.

Air-cured Tobacco Barns in Minnesota

Cigar-tobacco production has all but ceased in central Minnesota. Only a few farmers still grow tobacco in Stearns County (see fig. 7.1 p. 127). The barns here are reminiscent of those in the northern Wisconsin district. Even though they now are put to alternative uses, the barns can be studied as markers or data points to reconstruct the regional limits to the old production area that thrived during the early 1900s (Vogeler and Dockendorff 1978).

Conclusion

At the turn of the nineteenth century the middlewestern farmstead was a group of specialized buildings clustered near a house. Most farms were diversified, growing a variety of crops and raising different kinds of poultry and livestock, each associated with its own structure. Barley and wheat were stored in the granary; ear corn dried in a corn crib; hens laid eggs in a hen house; pigs fattened in a

143

hog house; and the farmer milked cows in "the barn." Work horses often were stabled in the barn and their main food, oats, was stored in a nearby bin, or perhaps in the barn itself.

A tobacco barn also fit into this organization of a specialized building dedicated to one major function. Nonetheless, many farmers used their tobacco barns for other purposes. In Kentucky, some farmers kept cattle in their tobacco barns after the crop had been taken down and sold. Ohio and Wisconsin tobacco barns stored machinery, the transplanter, and farmstead odds and ends. However, these uses were not part of the rationale for building the original structure; they were later adaptations.

The tobacco barn is usually the second largest building on the farmstead. The Kentucky burley and fire-cured barns often do stand in the field some distance from other farm buildings but, elsewhere, the tobacco barn is an integral unit of the farmstead. If we employed the jargon of suburban shopping-center developers, we could say that the tobacco barn is an "anchor" building, a place where activity centers, with the smaller structures subservient in function and image, as well as size. Activity in the hen house may have put meat on the table and egg money in the wife's pocket for the Saturday grocery-shopping trip to town, but the tobacco crop was often the source of cash that kept a farm family solvent. Wisconsin farmers talk fondly of the crop as a "mortgage lifter"; many paid for their property with a few harvests. So, the barn also represented security and well-being. Some farmers viewed their barns as strictly functional and made little effort to maintain or embellish them. Others kept them painted, often in the same colors as the other outbuildings. Some even used contrasting colors on ventilator doors and for door trim—red and white in Ohio and Wisconsin, creosote black and white in Kentucky.

TOBACCO BARNS AS SYMBOLS

The tobacco barn also provides the farm family a nostalgic signpost to seasons past. Few may reminisce about the hard work that producing a crop of tobacco demands: the drudgery of cutting tobacco on a hot August day; the heavy labor and danger of lifting sixty-pound tobacco sticks tier above tier, to be hung under the roof thirty-five feet above the floor; the long hours of stripping and grading; the uncertainty over whether the auction price will cover expenses; or the agonizing sorrow brought by the hailstorm that takes a neighbor's crop yet spares others. Yet, to look at the barn is to be reminded of the fun and camaraderie of family and neighbors helping in the planting and harvest, to remember those tremendous twice-a-day country meals that the farmer's wife served to the work crew, and to recall the evening's hot shower to scrub off the tobacco gum before grabbing a clean shirt and a beer.

REFERENCES CITED

Arthur, Eric, and Dudley Witney. 1972. *The barn: A vanishing landmark in North America*. Boston: New York Graphic Society.

Axton, W. F. 1976. *Tobacco and Kentucky*. Lexington: Univ. Press of Kentucky.

Billings, E. R. 1875. Tobacco houses. In *Tobacco: Its history, varieties, culture, manufacture and commerce,* edited by E. R. Billings, 405–14. Hartford, CT: American Publishing.

Bufton, V. E., A. J. Hintzman, and M. R. Goodell. 1951. *Wisconsin tobacco production and marketing*. Wisconsin State Department of Agriculture, Bulletin No. 305 (Madison).

Duncan, George A. 1991. *Recommended tobacco barn construction features*. Univ. of Kentucky, College of Agriculture, Cooperative Extension Service, AEN-58 (Lexington).

———, and Linus R. Walton. 1991. *Curing burley tobacco*. Univ. of Kentucky, College of Agriculture, Cooperative Extension Service, AEN-59 (Lexington).

Eastwood, Susan C. 1989. *Sowing down the ground: An ethnographic description of tobacco farming in Montgomery County, Kentucky*. Master's Thesis, Department of Anthropology, Univ. of Kentucky.

Fergus, E. N., and Carsie Hammonds. 1942. *Field crops management*. Chicago: Lippincott.

Gage, Charles E. 1933. *American tobacco types, uses, and markets*. Washington, DC: U.S. Department of Agriculture, Circular 249.

———. 1937. Historical factors affecting American tobacco types and uses, and the evolution of the auction market. *Agricultural History*, 11(1):43–57.

Garner, Wrightman W. 1951, rev. 1st ed. *The production of tobacco*. New York: Blakiston.

Hart, John Fraser, and Eugene Cotton Mather. 1961. The character of tobacco barns and their role in the tobacco economy of the United States. *Annals of the Association of American Geographers* 51(3):274–93.

Hudson, John C. 1984. The middle west as a cultural hybrid. *PAST-Pioneer America Society Transactions*, 7:35–45.

Hunt, Russell A., and Jesse B. Brooks. 1937. *Ventilation of tobacco barns*. Univ. of Kentucky, College of Agriculture, Extension Division, Circular No. 299 (Lexington).

Hull, William. 1991. Interview, July 5, Weston, Missouri.

Killebrew, J. B., and Herbert Myrick. 1909. *Tobacco leaf: its culture and cure, marketing and manufacture*. New York: Orange Judd.

Long, Amos. 1972. *The Pennsylvania German family farm; A regional architectural and folk cultural study of an American agricultural community.* Breinigsville: Pennsylvania German Society.

McMurtrey, J. E., Jr. 1961. *Tobacco production.* Washington: U.S. Department of Agriculture, Agricultural Research Service, Information Bulletin 245.

Martin, Lawrence. 1965, 3d ed. *The physical geography of Wisconsin.* Madison: Univ. of Wisconsin Press.

Montell, William L., and Michael L. Morse. 1976. *Kentucky folk architecture.* Lexington: Univ. Press of Kentucky.

Noble, Allen G. 1977. Barns as elements of the settlement landscape of rural Ohio. *Pioneer America* 9(1):62–79.

Oldum, George M. 1905. *The culture of tobacco.* Salisbury, Southern Rhodesia: British South Africa Company.

Raitz, Karl B. 1970. The location of tobacco production in Wisconsin, Ph.D. dissertation, Department of Geography, University of Minnesota.

_____. 1971. The government institutionalization of tobacco acreage in Wisconsin. *Professional Geographer* 23(2):123–26.

_____. 1973. Ethnicity and the diffusion and distribution of cigar tobacco production in Wisconsin and Ohio. *Tijdschrift Voor Economische en Sociale Geografie* 64(5): 295–306.

_____. 1975. The Wisconsin tobacco shed: A key to ethnic settlement and diffusion. *Landscape* 20(1):32–37.

_____ and Cotton Mather. 1971. Norwegians and tobacco in Western Wisconsin. *Annals, Association of American Geographers* 61(4):684–96.

Rawson, Richard. 1979. *Old barn plans.* New York: Mayflower Books.

Rowe, Harold B. 1935. *Tobacco under the AAA.* Washington, DC: Brookings Institution.

Smith, William E. 1964. *History of southwestern Ohio: The Miami Valleys,* vol. 1. New York: Lewis Historical Publishing Company.

Steed, Virgil S. 1947. *Kentucky tobacco patch.* Indianapolis: Bobbs-Merrill.

Vogeler, Ingolf, and Thomas Dockendorff. 1978. Central Minnesota relic tobacco shed region. *Pioneer America* 10(2):74–83.

Whitaker, J. Russell. 1929. The development of the tobacco industry in Kentucky: A geographical interpretation. *Bulletin of the Geographical Society of Philadelphia* 27(January):15–42.

_____. 1939. Human migration as a factor in the distribution of tobacco cultivation. *Geographical Review* 29(4):684.

Wilhelm, Hubert G. H. 1983. Tobacco barns and pent roofs in western Ohio. *PAST-Pioneer America Society Transactions,* 6:19–26.

Williams, M. F., and Stuart Brabant. 1934. *Curing fired tobacco.* Nashville: Cullom and Ghertner.

8

WITHIN THE REACH OF ALL: MIDWEST BARNS PERFECTED

Lowell J. Soike

LIGHT-FRAMING TECHNIQUES combined with advanced wood milling machines after the mid-nineteenth century to shape midwestern house building, enlarging their possibilities and bringing to their design all sorts of ornamentation, angles, and curves. Barns, however, continued to be built as before, with carpenters fashioning costly, heavy timber frames (see chapters 3 and 4). As large framing timber became ever more scarce and expensive, a new innovation called plank framing made its appearance. It would soon become a key transition on the way to building even lighter frames for barns.

The core feature of plank framing lay in devising ways to substitute heavy, long, square timbers with plank lumber. Once achieved, the lower priced, lighter frame techniques expanded the opportunities for farmers of moderate means to obtain barns. Thousands in both the eastern and western Midwest undertook the task of adding a new or replacement barn to their farm.

Ohio was fertile ground for plank-frame ideas to take root. Here a powerful agricultural paper editorially joined in common cause with several innovative and articulate barn builders to endorse, promote, and answer queries about the new techniques, and, overall, give voice to ideas for better barns. Between 1894 and 1903, the *Ohio Farmer* opened its columns to a quartet of vocal plank-frame enthusiasts: Joseph E. Wing (Champaign County), John L. Shawver (Logan County), Charles H. Hickox (Geauga County), and J. H. Fisher (Jefferson County). Of these, Wing and Shawver became plank framing's most persuasive and prominent advocates.

Each proponent had his own ideas about the right kind of plank-frame barn. They mutually understood two things, however. Farmers wanted to have barns with an open center to take full advantage of the new hay carrier's potential, and according to John Shawver (1896), "the growing scarcity of timber has demanded that some improvement be made in barn architecture that would require less timber" (104).

Two major forms of plank-frame construction emerged (fig. 8.1). The first, associated with Joseph Wing, took dimension plank lumber and imitated heavy timber framing, carrying the loads through posts and beams, but did away with crossbeam ties across the center of the bent. This made each part of the bent act as a cantilever. On each side of the drive floor, a long post reached from the floor straight up to the purlin plate. From this post to the outer wall ran a horizontal tie at the mow floor level, and a diagonal brace went down to the floor sill, both acting as sinews—the purlin post in tension and the bracing in compression—to hold the building from spreading. The second type, most closely associated with John Shawver, opened up the center of the barn by using at the bent, a truss of spliced plank lumber that ran from the floor sill to the roof ridge, supporting both the roof and purlin and restraining the outward thrust of rafters and pressures against the plate and walls. Since these became the two standard types from which numerous variations resulted, their origins merit discussion.

In 1893, Joseph E. Wing had carpenters erect a new type of barn on his family farm in Champaign County, Ohio. Making posts and beams of dimension plank lumber, but without a crosstie to attach one side of the bent to the other, Wing termed his open-center creation the *joist-frame barn*. His carpenters, unfamiliar with such a barn, had been "quite anxious for fear something would give way and the thing wreck itself" (Wing 1898a, 1). Wing was untroubled. His barn was soon accepting as much as one thousand pounds of hay in a single lift with the hay carrier. In the meantime, Wing began publicizing the merits of his joist-frame barn. While its substitution of spiked planks for heavy timbers saved time and money, its familiar resemblance to the older post-and-beam type of frame quickly attracted popularity (fig. 8.2).

Wing assumed that he had invented the frame. But within five years he realized from his travels that he had not been alone, for he had "seen more than one barn built on exactly the same model and built before our barn was planned" (Wing 1898a, 1). In fact, years later, one old carpenter reported having built a similar barn in 1877, although it had been from a combination of plank and heavy timber (Cox 1922, 36). Be that as it may, the barn's joist-frame name and subsequent popularity owed itself largely to Wing's promotion of the form. He found his joist frame gaining new friends every day, for it was "easily understood, all square work, and all weight borne on direct thrust of posts" (Wing 1898b, 104; 1899b, 49). He dismissed the traditional big, center-beamed barns as being outdated: "Any design that puts a cross-tie through the center of a barn is to be condemned, no matter what its other excellences may be," because it obstructs "the free movement of modern hay carriers and the use of slings" (Wing 1899a, 42).

John L. Shawver, on the other hand, took plank framing in a different and more lasting direction (fig. 8.3). A persuasive and unpretentious man with much construction experience and good writing ability, Shawver, after 1893, steadily brought forth his ideas on framing bents. He admitted "There is no harm in a little controversy when conducted in a friendly spirit." He offered his kind of barn not as "*better* than those illustrated by our worthy brothers of the square and compass (though I frankly confess that I believe it is), but [I] invite them to compare its merits with their own" (Shawver 1894, 341). His article on this frame in 1896

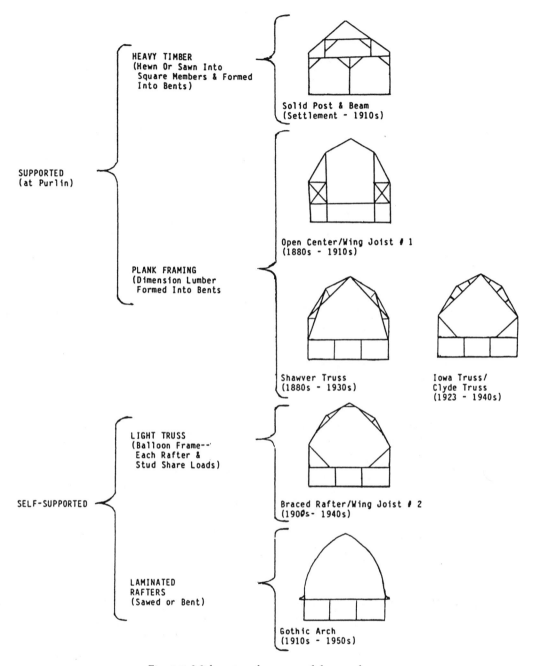

Fig. 8.1. Midwestern barns: roof-frame phases

pointed out how "the principle of its construction has been in use many years in bridge engineering" and how only a few points of weakness and instability had to be "overcome in order to adapt it to general barn building" (104).

In the face of growing timber scarcity and low prices for farm products, the plank frame, Shawver held, had come to the rescue of farmers needing economical shelter for stock. He touted seven advantages: saving of timber by using two-inch

149

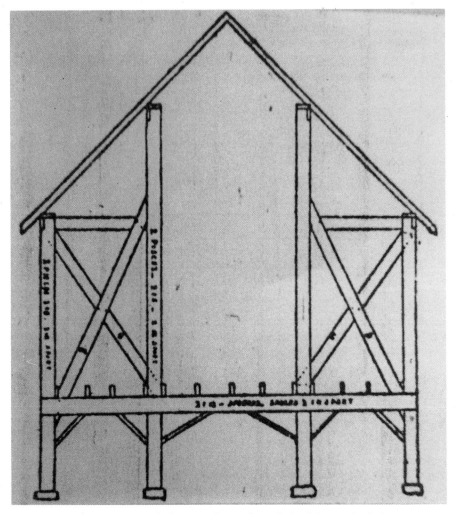

Fig. 8.2 Joseph E. Wing's popular joist-frame barn helped bring plank framing into favor. Readers of the *Ohio Farmer* regularly saw his illustrations, articles and correspondence.
Source: *Ohio Farmer*, August 18, 1898, p. 104

planks of varying widths, less chance of decay from water accumulating in mortises, no timbers in the way of hay fork or sling operations, saving of time in construction, saving of cost, less heavy lifting required during construction, and strength. "The time is coming," he prophesied, when plank barn framing "will be generally adopted, though people hesitate now, just as they did thirty years ago about building balloon frame houses." And, he added sarcastically, "I *urge* no one to build in this way. If he is one of these prejudiced fellows it would be better for him to build in the old way, so he can put three or four hundred dollars more money into circulation" (Shawver 1896, 104).

The distinguishing feature of Shawver's new plank frame was a truss arrangement which contained a long support post of two members extending from where the mow floor met the sidewall up to the purlin plate that held the roof.

150

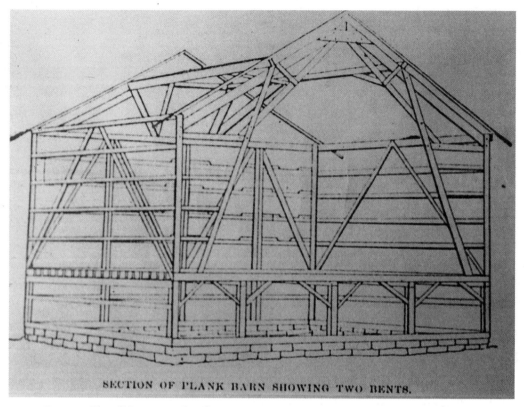

SECTION OF PLANK BARN SHOWING TWO BENTS.

Fig. 8.3. This illustration of a Shawver truss as applied to two bents of a gable-roof barn accompanied a major article on the plank-frame barn written by John L. Shawver. Source: *Ohio Farmer*, February 6, 1898

Supporting this double-member post was a single-member principal rafter that ran from the plate to the ridge. Each truss, typically spaced twelve feet apart, supported the purlin plate that carried the lower end of the upper rafter and the upper end of the lower rafter. The resulting Shawver truss gave a rigid and strong frame well suited for large barns, wide barns, and those with vertical siding (Shawver 1904; Strahan 1918).

From its early beginnings in the 1880s in Shawver's home territory of central Ohio, his plank truss method evidently expanded rapidly. By 1902 he was advertising that more than 5,000 such barns were in use. Much of the success no doubt was due to Shawver's writings in the *Ohio Farmer* and in the columns of the trade publication, *Carpentry and Building*. Further publicity for the barn came with his 1904 book, *Plank Frame Barn Construction*.

Plank-frame builders combined advocacy of their barns' virtues with attacks on what they termed "old-fashioned timber frame" barns (fig. 8.4). In comparing the construction cost of the traditional barn with his plank-frame barn, Shawver bragged, "We will use 40 percent less timber, and do the work of putting the frame together in one-third of the time" (1902a, 1; 1902c, 1). C. H. Hickox (1902) echoed the promise: "A man and a boy can attain the same results that ten men could on an old-fashioned timber frame" (1). Equally important, the apparent strength of square

Fig. 8.4. Plank-frame builders supplanted solid timber posts because the latter became too expensive to use. Overall view of framing; close-up of lumber posts.

Source: Franklin H. King, *A Textbook of the Physics of Agriculture*, 1914

timber construction was a myth, Hickox charged. Unlike solid framing, plank framing "preserved the full strength and quality and security so generally accorded the old fogy' principles of timber framing," by keeping its light sticks "uninjured by cutting mortises and tenons" (Hickox 1902, 184). In particular, Shawver challenged: is the builder's "6x6 post any better than one made of two 2x6s after he cuts away one-third of it for mortises and two-thirds for tenons?" For although "the large timbers look strong" the frame is "not one whit better" and "costs the farmer three to six times as much" from the extra work required to cut away so much in mortise and tenons, effectively "wasting the timber" as well as its strength (*Ohio Farmer* 1902a, 1).

Another plank-frame builder summed up their case:

> As I drive over the country this spring about my work and see timber barns building, with carpenters hewing, boring, mortising, day after day, and week after week, all that a show of strength may be made, held together by a few little wooden pins through timbers half mortised away, I say to myself, "You poor foolish farmer; you who can least afford it are wasting your money for that which is not strength, simply because your father, who had the virgin forest to draw from built in that way." (*Ohio Farmer* 1902b, 358).

While the attacks had their effect, eroding away at earlier justifications and traditional thinking about barn building, timber-framed buildings continued to be built well into the twentieth century, especially in forested areas such as the older Northeast (Marsh 1911). Nevertheless, by the turn of the century heavy-timber barns were fast giving way to light-framed varieties in midwestern prairie states, with only a few of them going up after 1910 (Kaiser 1953). On the prairie, the disappearance of the timber-frame barn seemed only a matter of time.

TAKING THE NEXT STEP

Plank framing represented a major departure from the past, but, as things turned out, it was only a transitional type in the development of light-frame construction. Within less than a decade, while plank framing was still drawing praise for being strong and good, many farmers decided that it also was too expensive and fit only for larger barns. In its place came forward a more economical barn, the balloon frame, that even greater numbers of farmers could afford.

Plank framers had not been of one mind about how far they were willing to take light construction techniques. While Joseph Wing, at the conservative end of the spectrum, had retained timber-frame methods as he replaced square timber with dimension plank lumber, Charles Hickox (1898) declared Wing's timbers "useless" in the purlin work and braces, ideas based on some "old-fashioned timber frames that were built twenty years ago." Instead he favored vigorous pursuit of balloon-frame barns (fig. 8.5). Such barns, Hickox knew, faced stiff resistance in 1898 because

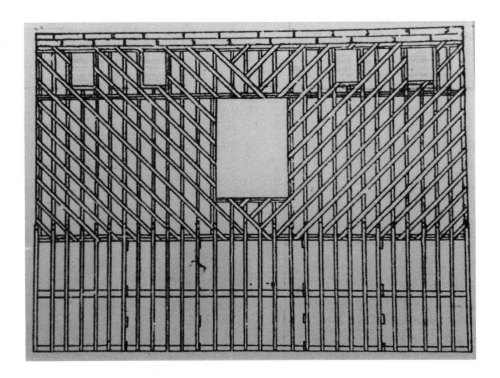

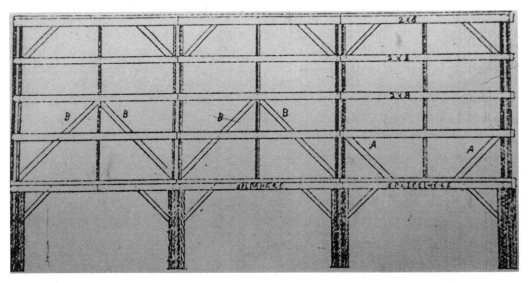

Fig. 8.5. Balloon-frame compared with plank-frame walls using posts and nailing girts.
Sources: Chas. Hickox, *Ohio Farmer*, October 20, 1898; Joseph Wing, *Ohio Farmer*, August 18, 1898

a balloon frame looks light and its name is given in contempt by those old fogy mechanics who have been brought up to rob a stick of timber of all its strength and durability by cutting it full of mortises, tenons and auger holes, and then supposing it to be stronger than a far lighter stick differently applied. (Hickox 1898, 1)

By the second decade of the twentieth century, Wing's joist-frame or "open-center" barn of cantilever design had fallen into disfavor, partly for the greater amount of lumber required, but mainly owing to the unwelcome diagonal bracing and ties which ran from the wall to the long, vertical, interior purlin posts (fig. 8.6). Specifically, reported one observer, these obstacles "hold up the hay badly, are apt to be bent or even broken by weight, and are unpleasant things to stumble over in the dark" (Marsh 1911, 120). Some innovators solved this by eliminating

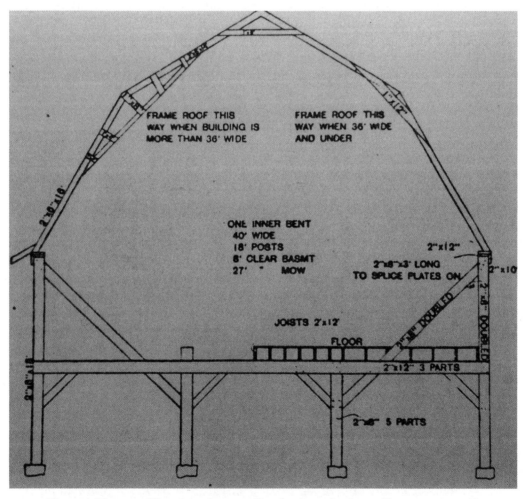

Fig. 8.6. The new Wing joist frame, offered a braced-rafter self-supporting roof. Wing did not yet glimpse that, when joined together with balloon-framed walls, a new generation of light-frame barns would result.
Source: *Farm Building*, 1907, p. 22

155

all ties and braces between wall and purlin post and, instead, substituting a form of Howe truss running lengthwise at the plate (and sometimes at the gambrel) to keep the plate from spreading (Marsh 1911).

When one spoke of plank framing after 1910, it meant Shawver truss design. A changing economy, however, now circumscribed even its range of competitiveness. Experience had showed the worthiness and acceptance of plank framing, but as lengthy pieces of large plank lumber for Shawver trusses grew ever more scarce and expensive, barn builders began to take the next step toward light construction, looking at the potential of balloon framing.

Balloon framing superseded plank framing in two respects. Stud walls replaced those of posts and nailing girts for handling loads, and light-truss, self-supported roofs replaced those heretofore supported at the purlin plates with posts from below. For exterior walls, light studs worked with horizontal siding/sheathing to broadly distribute through its framework the stresses from wind pressure, roof load, and weight of the building and its contents. This differed from both plank-frame and traditional square-timber work, the walls of which had supported loads with vertical posts at each bent, connected by horizontal timber girts onto which vertical siding was nailed. Such a method, argued a balloon-frame promoter, was costly and obsolete. Instead of having planks emulate walls of solid-frame construction, "The two inch lumber used in the plank frame" ought to be "treated as studding and the siding and sheeting . . . put on horizontally, and securely nailed," in which case "the whole covering of the barn then braces it from all sides and does double duty by largely dispensing with braces" (King 1914, 341). Barn walls would thus take on aspects of balloon framing, as they used, in Chas. Hickox's words, vertical studs in "a close, basket-like manner of construction, short bearings, a continuous support from the foundation to rafter and embracing and taking advantage of the . . . tensile and compressible strength of the timber" (Hickox 1898, 1). This studding, claimed its advocates, took "less lumber, less nails and less labor."

Similarly, self-supporting roofs spread stresses and loads through each and every set of rafters. Plank framers, like their predecessors, had traditional bents placed every twelve feet or so to support a purlin plate, relieving the weight and outward thrust of the roof from the walls. This support across the barn's width either came from a Shawver truss, with its long compression member running from the purlin to the sill, or from a vertical post acting as a cantilever in Wing's joist frame. Light-truss builders saw a different way to do things that would make the roof self-supporting.

Here again appeared none other than Joseph Wing. While balloon framing seemed to him not yet "adapted to large modern barns," he recognized that the many and varied notions of designers were all tending toward some form of simple joist- or plank-framing, and that a simple, light, and strong form of self-supporting roof fit the times. Described as the new "Wing joist-frame" (see fig. 8.6 p. 155), but later better known as the braced-rafter roof, his design had become known to readers of *Breeder's Gazette* and other publications by 1909, and it quickly caught on (Wing 1909).

In Wing's new roof, each set of rafters forming the gambrel received two braces, one running from the wall at the mow floor up to the midpoint of the lower rafter and another extending upward from there across the gambrel, to near the ridge. With each angle of the gambrel rafters braced across, tying them together into a unit, and with each braced unit spaced two feet apart rather than resting on a purlin plate supported from below every fourteen feet, several advantages resulted. Each light, arch-rib unit could be constructed quickly on the mow floor and raised easily into place. Moreover, the braced-rafter unit required about 11 percent less lumber, and its materials were of a stock size and length that could be bought at any lumber yard. Cheap to buy and easily built, braced-rafter construction became the recommended standard for barns up to thirty-six feet in width, while the extremely strong Shawver plank truss was the preferred frame of choice for barns over thirty-six feet and less than forty-two feet wide (Committee on Farm Structures 1916; Foster and Weaver 1925; Louden Machinery Company 1915; Fish 1924; Kelley 1930; Gordon-Van Tine 1917, 1926).

By 1926, braced-frame, balloon construction had become the most popular new barn type, even though Shawver plank framing, with its longer period of popularity, accounted for about "one-half of the better class of barns built in the North Central States" (Gordon-Van Tine 1926). For medium-sized and smaller barns, Joseph Wing's self-supported, braced-rafter construction clearly had joined with horizontal siding to become synonymous with the acceptance of balloon framing.

In this new era of balloon framing and self-supported roofs, the gambrel roof soared in popularity. Earlier called the curb roof, it had been around and growing in numbers during the latter half of the nineteenth century, encouraged by greater height and storage possibilities offered by the hay carrier. But its reputation for spreading rafters and settling roofs had denied it widespread popularity during these years. One could still affordably get extra loft space by building higher side walls with a cheaper gable roof. Light-lumber frames changed all that. The gambrel's angle lent itself to a self-supported truss for opening up the loft and, once achieved, the gambrel roof accompanied light-construction methods to the forefront of popularity.

Outside Services Arrive

Up to this point in the story of midwestern barns, the prime innovations had originated from the work of inventors, barn builders, and other individuals who had glimpsed a better way to do things. During the opening decade of the twentieth century, however, new influences on, and sources of, barn-building ideas emerged; agricultural engineers and experiment-station researchers, as well as commercial farm planning services, now entered the field. Together, amid their diverse voices, views, and experimental designs, they endorsed light-frame barn techniques and made possible the acceptance of new experimental forms.

With few exceptions, engineers and researchers at agricultural experiment stations had ignored the study of barns and their improvement during the nineteenth century. Farm structures began attracting some interest, however, during the opening decade of the new century, stimulated in part by the studies of Franklin H. King of the Wisconsin Agricultural College and Experiment Station. King, who gained leadership among agricultural engineers from his 1890's research and related publications concerning silo construction, also had authored a pioneering 1890 piece on a circular barn with a silo in the center. (see chapter 10 for further discussion of King's work with round barns.) But King's most notable achievement in barns came in his subsequent search for an improved system of barn ventilation. Dubbed the "King System" of natural gravity ventilation, it had become the accepted standard by 1910.

By 1905 agricultural engineers had formed the American Society of Agricultural Engineers (ASAE), which soon contained a committee on farm structures. However, little engineering knowledge existed on barns. Agricultural engineers seemed disinterested, and F. L. Marsh reported to his colleagues in 1911 that "there has been very little intelligent, definite thought given to the subject, generally speaking" (116). Instead, barn building had amounted to precedent being "blindly followed," with "much incorrect practice and waste" as a result. The reason why such things endured, Marsh concluded,

> is the farmer's custom of seeking advice from his neighbors in building matters, and at times it seems as if the less they know about building, the more readily he accepts their opinions. Even when the advice of local mechanics is followed, the defects of neighborhood practice are perpetuated (117).

Another society member disagreed. Although he admitted that farmers lacked knowledge about barn framing, he judged that the various agencies responsible for educating the farmer also shared blame for having given little attention to the subject (Marsh 1911). Gradually, however, engineers widened the variety of barn-building plans available to farmers, encouraged improved building standards, and took barn building in new directions.

Barn construction also felt the influence of new commercial farm-building sales and plan services. Various firms, such as Aladdin, Sears, Gordon-Van Tine, and Montgomery Ward, were getting into the business of producing ready-cut, build-it-yourself houses. Advertising their catalogs in magazines of large circulation, they met with good success in selling pre-cut, light-framed houses. As lumber-framing techniques became applied to barn construction, a new market opened up to them. A few barns showed up in building catalogs (Aladdin, Sears, Montgomery Ward), but when it came to making barns a major part of their sales operations, two Iowa firms moved to the fore, one selling barn equipment and the other, the barn itself.

The Louden Machinery Company, capitalizing on William Louden's inventions of the hay carrier in 1867 and the litter carrier in 1898, as well as the first automatic water bowl and first flexible sliding-door hanger, began its self-proclaimed "first free planning service" in 1907. Headquartered in Fairfield, Iowa, its catalogs, filled with sample plans and available barn equipment, invited farmers to simply "tell us about what you have in mind in the way of a barn" and then "we'll draw you a floor plan giving you our recommendations" without charge (Louden Machinery

Company 1940, 154). The plan service helped gain entry for the firm to advise farmers, especially dairymen, on ways to modernize and equip the barn with Louden's main stock-in-trade, which included ventilation systems, hay and litter carriers, windows, stalls, and pens. For a nominal charge, Louden's architectural department would furnish the farmer with a barn's complete working plans and contractor's specifications. By 1940, the company claimed it possessed "easily the largest" barn-plan department from which "more than 25,000 barns have been planned the world over" (Louden Machinery Company 1940, 154).

A second leader, the Gordon-Van Tine Company of Davenport, Iowa, advertised its plan services less as a way to sell barn equipment and supplies than to help sell pre-cut barns along with their ready-cut homes. "We are the largest single concern selling complete buildings," stated their 1917 catalog, with the great difference between themselves and other barn plan services being that "Gordon-Van Tine furnish the *actual barn*—every stick and nail and fixture needed to build and equip it" (3, 5). Gordon-Van Tine originated, so they claimed, the time- and money-saving approach of selling, in one transaction from producer direct to consumer all the building materials needed for the barn. Moreover, the ready-framed barn brought additional savings, because, as the company advertised, "we cut all this material to fit at our factories, and ship it, all bundled and marked, so that it reaches you all ready to nail in place" (6). The farmer or his carpenters then would simply follow the plans, which "show you exactly where each piece goes, the piece on the plan and the stick of lumber itself are marked exactly the same" (6) Then, appealing to the buyer's wife, Gordon-Van Tine reminded the farmer that, by buying a ready-cut barn, his "high-priced carpenter" and men, "instead of being on your place for weeks, for you to board and keep and your women folks to cook for, . . . go right to work building as soon as they get there, and in a few days they are gone, leaving your barn solid, substantial, well made" (Gordon-Van Tine 1917, 6).

Commercial plan services fit the time of plank- and balloon-frame construction, when the farmer no longer needed to make his barn-building decision based upon either the kinds of heavy timber locally available or the framing specialists who worked it into barns. Easy delivery for easy construction was possible anywhere, with the dimension plank lumber and fixtures for a Gordon-Van Tine barn of thirty-two by thirty-six feet being sent in a single train carload shipment. The main market for the number and kinds of commercially promoted plans was Corn Belt farmers, particularly those specialized in dairying. The company included different types of plans for other farming localities as well, recognizing as that "the western wheat grower needs a barn only for his teams and a cow or two, shelter for his implements and perhaps a tractor," whereas "the New England farmer grows a variety of crops and stock and puts everything he grows in a barn that is high, wide and frequently has a basement." Similarly, within the Midwest, "the barn that was just right for the Iowa farmer raising corn and blue grass—hogs and beef cattle, would not do at all for the Wisconsin dairyman" (Gordon-Van Tine 1917, 3).

Engineering research also benefited framing of gambrel roofs, culminating in the Clyde truss, known also as the Iowa truss (fig. 8.7). About 1920, A. W. Clyde, extension engineer for Iowa State College, conducted a series of tests on

Fig. 8.7. A. W. Clyde devised his strong new truss after it proved impossible to do a stress analysis of the Shawver truss. The result, also known as the Iowa truss, provided an attractive alternative to Shawver framing, using much less lumber, being of simple design, and built with materials easily available.
Drawing: From Wooley, 1941, p. 101

barn roof trusses (Clyde 1923). His resulting truss, built up every twelve feet or so at each bent, offered a stiff frame at far cheaper cost than did the Shawver truss, which required expensive extra-length material. The design, using gas pipe for shear pins at the ends of the truss, tied the ridge, the purlin, and the plate into a single uncomplicated truss to carry the intervening rafters. In 1937, the barn drew the praise of the American Society of Agricultural Engineers for being "amply strong" with "very rigid construction" and perhaps "more economical of materials than any of the methods of barn roof construction" (ASAE 1937; Giese 1946, 251; Wooley 1941, 99–100). Clyde's Iowa truss constituted the final innovation in the plank-frame tradition.

THE OPEN LOFT ACHIEVED

If any barn improvement's popularity was fostered through the mutually reinforcing activities of agricultural engineering and the commercial and govern-

160

mental services, the curved gothic roof certainly was. An unobstructed loft, free from interior braces, had long been an ideal, and it reached perfection in the laminated gothic roof, a visually impressive structure.

On the way to becoming the roof construction of choice after the mid-1920s, the gothic roof passed through more than two decades of experimentation as new ways of building and using curved rafters in barns evolved. In fact, curved-gothic laminated-roof construction in barns dated back into the nineteenth century. Joshua Secrest's curved-rafter octagon barn, built in 1883 near Iowa City, the huge 1878 barn of Muscatine lumber baron B. J. Hershey also in Iowa, and the curved rafter barns in Isabella County, Michigan, which dated as early as 1885, come to mind (Soike 1983; Giese 1946; Fogle 1927). Other gothic roof experiments showed up here and there, but not until the 1900s did they begin to attract wider interest. In the Central states, large-scale popular interest came after 1916, when architectual plans were published for a bent-rafter version near Davis, California (Kirkpatrick 1920).

In the evolution of methods used to create curved rafters, sawed construction became common first. This type, which reputedly came into use in the plentifully timbered Northwest, typically used one-inch boards eight-to-twelve-inches wide and three-to-four-feet long, from which the outside edge was sawed to the needed curvature. Three or four plies were laminated together side by side with nails, with the splices staggered to get the curve needed. Placed two feet on center, sawed laminated rafters gave strong support. However, due to the expense of material wasted and the labor consumed in sawing and nailing, midwestern farmers and builders were slow to adopt the rafters.

Bent or sprung rafters, the second major type of curved-rafter construction, attracted particular attention after a 1916 experiment in Davis, California brought them publicity (Kirkpatrick 1920; Fenton 1922). The perceived savings in material and labor required to produce the same contour, by bending instead of sawing, brought the rafters quickly into favor.

Although makers of bent rafters differed in the number of plies and the width of the one-inch boards employed, they usually built up four or five plies of one-by-four-inch strips. Tightly clamping the strips in the curved form with the joints staggered at least four feet apart, the builder then nailed them together from top and bottom with twelve- to sixteen-penny nails. Sometimes the builder added a three-eighths inch bolt with washers every three to four feet. Before 1916, bent rafters might have been used as a self-supporting roof, or built over a Shawver truss frame for extra rigidity and added confidence in strength.

The roof's pleasing appearance and brace-free haymow seized the farmers' interest. Soon, the head of Gordon-Van Tine's farm-buildings operation noticed that many were being built despite a "comparatively new design" (Kirkpatrick 1920, 90). Commercial plan services stood well positioned to take advantage of and to promote this development because, with the curved rafters seemingly more complicated to build than the quick-and-easy components of home construction, people willingly turned to professionals for guidance.

Gordon-Van Tine moved quickly to satisfy this large potential market for prefabricated curved rafters, featuring a gothic-roof barn in its 1917 catalog, along with predictions for its "wide popularity" (1917, 24). It was right. Its 1926 catalog sported the claim, "This Company was the first to design and ship barns using Bent Rafters. More than 25,000 such rafters are in use today" (11). Playing on farmers' uncertainty about making the rafters themselves, the company mixed caution with encouragement to the do-it-yourselfer: "The rafter radius must be very carefully figured" because exactitude will be reached "only by a trained engineer." To the brash but inexperienced carpenter, Gordon-Van Tine warned, gothic construction may look easy "but unless you care to risk the chances of structural weakness, order this barn from us and let us assume the responsibility." And, to the person who liked gothic roofs but worried about trying to build them himself to reduce costs, the company pointed out, "It is not that they are difficult to build on the job, for they are not," but at a "small charge for this service," the customer would find that "we can make them so much faster and better at the factory than can be done on the job" and all the customer would have to do would be to join together the two shipped parts (Gordon-Van Tine 1926, 11, 17).

Bent-rafter gothic construction, although more economical in labor and materials, proved less rigid than the more expensive sawed type. For this reason, many farmers adopted a combination of the two, with the sawed type spaced every eight-twelve feet and the bent rafters spaced between, twenty-four inches on center (Fenton 1922; Fish 1924; Foster and Weaver 1925; Wooley 1941). More improvements to offset weaknesses came from the Louden Machinery Company. In place of the sawed, curved rafter, Louden substituted every eight feet a patented, curved, reinforcing truss that ran continuously from plate to plate (fig. 8.8). This early 1920s truss, which Louden claimed was economical to build and simple to raise, lent "enormous strength" every third or fourth rafter. The interior braces of each truss could easily be cut from pieces of waste lumber at the construction site (Louden Machinery Company 1929, 1940). Louden also introduced the idea of having rafters extend all the way from the foundation sill on one side to the foundation sill on the other. This avoided the weak point where the bent rafters joined the upper wall plate, which often had been mounted to the plate by merely toe-nailing, sometimes with the help of braces running from the rafter to the mow floor joist (Fenton 1922).

The gothic roof entered its final phase of innovation during the 1930s. Here, the pivotal role of Henry Giese, a leader among agricultural engineers, cannot be discounted. At Iowa State Agricultural College, Giese tested existing types of laminated bent rafters in an attempt to solve their shortcomings. Special study went into ways to extend the life of nailed or bolted laminations which, under constant pressure, occasionally gave way and caused the roof to sag (Giese and Anderson 1932; Giese and Clark 1933).

Working in collaboration with the Rock Island Lumber Company, distributor of Weyerhaeuser Forest Products, Giese sought the best curve for the Gothic barn to withstand wind forces and to reduce back pressures from forming on the roof's opposite side. In particular, they explored the potential of modern glues to yield a stronger bent rafter. Using bents selected of Douglas fir clear of knots and defects and then glued under approximately 100 pounds per square inch of pressure, they shaped a rafter stronger than those laminated conventionally with nails

Fig. 8.8. The truss rib for reinforcing gothic arch barns became the featured cover illustration of Louden Company's catalog issued in the late 1930s.

and bolts, whether of sawed- or bent-lumber techniques. The rafter included a better and stronger connection, in the form of a two-inch dowel through which passed a bolt, for joining the rafter to the floor joist. By 1938, Weyerhaeuser was marketing these factory-built rafters under the trade name Rilco (*American Builder* 1938; Keith 1944).

What these ideas may have owed to the work of others is unclear. By the

163

summer of 1936, G. N. Brekke, a structural engineer from Rock Island, Illinois, had combined with the O.I. Kleaveland Lumber Company to produce a similar glued rafter, and "a great many experimental rafters" were delivered to customers that year (Brekke 1937, 74). Brekke had spent two years experimenting with laminated structures and American woods, utilizing "extensive experience in the Scandinavian countries" (74). The result bore a strong resemblance to the Rilco variety, including the use of hardwood dowels for strengthening the joint where rafters connected to the floor joists. Furthermore, Brekke fabricated three different types of rafters: type 1 "going down to the foundations, type 2, to the mow floor, and type 3, to the plate, which may be located some feet above the mow floor." This was the very same classification of types later advertised as available from Rilco (Rock Island Lumber n.d.; Rilco Laminated Products n.d.).

The United States Forest Products Laboratory evidently played a role as well. In 1935, after studying glued laminated construction during its more than thirty years of use in northern Europe, the laboratory had glued-laminated arches fabricated for its Madison, Wisconsin, service building by a company that, "together with another specializing in farm structures, has supplied glued laminated rafters for Gothic-style dairy barns and other farm buildings in the upper Mississippi Valley" (Wilson 1939, 5). In the laboratory's tests of the strength of glued-laminated construction, they found such rafters to be two to four times stronger than ordinary bent and sawed rafters laminated with nails. Laminations that had been glued and then nailed also proved less strong than those glued and pressed together to dry in clamps (Witzel 1941; Wilson 1939). These design influences notwithstanding, it was the Rilco gothic rafters that came to dominate the commercial laminated-rafter market, mainly among dairymen, during the final days of the two-story loft barn.

The agricultural engineering, plan service, and factory barn-production people had made an influence by the late 1920s, but many college extension men still saw other important inadequacies to correct. Uneven advice on building barns and farm buildings emanated from bulletins and circulars that agricultural experiment stations distributed, as well as in the farm buildings catalogs sent out from commercial farm-building services. One engineer decried at a 1929 ASAE meeting that "confusion and ineffectiveness" prevailed, owing to "differences of opinion and lack of cooperation between states." Should not, he asked, dairy barn designs for example, "follow climatic belts rather than state lines?" Let us, he pleaded, "forget personal differences and the idea that we must have something which is distinctively Iowa, Minnesota or Dakota" and "pool our interests and resources, eliminate useless duplication of effort and build a real cooperative plan service" (*Agricultural Engineering* 1930, 337–38).

By 1932, the idea had blossomed among agricultural colleges in fifteen midwestern states, an area within which more than one-half of the nation's farm-building investment occurred. The Mid-West Farm Building Plan Service was organized under the wing of the Farm Structures Division of the American Society of Agricultural Engineers (Giese 1949). In 1933, the new cooperative service produced its first illustrated catalog, with descriptions of farm buildings climatically suited to the region's needs. Prospective builders who saw something to their liking in the catalog could obtain a set of blueprints at a nominal price from the extension engineer or agricultural engineering department at a participating state college or university. The ninety-six-page catalog contained 113 plans, eleven of them barns, selected and revised from among the more than fourteen hundred then in circulation among the fifteen states. The Midwest Plan Service, headquartered at Iowa State University, followed this success with a second, revised edition in 1937. Thereafter, the service became a leading institutional outlet for applying the knowledge of accumulated standard practice and engineering design to barn and farm buildings, and it became a regional influence on modern farm construction (Giese 1957; Mid-West Farm Building Plan Service ca. 1933; Gray 1955).

THE ELUSIVE DREAM

The various kinds of plank and balloon framing being proposed for barns during the early 1900s indicate that framing methods were by no means set. New ideas had opened a larger sphere of experimental possibilities to barn builders than they had heretofore known. Similarly, uniformity evaded the efforts of agricultural structures engineers to promote braced-frame, Shawver-frame, or gothic-arch designs, both in how they used these terms and in their recommended materials and methods of construction. It might be said that dissimilarities in the right way of doing things ended only after World War II, when the two-story loft barn disappeared from the construction scene.

The agricultural engineer's influence in barn construction, with the exception of gothic arch developments, proved minimal. "If we look at the facts squarely," stated A. W. Clyde bluntly in 1923, "we must admit that little real engineering knowledge has ever been used in barn roof design. The common styles of self-supporting roofs were developed by so-called practical builders rather than by engineers." In fact, not only have we "followed their plans with little knowledge of what we were advocating," but "in the case of the wing-joist or braced rafter framing, we have even recommended changes which have weakened the original plan" (Clyde 1923, 107).

As late as 1949, Henry Giese still saw the standardization of buildings as an unmet challenge. With farm building design an unprofitable field for the professional architect and farmers finding that "the contractor in the usual sense is frequently not present," Giese pointed to the yet-continuing influence of the country builder. "Much farm building is done with farm labor and most of the remainder by country carpenters who must be jacks-of-all-trades" (566, 568).

CONCLUSION

During the era of barn building, standardization represented but a distant goal to contemporaries arguing for their own particular ideas. Things obviously were moving in the direction of building lighter-frame barns. Nevertheless, historical distance can easily lead the unwary modern observer into thinking that barns represent merely fading neighborhood traditions pushed into oblivion by a singular and indifferent industrial technology. This robs the past of its human complexity. The midwestern farmer and builder alike adapted and adjusted their practices in a multitude of ways during times of unfolding agricultural change and rising subregional specialties. Barns fashioned for dairymen, pole-frame barns embraced by beef producers, the silo's impact on barns, and new ideas about ventilation and lighting of barns—accounts of which cannot be given in the space of this chapter— richly illustrate the evolving history of such barn building in the Midwest.

Perhaps, Midwest barns, variously built as persons adapted to these new developments, contain a story of complexities never to be told. The pace of things is quickening today, as multitudes of farmsteads are swept away in farm consolidation. If the owner of the larger, absorbing farm decides to keep a building or two, the barn is rarely one of them.

REFERENCES CITED

American Builder. 1938. Gothic rafter barns. 60(August): 58–59.

Agricultural Engineering. 1930. How the engineer can help the farmer build good farm buildings. 11:337–38, quoted in Henry Giese, The Midwest plan service, Unpublished paper.

American Society of Agricultural Engineers. 1937, 2d ed. *Midwest farm building plan service.* Ames: Midwest Plan Service.

Brekke, G. N. 1937. Bent, Glued Rafters Make Strong Barns. *American Builder,* 59(May): 74–75.

Clyde, A. W. 1923. Tests of self-supporting barn roofs. *Agricultural Engineering.* 4(July): 107–08.

Committee on Farm Structures, ASAE. 1916. Report of committee on farm structures. *Transactions of the American Society of Agricultural Engineers.* 9(March 1916): 202–29.

Cox, H. E. 1922. Farm barn frames past and present. *Rural New-Yorker.* 81(January 14): 36.

Fenton, Fred C. 1922. Recent developments in farm buildings. *Agricultural Engineering* 3:28–33.

Fish, N. S. 1924. *Building the dairy barn.* Wisconsin Agricultural Experiment Station, Bulletin No. 369 (Madison).

Fogle, F. E. 1927. The gothic barn roof with sprung rafters. *Agricultural Engineering* 8:13–14.

Foster, W. A., and Earl Weaver, 1925. *Dairy barns and equipment,* Iowa State College of Agriculture and Mechanic Arts Circular No. 93.

Giese, Henry. 1946. Trends in farm structures. In *A century of farming in Iowa, 1846–1946,* 250–61. Ames: Iowa State College Press.

_____. 1949. Farm structures—a forward look. *Agricultural Engineering* 30(December): 565–68.

_____. 1957. The Midwest Plan Service: remarks by the chairman, Henry Giese, at the meeting held in Ames on 15 January 1957. An unpublished paper.

_____ and F. D. Anderson, 1932. Tests of laminated bent rafters: Part 1. *Agricultural Engineering* 13(January): 11–13.

_____ and E. F. Clark, 1933. Tests of laminated bent rafters, Part 2. *Agricultural Engineering* 14(September): 248–51, 255.

Gordon-Van Tine Company. 1917. *Farm buildings.* Davenport: Gordon-Van Tine.

_____. 1926. *Farm buildings.* Davenport: Gordon-Van Tine.

Gray, Harold E. 1955. *Farm service buildings.* New York: McGraw-Hill.

Hickox, C. H. 1902. Improved barn building. *Ohio Farmer* 101(February 6): 1.

Hickox, Charles H. 1898. An improved balloon frame. *Ohio Farmer* 94(October 20): 1.

Kaiser, W. G. 1953. A century of progress in farm housing and storage structures. *Agricultural Engineering* 34:34–36, 46.

Keith L. P. 1944. Applications of new developments in timber construction to farm buildings. *Agricultural Engineering* 25:461–62.

Kelley, J. B. 1930. *Building plans for the dairy farm.* Kentucky College of Agriculture Extension Division Circular 128.

King, Franklin H. 1914. 6th ed. *A text book of the physics of agriculture.* Madison, WI: privately printed.

Kirkpatrick, W. 1920. Gothic roofs for barns. *Transactions of the American Society of Agricultural Engineers* 14:87–91.

Louden Machinery Company. 1915. *Louden barn plans.* Fairfield, IA: Louden Machinery.

———. 1929. *Louden general catalog No. 54* Fairfield, IA: Louden Machinery.

———. 1940. *Louden farm building plans & equipment, seventy-three catalog* Fairfield, IA: Louden Machinery.

Marsh F. L. 1911. The principles of barn framing. *Transactions of the American Society of Agricultural Engineers* 5:116–29.

Mid-West Farm Building Plan Service. ca. 1933. *Catalog,* Ames, IA: Mid-West Farm Building Plan Service.

Ohio Farmer. 1902a. Plank-frame barns. 101(March 20): 1.

———. 1902b. Plank-frame barns—cost and strength. 101(April 17): 358.

———. 1902c. Experiment farm notes. 101(June 26): 1.

Rilco Laminated Products Company. n.d. Non-sag gothic rafters. *Catalog,* Albert Lea, MN: Rilco.

Rock Island Lumber Company. n.d. Mill fabricated gothic rafters. *Catalog,* Albert Lea, MN: Rock Island.

Rural New-Yorker. 1922. H. E. Cox, Farm barn frames past and present. 81(January 14): 36.

Shawver, John L. 1904. *Plank frame barn construction.* New York: David Williams Company.

———1894. Framing that barn. *Ohio Farmer* 85(May 3): 341.

———1896. The plank barn frame: The "Shawver" frame. *Ohio Farmer* 89(February 6): 104.

Strahan, J. L. 1918. Barn roof design. *Transactions of the American Society of Agricultural Engineers* 12:57–75.

Soike, Lowell J. 1983. *Without right angles: The round barns of Iowa.* Des Moines: Iowa State Historical Department.

Wilson, T. R. C. 1939. *The glued laminated wooden arch.* Technical Bulletin No. 691 Washington, DC: U.S. Department of Agriculture.

Wing, Joseph E. 1899a. A barn question. *Ohio Farmer* 95(January 19): 42.

———. 1898b. The joist frame again. *Ohio Farmer* 94(August 18): 104.

———. 1898a. The "open center" barn-frame. *Ohio Farmer* 93 (March 24): 1.

————. 1909. Other types of barn construction. In Vol. 1, *Farms, cyclopedia of American agriculture,* edited by Liberty Hyde Bailey, 258–60. New York, 1909.

————. 1899b. Plank barns. *Ohio Farmer* 96(July 27): 49.

Witzel, S. A. 1941. Laminated rafters. *Successful farming.* 39(March): 16, 52.

Wooley, John C. 1941. *Farm buildings,* New York: McGraw-Hill.

9

CORNCRIBS TO GRAIN ELEVATORS: EXTENSIONS OF THE BARN

Keith E. Roe

CORNCRIBS REMAIN a dominant element on many Midwest farms, especially those in the heart of corn country, where they often surpass the barn itself in size. Today's corn belt is still distinguished by the size of its corncribs, though modern harvest and storage technologies have significantly reduced the importance of cribbing ear corn. Grain-handling systems, with their steel bins, driers, and auger conveyers, represent modern on-farm storage, while grain elevators identify both the agricultural economy of a region and the towns in which they are located. The massive concrete grain elevator, sometimes called the "skyscraper of the plains," symbolizes the industrialization of Midwest agriculture in the twentieth century.

EVOLUTION OF THE CORNCRIB

Pioneer farmers frequently built log corncribs during their two centuries of migration into and settlement of the Midwest (fig. 9.1). Crude frontier log cribs were little more than bins, loosely constructed of saplings or split rails and laid up with saddle notching to hold them together (Blegen 1955; Schimmer and Noble 1984). The bin-like crib might have been covered with thatch or cornstalks to help shed rain; a board and shingle roof took more effort, required nails, and thus was more expensive. Unfortunately, thatch roofs served as housing for rodents, and the crib became their pantry.

Considering the primitive nature of family living quarters on pioneer farms of the Midwest, it is little wonder that corncribs remained crude utilitarian bins until relatively recently (Bogue 1963). The simple rail corncrib, adopted from the popular log cribs of Appalachia, was one origin of the midwest corncrib (Hart 1991).

Log construction of corncribs remained popular through the 1800s in areas where timber resources proved readily accessible, such as in the northern Mid-

Fig. 9.1. Log corncrib typical of pioneer farm
Drawing: M. Margaret Geib

west and the South. Some log corncribs were built much more substantially, out of hewn logs and with dovetailed notching. A few of these have weathered the century or more since their construction and are now preserved mostly on living history farms. Like other pioneer buildings, however, they are rare survivors rather than the norm (Main 1982).

The size of corncribs remained small, even as corn production rose, during much of the nineteenth century, in part due to the practice of corn shocking. Corn could be gradually "shucked out" as needed and hauled to the crib or barn for milling or feeding to livestock (Hardeman 1981; Parker 1972). Large corncribs were unnecessary since farmers could leave much of their corn in the field until spring. By 1870, however, in the expanding corn belt, picking and husking in the field were favored, along with cribbing the corn (Bogue 1963; Schimmer and Noble 1984). Even so, the crop might be left standing in the field all winter if harvest was delayed because of rain. Such practice is still encountered in some eastern states and where the crop is gradually harvested for feeding livestock on the farm.

THE SINGLE CORNCRIB

The single crib is the simplest type of corn-storage building, ranging from the lean-to covered bin to the gambrel-roofed, keystone-shaped corncrib. It has

171

been popular with farmers for three centuries. The most recent versions use pole and two-by-four framework with wire-mesh siding for economy and ease of construction. Most often the crib is five to eight feet wide and is covered with a slanted or lean-to roof. Crib width is influenced by the climate of a region; drier conditions allow for wider cribs with no increased loss of corn due to mold.

A classic type of corncrib in the northern states has a keystone shape, with side walls flaring outward toward the roof, giving the appearance, in end view, of a coffin (fig. 9.2). These cribs are generally quite small, rather top heavy because of their shape and thus somewhat unstable. They may hold only 50 to 100 bushels, though many double cribs of this sort in Wisconsin and Minnesota are much larger, of 1,000 to 2,000 bushel capacity. The sloped walls presumably aid in emptying the crib, and they help to shield against rain. This latter feature was more important before the days of self-draining corncribbing, a milled-lumber pattern with tapered edges that dates from the late 1800s (Roe 1988).

THE DOUBLE CORNCRIB

If two straight-sided single cribs are built near one another and roofed over, the result is a double corncrib (Hart 1991; Roe 1988; Schimmer and Noble 1984).

Fig. 9.2. Example of a coffin-shaped single corncrib, Wayne County, Ohio. The upper side walls have openings for filling.
Photo: A. G. Noble, 1987

It may have a narrow ventilator space between the cribs, or, if the space is wider, a shed is created which can provide protection from the weather, for unloading corn into the bins or for storing wagons and machinery. The double crib shed became a ubiquitous feature throughout and beyond the corn belt during the nineteenth century (fig. 9.3). Its popularity may have been stimulated by the Homestead Act of 1862 which resulted in a growing number of tenant farmers working for a share of the crop (Bogue 1963; Gates 1972; Shannon 1945; Saloutos and Hicks 1951). The matching cribs made dividing the crop easier (Long 1964).

Before machinery was invented to elevate grain, the practical height of corncribs was limited to that to which the average adult could pitch a scoopshovel-full of ear corn from a wagon—about ten feet. Doors for filling cribs by scooping were located on the sides near the top. Filling cribs this way meant that they could never be quite full; there was always some wasted space above the door level.

The driveway or alley formed by the double corncrib has long been used to store machinery. During the heyday of corncrib construction in the mid-twentieth century, wider alleys were desired to accommodate the growing size of farm equipment, whether for loading wagons from overhead grain bins or for bringing loads to an inside cup elevator for emptying. This became impractical, however, because of the extra cost of joist materials to span the alley with sufficient strength to hold the grain bins. The advent and popularity of machine sheds with high and wide doors coincided with the advent of large-scale machinery and reduced the

Fig. 9.3. Double-crib shed of keystone type and loft and drive-in alley, Chisago County, Minnesota
Photo: K. Roe, 1983

use of corncrib alleys as machine storage areas. Many of today's farm trailers find it a tight squeeze in yesterday's corncrib alley.

The roof of a double corncrib creates usable loft space over the alley or vent space, if the tops of the cribs are connected by a floor. This method of building corncribs became popular during the nineteenth century, as noted in farm magazines and books (Halsted 1903; Radford 1908). Lofts could be used for storage of bagged grain and other commodities, or, with the advent of portable elevators, they simply might provide overflow space for ear corn as the cribs became full (Long 1964). Corncribs have always been favorite homes for rats and mice, however, making it impractical to store valuable shelled seed corn and other bagged grain in lofts.

Roof design became an important factor in the construction of farm buildings during the latter years of the nineteenth century. Before then, the roofs of corncribs had been the simple lean-to or sloping kind, while the gable roof was used on most double crib sheds. The development of gambrel roofs for barns in the late 1800s significantly increased usable loft space (Schimmer and Noble 1984). This design innovation was carried over to corncribs, not to increase open loft space with self-supporting roofs as in barns, but to allow for creation of grain bins above the alley. Gothic roofs were used in the same way between the 1930s and 1950s. Granaries for shelled corn, oats, and other small grains had long existed as separate buildings, or they commonly occupied part of the barn or corncrib. Usually, however, they were situated at ground level for ease of use by the farmer needing only a bushel or so of grain at a time. Overhead granaries, on the other hand, allowed for easy emptying of the bins by gravity flow into wagons or portable grist mills located in the alley below.

The creation of larger corncribs and their overhead grain bins depended upon the invention of new methods to raise the grain and ear corn higher than a farmer could scoop it. The era of building Midwest corncribs, typically capped with cupolas for elevator access, coincided with increased grain production. High cribs were made possible by the commercial adaptation of the continuous belt-and-cup elevator for grain mills during the mid-nineteenth century, and by the portable grain elevator in the 1890s. Farmstead architecture changed as the industrial and agricultural revolutions marched in step and accelerated in the twentieth century.

MECHANIZATION AND TECHNOLOGICAL ADVANCES

The machine age in American agriculture began in the 1840s with new devices for harvesting and threshing small grains. However, because of its large and tough stalks, corn was not so readily adapted to machine harvesting. Mechanized corn pickers were manufactured in the 1870s, but were not commercially successful until the small gasoline tractor with power take-off became popular around 1929. New corn hybrids with stronger stalks and roots were created for mechanical picking (Wallace 1956). Still, before World War II, most corn was picked by hand.

The first machine to affect the building design and size of corncribs was the cup elevator. It was patented by Oliver Evans in 1785, and first used successfully in a commercial grain elevator in 1843 (Dart 1879; Schlebecker 1975). Transport of grain to and from the flour or grist mill had for centuries been a laborious, back-breaking task. The threshed grain or shelled corn was bagged and carried on barges, wagons, or draft animals. However, it was loaded or unloaded and carried within the mill on men's shoulders. As both a mill owner and inventor, Evans sought to eliminate this labor-intensive work and to expedite the shipment of grain and flour. He adapted for commercial use the well-known principle for lifting water: a series of buckets on a vertical wheel or continuous belt stretched between two pulleys and axles. This elevator could do the work of dozens of laborers in half the time. It also allowed for building taller mills and corncribs, and served as a namesake for the building called a grain elevator.

The term *grain elevator* has several meanings. It is properly used to identify the device used for lifting grain in a series of cups or buckets attached to a continuous chain or belt, made originally of leather but nowadays consisting of reinforced rubber, much like tire casing. Because this cup elevator is the key operational element of large grain-storage buildings and, indeed, made them possible, the name "grain elevator" also describes the storage structure itself or the integrated complex of such structures.

Many corncribs built in the twentieth century, especially the larger sorts, have a vertical cup elevator built-in along one side of the alley. The structure itself, if built for ear corn storage, is still properly called a corncrib. However, some farm granaries, built for shelled corn and small grain storage, are truly grain elevators, though usually small by commercial standards and rarely referred to by that term.

Confounding the identity issue still further is the *portable elevator*, which is commonly used to fill corncribs or storage bins. This machine came into production in the 1890s, but sales were slow until the second decade of the twentieth century. Increased crop production, stimulated by war needs and a scarcity of farmhands for the corn harvest, contributed to greater use of portable elevators to fill cribs. The portable elevator is basically a long trough made of wood or, more commonly, of steel, along the length of which is looped a continuous flat-link chain with blades or paddles attached at regular intervals. These blades serve to move the grain along the trough as the chain is rotated around spindle gears at both ends. The portable elevator was always a dangerous farm implement. Its exposed moving rods, gears, and chains frequently were responsible for the loss of fingers or broken limbs. Portable elevators are held by cables inside a framework which allows for height adjustment to match the crib or bin permitting the elevator to be moved between storage structures.

Few chain-driven, open-faced portable elevators are manufactured or sold today for use on farms. Most farm grain-handling systems now use auger-type elevators. These consist of a long tube, inside the length of which a screw is turned to move the grain through. Before the days of machines for loading storage bins and cribs, grain handling was truly a hand-labor operation. Corn ears, picked by hand in the field and hauled in wagons to the farmyard, were scooped by the shovelful into cribs. Prior to power-driven shellers, corncribs were emptied gradually over the winter and following summer. The corn was fed to livestock as whole or chopped ears, or hand-turned shellers were used to strip the kernels from cobs.

Invention of the power-driven corn sheller in the late 1800s meant that entire cribs could be emptied quickly and the shelled grain sent to a local elevator, ground for feed, or stored on the farm as whole grain for subsequent feeding or grinding. Shelling out a crib is an event, not unlike that of earlier threshing days, though on a smaller scale, with several farmhands involved, along with considerable noise, work activity, commotion, and dust. The contrast with an otherwise serene building is dramatic: workers rake at the solidified mass of ears and husk to loosen and drop them into the dragline conveyer leading to the sheller. This drag is placed alongside the crib, or through the vent beneath it. Another worker levels the shelled corn being dropped via auger conveyer into a wagon or truck, and the operator controls the sheller, cob elevator, and husk blower, while keeping an eye out for problems and shutting down the machine as wagons are filled. In the meantime, rats and mice scurry for cover as they lose their nests.

ERA OF THE GRAIN ELEVATOR

The grain elevator of agricultural commerce grew up alongside developing transport systems during the second half of the nineteenth century (Riley 1977). Hundreds of branch or line elevators were built in grain country by the expanding railroads and owners of terminal elevators in the central market cities (Shannon 1945). Growth of facilities for grain storage and transport continued dramatically in the twentieth century, in step with increased crop production and processing of grain into food, feed, oils, and other derived products.

Early grain elevators were often associated with the flour mills they served. These were usually timber-framed structures, as were the mills themselves. In the nineteenth century, however, and up until the 1940s, most wood elevator bins were constructed by the cribbed method or with balloon (studded) framing. Less common was the wood-stave silo method by which vertical interlocking staves were encircled by steel rods to hold them into place. The studded method made economical use of materials, but often lacked the strength necessary to handle pressures generated by grain in deep bins. For larger country elevators of wood, the cribbed method of construction was employed, using two-by-eight planks at the base of the structure and six-inch stock above ten feet or so. Solid walls were built up by layering and overlapping the planks and spiking them together (fig. 9.4). Even so, collapsed walls or burst bins were not rare, and swollen walls and emergency reinforcing became characteristic of wooden elevators. Most such elevators subsequently were covered with galvanized steel sheeting for weatherproofing and to help prevent fires. This was especially of concern during the days of coal-fired locomotives, from which flying sparks were always a danger.

In the late 1800s, concrete drew growing attention as a construction material. The world's first cylindrical concrete grain elevator was built in Minneapolis in 1899 by Frank H. Peavy and Charles F. Haglin (Heffelfinger 1960). Originally eighty feet tall, with walls sixteen inches thick at the base, tapering to six inches at

Fig. 9.4. Derelict grain elevator of studded construction, Huron County, Ohio
Photo: K. Roe, 1990

the top, the so-called "Peavy's Folly" was predicted by skeptics to burst upon filling, but it did not. Being an experiment, it was filled only once, but it ushered in the era of massive grain storage in multiple-silo, monolithic, concrete grain elevators that have come to identify the grain-producing heartland of America.

GROWTH AND SPECIALIZATION: CORNCRIBS

The new century spawned dramatic events and discoveries that altered the course of agriculture and farm buildings. Wars, increased mechanization, growing use of commercial fertilizers, and improved strains of crops all stimulated production and, therefore, the need for expanded storage facilities. Family farms, which dotted each square mile of the corn belt at the beginning of the century, gradually began to disappear as individual farm operations specialized in fewer crops and grew in size through consolidation.

Both concrete and steel were promoted as alternative construction materials for corncribs and grain elevators in the early decades of the twentieth century (fig. 9.5). The use of hollow clay tile also was encouraged in those parts of the Midwest where they were manufactured, notably in Iowa, Illinois, and Indiana (fig. 9.6). Concrete had its advocates in the Portland cement industry, as well as in agricultural colleges and the United States Department of Agriculture, especially

Fig. 9.5. Double-bin concrete stave block corncrib, Hamilton County, Iowa. Smaller
steel grain bins to the right.
Photo: K. Roe, 1983

between 1900 and 1940. It could be a do-it-yourself material, poured into homemade forms, to build barns and other outbuildings, including corncribs though
few of these now exist. More adaptable, or at least saleable by manufacturers, was
the formed concrete-block corncrib.

The most common variety of concrete corncrib is made of interlocking stave
blocks which have been cast with ventilating slots in them (see fig. 9.5). In some
cases, steel wires or rods are incorporated in the vents to keep rats out. The blocks
are laid up in the form of circular bins. These are encircled with steel rods, enabling
the structure to withstand side pressures from the corn heaped within. Single and
double-bin corncribs of this type are most common, although four-bin ones are
not unusual. Most of these corncribs are found in Iowa and Illinois, in regions
where the blocks were made and along routes of the salesmen who promoted
them. Rectangular concrete block corncribs are rare but not unknown.

Hollow glazed tile, such as that used in silos, was promoted for construction
of farm buildings by manufacturers looking to develop new markets for their products during the lean economic years of the 1920s and 1930s (Giese 1946). For the
ventilated part of a corncrib, the tiles were laid down sideways, exposing their
slotted surfaces to the air. The openings in the tile were supposedly narrow
enough to keep out rats. A tile corncrib required the skills of both a mason and a
carpenter, who used round, rectangular, and square patterns. The distribution of

Fig. 9.6. Clay-tile corncrib with very limited ventilation area, Calhoun County, Iowa. Note bracing on the side.
Photo: K. Roe, 1982

these corncribs was restricted to areas of tile manufacturing and to where tile clays were found, mostly in parts of Iowa, Illinois, and Indiana. Like concrete corncribs, they were usually built near paved roads, essential for the transport of such heavy construction materials (Schimmer and Noble 1984). Another type of cylindrical corncrib, one associated more with commercial grain elevators than farms, was built with a combination of clay tile and concrete. Tiles were incorporated into the forms while the concrete was being poured, providing ventilating slots.

Metal construction for corn storage came into use early in the century and was promoted by the steel industry during World War I as a crop saver for the patriotic farmer (fig. 9.7). Flat, galvanized-steel sheeting with ventilation perforations was used to build rectangular or hexagonal corncribs. Corrugated, curved sheets created the more common cylindrical bin type, which was usually topped with a conical roof, much like the common steel grain bins of today. Nonetheless, a steel corncrib is distinguished by wall ventilation slits and, most times, by a roof ventilator at its peak.

Corncribs of steel rods or heavy wire mesh also became available by the 1930s. The wire-mesh type became extremely popular after World War II because of its low cost, ease of filling, and low maintenance (fig. 9.8). Indeed, it is still the principal kind of corncrib manufactured, although wood-and-wire or snowfence cribs are also available commercially. In bumper crop years between the late 1930s

Fig. 9.7. Steel crib still in use as shown by hand sheller and cob pile on the left, McLeod County, Minnesota
Photo: K. Roe, 1983

and 1950s, before manufactured wire-mesh cribs became widely available and affordable, farmers often threw up ordinary livestock fence or snowfence for temporary enclosures, rather than dumping the corn on the ground. Substantial wood-fence cribs of oak slats and heavy wire had been available in the 1890s from the mail-order firms of Montgomery Ward and Sears Roebuck, but the flimsier snowfence cribs do little more than help keep livestock from feeding on the corn. They are set on the ground or on boards, are large in diameter for maximum capacity, and seldom roofed, all of which lead to losses by mold and small animals. Often the hoops of fence are piled two or three high and may collapse under the pressure. These simple corncribs are of little architectural significance, but they do serve as indicators of excess corn production and the farmers' expediency in dealing with it.

No suitable alternative to a wood crib, or a roofed wire-mesh type, has been found for ear corn storage. Concrete blocks absorbed and held moisture, the bins of circular masonry corncribs are too big to promote drying, and the perforations in steel cribs do not provide adequate ventilation to dry the crop. Nearly all these structures now stand empty, abandoned.

Rising lumber prices in the late 1950s began to make wood-frame crib construction less affordable. At the same time, midwestern corncribs required heavier studding and timbering to support the greater weight of soybeans, the production

Fig. 9.8. Wire mesh corncrib beside a bank barn, Jefferson County, Wisconsin
Photo: K. Roe, 1983

of which was increasing as farmers switched to a crop rotation based primarily, if not solely, on corn and beans. The dilemma of building expensive wood corncribs was solved with the change from ear-corn harvesting and storage to field shelling using combines with corn heads and storing the grain in bins.

GROWTH AND SPECIALIZATION: GRAIN ELEVATORS

Grain elevators had been constructed of wood during their first fifty-odd years but, as with corncribs, the turn of the century brought experimentation with fireproof materials, notably concrete, steel plate, and clay tile (Ketchum 1907). Steel bins or silos often were used in an elevator complex to expand storage capacity. During the first half century, clay tiles were used to construct bins and to enclose headhouse and scale operations. The use of concrete blocks for grain elevator bins was less popular than steel or tile. Poured concrete, reinforced with steel, became the material and method of choice for all such large projects.

FUNCTIONS, PROBLEMS AND HAZARDS

Corncribs developed in close association with barns, both functionally and spatially. Barns had performed the function of storing and drying corn before

181

there were separate corncribs. Even at the turn of the twentieth century, barn plans often included corncribs as either a part of the structure or as an attachment to it (Radford 1908, 33ff). As a functional part of the farmstead, corncribs usually were situated for easy access in loading and shelling or for feeding livestock. When these functions conflicted, farmers often had to shoulder and carry bushel baskets of chopped or shelled corn from crib to barn or hog house. Even though it would have been more practical to locate farm buildings in close proximity, spacing helped prevent the spread of fires and the consequent loss of more than one building. Damp hay in the barn was prone to spontaneous combustion, and there was always a risk of an accident with a lantern or an electrical short circuit.

Grain elevators and corncribs have been closely associated since the mid-nineteenth century. Large corncribs were being put up next to grain elevators, to hold surplus corn for drying and later shelling, as recently as the 1940s. Most of these have since been removed, especially those of wood. Even today, in areas where mechanical corn pickers are still used, farmers may haul their ear corn to local grain elevators for shelling, rather than storing it on the farm. The tell-tale sign of ear-corn processing at an elevator used to be a husk and cob burner which was located a safe distance away from the storage complex (Richey and Johnson 1952). Husks and chaff are still commonly burned, but cobs are often retained and sold for secondary processing as feed supplements or fertilizers.

As corncribs grew in size, strain increased on the sides of the bins and on load-bearing walls, leading to frequent construction failures (Giese 1946). Foundations sagged, studding gave way, or the overhead grain bins split near their bases. Reinforcing tie rods and additional framing often were used to avoid some of these problems. Evidence of such preventative measures can usually be seen on the exterior of cribs or bins of both corncribs and grain elevators.

TECHNOLOGICAL ADVANCES AND ECONOMIC CHANGE

During the first sixty years of the twentieth century, a combination of new inventions, technical adaptations, and scientific discoveries combined to change the complexion of farming methods, as well as the appearance of farm buildings. Most influential in changing corn production and the size and types of storage facilities were the gasoline tractor, portable elevator, mechanical corn picker, hybrid seed corn, power take-off for tractors, commercial fertilizers, including anhydrous ammonia, and the corn head for combines. The switch from horse power to tractors, which got into full swing in the 1920s and 1930s, freed up vast acreages that had previously been devoted to oats for more corn production (Cochrane 1979; Johnson 1978). The change, however, reduced the economic independence of farmers, who now had to purchase fuel. The shift to cash cropping and specialized farming in the Midwest, which began with mechanization in the nineteenth century, was hastened by each new development. Since the introduction of field shelling by combine and corn head in 1956, the proportion of corn harvested as ears has dropped steadily, and with it the number of corncribs in use (Leath, Meyer and Hill 1982).

Hybrid seed corn was available commercially before 1930, but farmers were reluctant to try it. The drought years of the mid-thirties helped prove the superiority of hybrids, but it took another ten years to convince the last skeptics of their yield-raising value (Drache 1976; Wallace 1956). After World War II the use of anhydrous ammonia as a nitrogen fertilizer helped boost production, resulting in a need for more crib storage (Schlebecker 1975).

The development of early-maturing corn hybrids not only increased overall production but also, since the 1950s, expanded the corn belt north and west beyond the traditional heartland of Iowa and Illinois (Leath, Meyer and Hill 1982; Roepke 1959). Likewise, the use of irrigation systems brought corn farming back to areas of Kansas and Nebraska that had not seen much of the crop since before the Dust Bowl days of the 1930s. In regions such as these, where large-scale corn production either was renewed or became a relatively new event, harvest and storage technologies usually skipped over the era of large wood corncribs. Corn shelled by combine in the field is stored in grain bins and elevators, and farmers using corn pickers generally store their corn in large steel-mesh corncribs.

The wave of technological, social, and economic changes that swept through the Midwest grain country after World War II altered not only the methods of grain harvest and transportation, but also the sizes and types of grain storage facilities (fig. 9.9). Living standards and lifestyles, and rural population patterns and

Fig. 9.9. Multisilo, monolithic concrete grain elevators (Starke County, Indiana) identify Midwest towns. Note elevator legs and heads outside main structure to help prevent catastrophic dust explosions.
Photo: K. Roe, 1990

183

densities, also have changed. The small town, struggling for economic survival, has lost its businesses and residents to urbanization, consolidation of schools, regional city merchandising, commodity price depressions, bankruptcies, and the greater mobility of townfolk and local farmers alike. In many cases, only the grain elevator remains as a viable business, and that may depend on continued rail access. Consolidation of elevator operations has left numerous small mills and storage facilities abandoned, even along high-volume rail lines, since it no longer pays to stop at every small town along the way.

OBSOLESCENCE AND ALTERNATIVE USES

Few grain elevators have been adapted for other uses, but heavy-timbered feed or flour mills, which often date from the nineteenth century, have the roominess and character to be used as restaurants or shops. Though not so adaptable as barns for business or domestic uses, corncribs have been converted into granaries, machine sheds, and even houses. During the 1960s, when they were still relatively new, some cribs were lined or covered with siding to make tighter bins for shelled corn or other grain. Conversions to alternative functions, however, frequently cost more than new structures. Sometimes, though, as with houses, the gain was measured in uniqueness or character, not dollars. Smaller corncribs often found new use as storage sheds for baled hay, firewood, tools, and various potentially useful junk.

The great amount of heavy construction lumber used in a large corncrib, especially one in good condition, is worth salvaging. This is rarely the case with grain elevators. The studded types are usually too dilapidated, with the lumber bent out of shape, while the cribbed varieties are so laced with spikes that salvage is impractical.

Not all corncribs have been swept aside in the changeover to shelled corn drying and storage (fig. 9.10). Some farmers who continue to pick their corn by machine use crib storage because it is economical and familiar. Livestock farmers may grind whole ear corn, the cobs serving as roughage in the animals' diet.

The midwestern corn country of the past generation was identified by the size and numbers of its corncribs, especially the large double type with an overhead granary and a cupola on top. Today's grain-producing regions are characterized by their monolithic concrete elevators. Corncribs and grain elevators are indicators of change in the agricultural landscape and life of the Midwest.

184

Fig. 9.10. Small wood-grain elevator no longer served by rail, Marshall County, Indiana. Many such operations have been abandoned, while others, like this one, continue in the feed business by relying on truck transportation and local sales.
Photo: K. Roe, 1990

REFERENCES CITED

Blegen, Theodore C. 1955. *Land of their choice*. Minneapolis: Univ. of Minnesota Press.

Bogue, Allen G. 1963. *From prairie to corn belt: Farming on the Illinois and Iowa prairies in the nineteenth century*. Chicago: Univ. of Chicago Press.

Cochrane, Willard W. 1979. *The development of American agriculture*. Minneapolis: Univ. of Minnesota Press.

Dart, Joseph. 1879. The grain elevators of Buffalo. *Publications of the Buffalo Historical Society* 1:391–404.

Drache, Hiram M. 1976. *Beyond the furrow*. Danville, IL: Interstate Printers and Publishers.

Fite, Gilbert C. 1966. *The farmer's frontier 1865–1900*. New York: Holt, Rinehart and Winston.

Gates, Paul W. 1972. Problems of agricultural history, 1790–1840. In *Farming in the new nation: Interpreting American agriculture 1790–1840*, edited by Darwin P. Kelsey, 33–58. Washington, DC: Agricultural History Society.

Giese, Henry. 1946. Trends in farm structures. In *A century of farming in Iowa 1846–1946*, 250–61. Ames: Iowa State College Press.

Halsted, Byron D. 1903. 2d ed. *Barn plans and outbuildings*. New York: Orange Judd.

Hardeman, Nicholas P. 1981. *Shucks, shocks, and hominy blocks*. Baton Rouge: Louisiana State Univ. Press.

Hart, John Fraser. 1991. *The land that feeds us*. New York: W. W. Norton.

Heffelfinger, Ruth J. 1960. Experiment in concrete: A pioneer venture in grain storage. *Minnesota History* 37(1): 14–18.

Johnson, Paul C. 1978. *Farm power in the making of America*. Des Moines: Wallace-Homestead.

Ketchum, Milo S. 1907. *The design of walls, bins and grain elevators*. New York: Engineering News.

Leath, Mack N., Lynn H. Meyer, and Lowell D. Hill. 1982. *U.S. corn industry*. Washington, DC: U.S. Department of Agriculture, Economic Research Service.

Long, Amos. 1964. Pennsylvania corncribs. *Pennsylvania Folk Life* 14(1): 16–23.

Main, Gloria L. 1982. *Tobacco colony: Life in early Maryland, 1650–1720*. Princeton, NJ: Princeton Univ. Press.

Noble, Allen G. 1984. *Wood, brick, and stone*. Vol. 2, *Barns and Other Farm Structures*. Amherst: Univ. of Massachusetts Press,

Parker, William N. 1972. A note on regional culture in the corn harvest. In *Farming in the new nation: Interpreting American agriculture 1790–1840,* edited by Darwin P. Kelsey, 181–89. Washington, DC: Agricultural History Society.

Radford, William. 1908. *Radford's combined house and barn plan book.* Chicago: Radford Architectural.

Richey, Perry A., and Thew D. Johnson. 1952. *Factors to be considered in locating, planning, and operating country elevators.* U.S. Department of Agriculture Marketing Research Report No. 23. Washington, DC.

Riley, Robert B. 1977. Grain elevators: Symbols of time, place and honest building. *AIA Journal* 66(12): 50–55.

Roe, Keith E. 1988. *Corncribs in history, folklife, and architecture.* Ames: Iowa State Univ. Press.

Roepke, Howard G. 1959. Changes in corn production on the northern margin of the corn belt. *Agricultural History* 33:126–32.

Saloutos, Theodore, and John D. Hicks. 1951. *Agricultural discontent in the Middle West 1900–1939.* Madison: Univ. of Wisconsin Press.

Schimmer, James R., and Allen G. Noble. 1984. The evolution of the corn crib with special reference to Putnam County, Illinois. *PAST—Pioneer America Society Transactions* 7:21–33.

Schlebecker, John T. 1975. *Whereby we thrive: A history of American farming, 1607–1972.* Ames: Iowa State Univ. Press.

Shannon, Fred A. 1945. *The farmer's last frontier: Agriculture, 1860–1897.* Vol. 5, *The Economic History of the United States.* New York: Rinehart.

Wallace, Henry A. 1956. Corn and the midwestern farmer. *Proceedings of the American Philosophical Society* 100(5): 455–66.

10

Barns of Nonorthogonal Plan

Keith A. Sculle and H. Wayne Price

ROUND BARNS, octagonal barns—any of those kinds of barns that do not employ right angles—are preeminently barns of the Midwest. More barns of nonorthogonal plan were built in the Midwest than in any other region of the United States (figs. 10.1 and 10.2). Although they were not successful in the sense that they supplanted previous barn types to become much in demand by farmers, they represented essential values of the Midwest. They are not failed quirks deserving less attention than more representative barns, but worthy subjects for material culture study. Barns of nonorthogonal plan were the result of a unique constellation of factors that aligned in midwestern agriculture during the period 1880–1920.

GENERAL BACKGROUND

Economic factors conditioned the alignment. An agricultural revolution based in the Midwest got underway in the 1860s. Land was plentiful. Farming spread rapidly. Settlement of the trans-Mississippi West accounted for most of the new agricultural land, including the eastern parts of the Dakotas, Nebraska, and Kansas—the western perimeter of the Midwest. While cultivation of these areas was the most dramatic aspect of the agricultural revolution in the coalescing Midwest, many areas of the Old Northwest also opened to farming (Paullin 1975). Soon the Midwest became the breadbasket for an international market.

Capital and labor were relatively scarce and expensive. The farmer was caught in a cost-price squeeze. He paid out more than he earned and he could not make up the difference by increased production. Technology, the mainspring of increased profit (Bogue 1963), effected an endless spiral. As technology was introduced to increase farm production and to replace manpower, it also increased operating costs (Baltensperger 1985). Any technology that promised to cut costs, such as a barn which not only was cheaper to build but also saved labor, was welcome (fig. 10.3). Nonorthogonal barns held appeal. Although in the long-run,

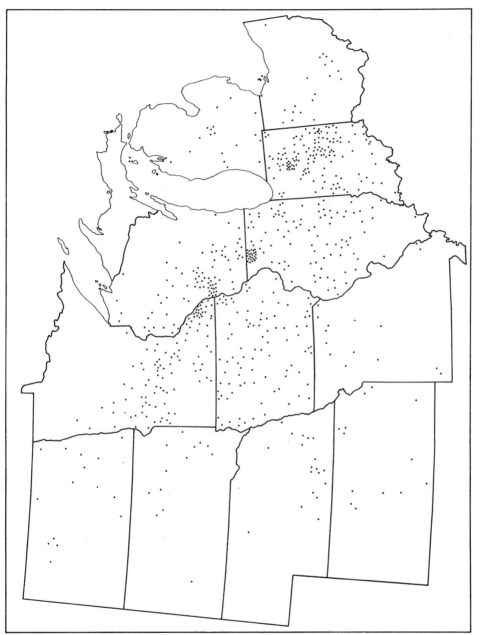

Fig. 10.1. Round barns in the Midwest. Nonorthogonal barns are concentrated in the prime dairying and corn belt areas, while only scattered examples exist on their margins. This figure and fig. 10.2 together show 1,048 nonorthogonal barns. Not included are barns whose perimeter wall shape is uncertain.

Sources: State Historic Preservation Offices and for the following states: Illinois: authors' field survey, William Clark; John Drury; Indiana: John T. Hanou; Iowa: Lowell J. Soike; Michigan: Eric A. MacDonald, Jack Worthington; Minnesota: Roy W. Meyer; Missouri: Joetta Davis Cornett; Nebraska: Roger L. Welsch; North Dakota: L. Martin Perry; Ohio: Mary Ann Brown; Wisconsin: Timothy L. Ericson, Larry T. Jost.

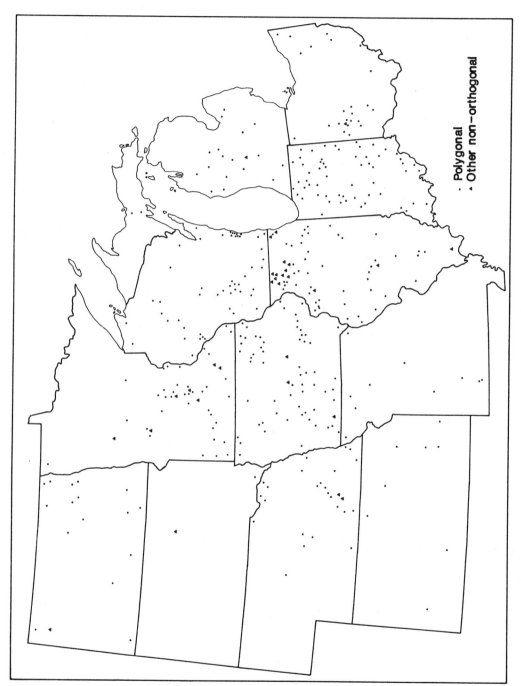

· Polygonal
◄ Other non-orthogonal

Fig. 10.2. Polygonal and other nonorthogonal barns in the Midwest. (See fig. 10.1 for sources.)

Fig. 10.3. Two round barns as they looked shortly after construction at the Sanders farmstead near Stockton on the Kansas prairie. Benton Steele built the barn on the left and began the one on the right.
Photo: Courtesy of George W. Colburn, 1914

farmers have continued to put faith in their individual application of technology to increase their income, they never perceived non-orthogonal barns as more than slight help (Farrell 1977).

Values were also at work within the economic alignment to legitimatize nonorthogonal barns as economic expedients. The vast majority of those who farmed in the Midwest did so for financial profit (Bogue 1963; Hart 1972). They exploited the land to its maximum capacity and readily innovated, so long as it promised increased income. For most midwestern farmers, commercial farming was their way of life.

Scientific and industrial values also aligned. Industrialism demanded specialization of functions to generate the highest profit rather than generalized operations for subsistence. Scientific and industrial farming techniques meant, after calculation of a farm's resources, such as soil type and transportation proximity, a farmer specialized in a few commodities, rather than relying on general farming to feed only his family.

Scientific agriculturalists were the first to broadcast the benefits of the new farming. They did so occasionally through model farms but, later and more frequently, through the agricultural press (Schlebecker and Hopkins 1957; Marti 1980). Their advice included a wide range of technology, including new building

191

types. Another group, the agricultural scientists, later emerged at land-grant colleges, where they at first were more interested in the discovery of a body of agricultural knowledge than mass implementation. They eventually worked to fulfill the legislatively mandated promise of the Morrill Act (1862) by establishing and teaching in colleges of agriculture, and, later, under the Hatch Act (1887), extended their teaching through agricultural experiment stations. Systematic farmers adopted, adapted, or rejected the preachments of the two scientific groups, depending on the perceived financial prospects (Marcus 1985; Rome 1982). As the owner of a large Missouri livestock farm with an octagonal barn explained:

> When my farm practice is in harmony with scientific theory, it is because I have found that the theory brings profit in practice. Where I depart from theoretical practice, or stop short of following out an accepted theory to its extreme, it is because I can make more money the other way. (Rankin 1902, 293)

By 1880 the foregoing factors had aligned to help formulate the Midwest's three major combinations of livestock and grain: the northern dairyland, the central corn belt, and the western wheat region (fig. 10.4). In each, nonorthogonal barns found a tentative audience for reasonable entrepreneurial risks. The economic framework of this general background is more fully developed in Fite and Reese (1973).

EARLY ADVOCATES AND EXAMPLES

Barns of nonorthogonal plan appeared first in the Northeast and South. Most were showpieces of gentlemen farmers, such as George Washington, who had a sixteen-sided barn built in late eighteenth-century Virginia (Haworth 1915); Leonard Bronk, with his thirteen-sided barn in early nineteenth century New York (Beecher 1991), and Charles B. Calvert and his octagonal barn in mid-nineteenth-century Maryland. These barns apparently lacked influence despite one agricultural journalist's recommendation of a smaller version for the average farmer (*Genessee Farmer*, 1854). Nonetheless, Calvert (1854) was a theoretical forerunner of those who later advocated nonorthogonal barns for efficiency.

Contemporary newspaper accounts of local, nonorthogonal barns so often cite the well-known, round Shaker barn built in 1826 in rural Berkshire County, Massachusetts, as America's first example. However, it was not a seminal model from which Americans quickly took inspiration to build others. The fact is that the first Shaker barn is readily distinguished from later mass-produced examples in the Midwest by its extraordinarily large (ninety foot) diameter relative to its small capacity (fifty-two cattle), stone walls which defied engineering efficiency, and lack of influence on subsequent structures. It was the barn rebuilt after a fire in 1864 whose publicity may have spurred wider interest among farmers (Robinson 1868; Soike 1983).

Orson Squire Fowler's *A Home for All*, the first of whose many editions was published in 1848, was the first widely disseminated argument for the octagon

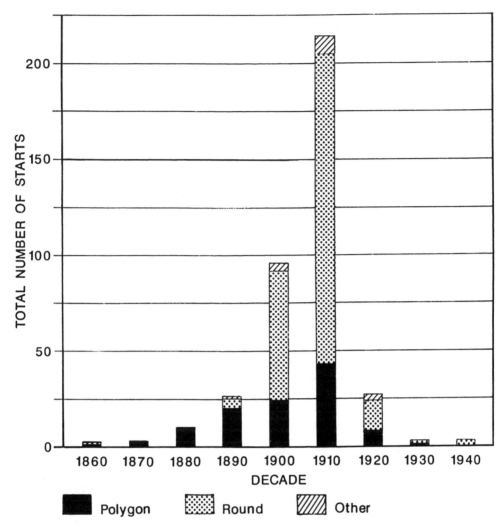

Fig. 10.4. Chronology of nonorthogonal barn building in the Midwest. This graph shows the year in which 376 polygons, round, and barns of other nonorthogonal plan were started. Barns built over a span of years are shown as built in the first year of construction. Polygons are underrepresented because many, probably nineteenth century in origin, could not be dated. Fewer barns are represented in this graph than on the maps in this chapter because the construction year is harder to determine than shape of plan and location.

form (1853). In it, Fowler criticized the impractical nature of the round plan. Although theoretically the round barn cost the least of all the shapes because it enclosed the most space per linear feet of wall—and despite the fact that Fowler regarded it as the most beautiful form—the barn nonetheless was harder for the average carpenter to build (Fowler 1853). Consequently, it was in practice more expensive. Thus, Fowler's championed octagon was actually a compromise, easier to build because it relied on straight wall construction, yet approximating the circular shape. The octagon barn enclosed more space than a building based on square corners. Although the influence of Fowler's widely read book on the construction of houses is commonly acknowledged, its influence on barns is largely discounted. Several barns, however, may be attributable to the brief treatment he gave to the octagonal barn plan (Fowler 1853).

Before the early period of gentlemen farmers' grand but isolated models ended in the 1860s, at least two similar barns were built in the Midwest. Perhaps the region's first was the 100-foot-diameter round brick barn which A. C. Jennings built in 1861 for his estate at Urbana, Ohio (Taft 1976). This landmark still stands; little is known of its origins. Possibly, it is as yet another work of a gentleman farmer, whose wide circulation likely introduced him to progressive ideas, and whose wealth permitted the luxury of experimentation. The other early midwestern case is the sixty-eight-foot-diameter octagonal barn built in 1867 by Lorenzo S. Coffin for his model stock-breeding farm near Fort Dodge, Iowa. In 1882 Coffin wrote a series of publications lauding his barn's convenience, strength, and ease of construction. By that time Elliot W. Stewart, a more influential publicist in New York, already had launched the nonorthogonal barn's period of greatest popularity (Soike 1983).

THE THEORETICAL FOUNDERS

Need fostered both theory and practice. Theoretical presentations laced with descriptions of how to build nonorthogonal barns began to appear in the 1870s. Thereafter, the fullest reasoned justifications and most elaborate descriptions for nonorthogonal barns were published, then reinforced through repeated publication. The barns arose in the dairying community, where their labor-saving promise was especially welcome in the most labor intensive of all the developing agricultural specialties (Alexander 1963), and were clarioned at approximately ten-year intervals beginning with Elliot W. Stewart in New York in the late 1870s. As the nation's primary dairying area emerged in the Midwest, with Wisconsin its center, Franklin H. King in 1890 first justified and elaborated a plan there; and, finally, Wilber J. Fraser did so in 1910 and 1918 as the corn belt undertook dairying for a variation on its developing farm system. Once popular interest beckoned and theory responded, the agricultural journals reinforced the reciprocal process by frequently describing plans and appending various brief rationale.

Elliot W. Stewart, the first theorist of the nonorthogonal barn, was a tireless scientific agriculturalist. He farmed, held a brief nonresident appointment in the fledgling college of agriculture at Cornell University, edited his *Buffalo Livestock Journal* (1872–76), was an officer and member of several local farm organizations, published one of the earliest agricultural textbooks, *Feeding Animals* (1883), which was frequently reissued (Dunn 1971, 19), and contributed regularly to several agricultural journals, especially *Country Gentleman* and *Rural New Yorker* (Stewart 1888). He deserves a more in-depth biography.

Scientific and industrialized dairying was under way in Erie County, New York, when Stewart farmed there near Eighteen Mile Creek. After four of his rectangular barns burned in the summer of 1874, Stewart took the loss as a

194

chance to build a barn in keeping with the "new agriculture." He constructed an eighty-foot-diameter octagonal barn as an integral part of the system for livestock breeding he had been developing for almost thirty years. Before building his octagonal barn, Stewart had assimilated the growing knowledge about specialized breeds and research on feeding and diseases, as well as housing. It is revealing that, in his treatise on scientific livestock farming, whose emphasis is reflected in its title, *Feeding Animals,* Stewart discussed the novel barn, not at the outset, but later in the text. Thus, from the very inception of the nonorthogonal barn's period of greatest popularity, it was not an architectural novelty built for its own sake, but was part of a far-reaching and complex strategy to modernize farming. It was not the barn alone, but the entire system of variables that was important to this mentality.

In conceiving the ideal barn to complement his scientifically managed farm, Stewart was driven by the quest for efficiency. He searched for the barn that would permit the fullest realization of all desired factors, including low construction and operation costs and great durability. Rectangular barns were easy and cheap to work with, Stewart admitted. However, when the new technology of the hay fork made it possible to increase production, taking more hay into a mow than was possible by hand, the resulting larger and higher rectangular barns required the introduction of interior posts, which obstructed operation. What Stewart termed "concentration" was another consideration. Following the lead of agriculture elsewhere in America (Hubka 1984; Herman 1987), Stewart was motivated to consolidate all the functions in one barn. "The shorter the lines of travel, the easier the work is done," he reasoned (Stewart 1888, 88). A round barn would better resist the wind, and, as Fowler had known, it would enclose more interior space with fewer linear feet of exterior wall. Nevertheless, while Stewart appreciated the round barn as the theoretical ideal, he rejected it in favor of the octagon barn. The round barn was too costly because builders were unfamiliar with it, whereas the octagon approached the true circle in all benefits, yet was almost as easily built as the square.

For twenty years after Stewart's initial explanation and description of his octagonal model in 1878, he campaigned for it, with considerable support in the agricultural press. In 1884, he reported that thirty to forty octagonal barns had been built in the nation, with approximately one-third of them in the Midwest: four or five in Illinois, three in Indiana, and two in Minnesota (*Cultivator and Country Gentleman* 1884).

Meanwhile, industrialized dairying with its propensity for nonorthogonal barns moved westward, and Wisconsin emerged as the nation's dairyland (see chapter 6). Not unexpectedly, New Yorkers were instrumental in this relocation. William D. Hoard, perhaps the most dramatic exemplar of the New York connection, founded and edited an agricultural journal, *Hoard's Dairyman,* which promoted the industrialization of dairying, and he achieved sufficient sway in his adopted state to be elected governor (Schafer 1992; Lampard 1963). The appeal of the nonorthogonal barn emerged next in this newly industrializing dairy scene.

Franklin H. King, son of a Wisconsin dairy farmer and a professor of "agricultural physics" at the University of Wisconsin, restated the rationale in terms heard before: efficiency, cost, and durability. In addressing old dairy-barn problems, King formulated a significantly new answer—the truly round barn. Responding in 1889 to an inquiry about the ideal dairy barn, he built and then tested a true round barn on his brother's farm near Whitewater, Wisconsin. He then advocated it in the university's annual experiment station report of 1890. King no doubt was aware of Stewart's writings on nonorthogonal barns, but he was convinced the round barn could be built more cheaply than the octagon. Stewart (1887) had insisted that his nonorthogonal ideal could be built only with heavy timber framing, yet King's experimental barn persuaded him that construction of a sturdy round barn was possible with the cheaper balloon framing. In taking a step further toward the ideal of efficiency, King "consolidated" a centrally located circular silo in the barn (Soike 1983). The silo was a technological device perfected only toward the end of Stewart's agricultural evangelism in the 1880s.

King's barn, like Stewart's, was founded on faith in scientific farming to increase profit. King had experimented with silos for a decade in order to extend dairy production into the winter, and the round barn augmented his effort. Such a structure was "greatly needed to insure the highest development of a large and profitable animal husbandry in a climate of long cold winters" (King 1890, 183).

In helping to found Wisconsin's national dairy leadership, King gained recognition as an expert on barn ventilation and published his accumulated knowledge on agriculture in a 1908 textbook (Soike 1983). A biography of King should be written. His influence on farmers wanting nonorthogonal barn plans came fairly quickly (Soike 1983). After all, he published from the eve of the agricultural boom of 1897 to 1912, and his ideas were widely disseminated by the agricultural press and several advice books on farm buildings. The shift in popular preference from Stewart's octagonal design to King's circular one can be traced in the agricultural press. Round dairy barns with King's characteristic central silo and balloon frame were reported widely in the 1890s (Sisson 1897; Benedict 1897; Curtis 1899).

Wilber J. Fraser, dairy specialist at the University of Illinois Agricultural Experiment Station, was the last theorist of nonorthogonal barns in their heyday. Like King, Fraser and his builder, H. E. Crouch, advocated the true round barn and not polygonal varieties. And, like King and Stewart's barns, Fraser's ideal barn was but one part of an overall scheme for scientific dairying to yield greater profit. He added nothing conceptually new to the appeal of the round barn, but just as important for its popularity, he published a bulletin on the round barn at the agricultural experiment station in 1910 and a revised one in 1918. By this period the station had established a tradition of reliable public service, and the agricultural boom made farmers willing receptors of the station's latest recommendation. Fraser's bulletins were further distinguished by more elaborate descriptions, including photographs and drawings, than his predecessors Stewart and King. This was probably to overcome the round barn's chief drawback—as Fraser saw it, the average carpenter's inability to build one easily.

Fraser's work virtually eclipsed his builder's, but their relationship merits further attention. Fraser, the theorist, relied heavily on Crouch to overcome the practical limitations which Fowler and Stewart pointed out in the round barn plan, and which King had almost ignored in his largely theoretical advocacy. Crouch's contribution as a builder permitted Fraser's bulletins to be implemented. Round barns, with a characteristic hip roof braced at the break, abound, especially in Illinois. They are silent testimony to Fraser and Crouch's fruitful teamwork.

THE BUILDERS

Builders of nonorthogonal barns were more important than traditional builders usually were, given the unusual problems nonorthogonal barns presented. Without capable or willing builders, nonorthogonal barns would never have become as popular as they were. Four categories of builders are identifiable: (1) builders who traveled throughout the Midwest to specialize in nonorthogonal barns; (2) builders who restricted their specialty to their home vicinity; (3) farmers or carpenters who built one nonorthogonal barn, or at most a few, in their immediate neighborhood; and (4) companies which supplied plans and materials and could furnish labor on request.

The itinerant specialists included a remarkable contingent of carpenters who started in Indiana. Benton Steele was foremost among these (fig. 10.5). Born near Warrington, Indiana, Steele was an exquisite draftsman who, alone among the itinerant builders, regularly wrote articles for the agricultural press advocat-

Fig. 10.5. "Ready for the rafters," written in Benton Steele's own hand above the upper right-hand margin of this photograph, proclaimed the stage at which Steele (extreme right) and his crew posed at an unidentified barn construction site. Photo: Courtesy of Shirley L. Koch

ing the round barn. He published at least sixteen articles on the subject in the *Indiana Farmer* between 1903 and 1909 and several others elsewhere in the Midwest as late as 1923 (Steele 1903, 1904a, 1904b, 1905a, 1905b, 1906, 1907a, 1907b, 1908a, 1908b, 1908c; 1915; Soike 1983).

Steele helped design barn equipment for an undetermined time for the Loudon Company of Fairfield, Iowa, which doubtless multiplied his influence (Steele MSS). In February 1909, Steele relocated to Halstead, Kansas, where he continued to advocate and build nonorthogonal barns. Although he is known to have built at least forty-four round barns in the Midwest—in Indiana, Iowa, Kansas, Missouri, Nebraska, and South Dakota (Hanou 1993; Soike 1983; Steele 1915), and possibly Minnesota (Gebhard and Martinson 1977)—the influence of his publications probably far exceeded these documented cases. His relocation to Kansas, where he had relatives, is largely due to his rivalry with another Indiana builder, Horace Duncan (Hanou 1993).

In 1903, Duncan and Steele had worked together on the 102-foot-diameter round barn for Frank L. Littleton near McCordsville, Indiana. Although the structure had been designed by Steele, the contractor Duncan not only earned praise for faithfully completing the challenging project according to the plans, but for "having suggested a number of new ideas which were adopted" (Steele 1904a, 1). These improvisations were not specified, but may have included the techniques for building the self-supporting roof. Duncan, with another carpenter, Isaac S. McNamee, and the help of Littleton, an Indianapolis attorney, were granted patent 804,427 for a "self-supporting conical roof" in 1905 (fig. 10.6). Vernacular builders thus made a signal contribution to the perfection of the round barn, which the theoretician King had introduced. In all Duncan is known to have built at least twenty-three round barns in Indiana, Illinois, North Dakota, and Ohio (Duncan 1912; Hanou 1993; Price and Sculle 1983).

Three builders are known to have built a large number of nonorthogonal barns only in their county of residence. Ernst Clausing, with his brothers, built at least one round and seven octagonal barns in Ozaukee County, Wisconsin, between 1892 and 1902. The Clausing barns account for half the county's unusually high number of sixteen nonorthogonal barns (Jost 1980; Whyte 1950). The Kindig brothers built at least nine round barns and one octagonal barn between 1910 and 1924 in Fulton County, Indiana, more than half of that county's sixteen nonorthogonal barns (Hanou 1993; Hood 1971).

The work of another local builder team, Jeremiah J. Shaffer and his five brothers-in-law, the Haases, is better known (fig. 10.7), and it illustrates how the interaction of one farm community and its set of local builders yielded a remarkable result. The principal market of the Shaffer-Haas team was Stephenson County, Illinois, where twenty-four round barns were built, one of the largest concentrations in the nation. Despite this impressive total, it should be noted that between 1901–07, 331 orthogonal barns had been started or adapted in Stephenson County (Sculle and Price 1983). For this prime dairying area on the Wisconsin border, the Shaffer-Haas team built at least fourteen round barns, including one in Wisconsin.

Fig. 10.6. Horace Duncan (left, foreground) with a crew at the site of an unidentified round barn. The sign at the right side of the barn's entrance makes a promotional stunt of this posed photograph and hints at the qualities which enabled Duncan to become a regional builder.
Photo: From the authors' collection

Jeremiah ("Jere") Shaffer was born in rural Stephenson County, attended college, and taught grade school. He was a voracious reader, often neglecting repairs on his house in favor of reading. In a speech to the county farmer's institute in 1905, he praised the round barn as cheaper to build, labor-saving, and more wind resistant (*Freeport Daily Bulletin*, Jan. 13, 1905).

Shaffer and his brothers-in-law had been building round barns for their neighbors since 1901. Shaffer, in the vanguard, advocated the product and arranged the contracts. Pride, pluck, and dramatics were assets in his neighborly appeals. For example, Shaffer persuaded one farmer to build a round barn with an ingenious demonstration. Seated at the farmer's kitchen table, he cut the bottom out of the cardboard tray from a box of kitchen matches. This left a rectangle which Shaffer filled to the top with oats. Upon reshaping the same cardboard into a circle, he demonstrated that the circle could hold more oats, even though it had the same perimeter as the original rectangle. Shaffer reasoned with customers about the other advantages of the round barn, applied his highly developed arithmatical skills to solve the novel problems of design, but worked with his crew only to start each barn.

Success of the product depended ultimately on Haas carpentry, the quality of which is a matter of local legend, due principally to the work of head carpenter

Fig. 10.7. Jeremiah J. Shaffer (center), a very prolific round barn builder, also constructed other buildings for his neighbors
Photo: From authors' collection

Omer Haas. He figured the cost and amount of materials and supervised construction, especially by laying out the essential framework. His brothers followed his instructions. The team built one round barn in adjacent Rock County, Wisconsin, but none in Stephenson County after 1914. The following year the Haases did build three in Albert Lea, Minnesota, and a roof for one in Winnebago County, Illinois, in 1917. Shaffer's last nonorthogonal barn was built that same year.

By far the greatest number of nonorthogonal barns were built by local carpenters or by the farmers themselves. Some bought plans and/or a kit from companies, but many others, apparently inspired by the minimal descriptions of particular barns in agricultural journals, sketched their own plans. A few of these simple plans, such as that for the octagonal barn A. C. Sherman built in 1908–09 south of Sleepy Eye, Minnesota, survive. They imply that most of the nonorthogonal barn's novel construction problems were solved as they arose on the job rather than having been foreseen and conveniently incorporated in detailed drawings (Akers, 1990a, 1990b).

Companies which sold combinations of plans and materials and recommended builders, when necessary, were the last to appear. The earliest of these were the outgrowths of individual builders whose hopes for large-scale profits led them to advertise their plan books. William E. Radford, founder of the Radford Architectural Company in Chicago, authored many do-it-yourself construction books, including *Radford's Practical Barn Plans* with discussions and drawings for round and octagonal barns (Radford 1909). William E. Frudden, of Charles City, Iowa, claimed in the foreword of his 1916 *Farm Buildings: How to Build Them:* "These farm buildings plans represent the practical results from ideas originated by farmers of the middle western states" (4). Photographs, brief descriptions, and a list of building materials for four variations on the round plan, two hollow-tile dairy barns, and a concrete and a hollow-tile barn for mixed farming demonstrate how versatile the nonorthogonal barn had become (Frudden 1916).

Meanwhile, Sears and Roebuck (fig. 10.8), from its midwestern headquarters in Chicago, mass-marketed pre-cut kits as but another of its many wares for farmers, available from mail-order catalogs (1914, 1915, 1916, 1917, 1918). Other companies, most notably Gordon Van-Tine of Davenport, Iowa, promoted the round barn to augment sales of their main products or services.

THE FARMERS

What kind of farmers had a barn of nonorthogonal plan built? The answer is not easily given; for even though correlations are possible by overlaying maps of various economic factors, such as farming regions or railroad net, historians of agricultural innovation have long known that adjacent farms can be very different. Each farm is an individual environment whose differences of terrain, size, ownership, and transportation proximity may seem subtle to the outside observer, but actually interact very differently to produce distinctive neighboring farms (Bogue 1963). Farmers who introduced nonorthogonal barns were not much above-average age, but were above-average in education, and operated above-average farms. However, many of the innovative barn owners, especially in Minnesota and Wisconsin, were not native born, and were of average means.

To be more specific, four Midwestern farmers from widely separated locations are presented as representative of those who built nonorthogonal barns. Profiles are offered of small-scale farmers because they had most of the nonorthogonal barns built. Yet, the patronage of the large-scale farmer, presented earlier, should not be overlooked.

Olof M. Titrud had a sixty-seven-foot-diameter round barn built in 1908. Titrud, a Norwegian immigrant, had settled in 1868 at the edge of Cokato, Minnesota, an area where diversified farming had supplanted small grain farming by

Fig. 10.8. Advertisement for an octagonal barn kit in the Sears, Roebuck and Company catalog of 1917
Source: Sears, Roebuck and Company archives

1900 (Boss 1912). Titrud selected two of the three local alternatives, dairying and livestock, but not grain production, with which to venture into commercial farming. To this end, his son, O. L. Titrud, a student of agriculture at the University of Minnesota, persuaded him to risk an innovative barn design. M. Carlsted, a respected carpenter from nearby Dassel, was hired to design and build the barn. Its central silo, King ventilation system, numerous windows, and reliable hay carrier marked Carlsted's work as state of the art, for which it was eagerly publicized in the 1910 issue of the *Minnesota Farmer's Institute Annual*. Titrud's barn may have helped reinforce the vicinity's inclination toward innovative barns because at least three other nonorthogonal barns were built before it, and at least two after, in Wright County, Minnesota (Meyer 1986). The cost was $3,000, with the finished barn housing eighteen cattle and nine horses (Titrud 1910). The barn survived without evidence of owner discontent (Hackett 1978).

On the western edge of one of Wisconsin's oldest dairying regions (Whitson 1912), Wesson J. Dougan, a young Methodist minister, had a sixty-foot round barn built in 1911 for the dairy farm he had bought five years earlier west of Beloit, in Rock County. Rock was a county apparently receptive to nonorthogonal barns. Dougan may have been inspired by the county's two earlier octagonal barns and he, in turn, may have inspired the county's two later round barns. His design was derived from King's of 1889, except for extensions and a secondary building. One extension was a nineteenth-century barn with characteristic hand-hewn frame which was joined to the balloon-framed round barn and initially adapted for horses, and then calves. Another extension was a shorter, ten-foot-long and steeply gabled wing devised as a sanitizing vestibule. It was fitted with a burlap flap through which the cows passed to remove flies before entering the barn. The pests were discharged into an ingeniously contrived cage for easy disposal. An approximately 100-foot-long shed nearby was where the herd awaited milking. Dougan, as his son later recalled, worked with carpenter Mark Keller in an adjacent field on various rafter arrangements to develop "an esthetically pleasing roof" for the main barn (Douglas 1978).

Dougan's adaptations of King's basic concept attest to two related characteristics of farming with special significance for nonorthogonal barns. First, many farmers were clever tinkerers who regularly adapted prescriptions of "book farming" to their own circumstances. Second, their ceaseless improvisation implies optimism as well as willingness to risk new devices or arrangements. The claim that farmers at the turn of the century generally ruled out the round barn as a matter of habit (Soike 1983) is doubtful.

In the established corn belt environment of Douglas County, Illinois, John McCarty had a sixty-foot round barn built in 1911 for the 240-acre farm he inherited north of Filson. McCarty, a 1904 graduate of the University of Illinois, was well aware of the round barn experiments in progress there. He wanted to take advantage of the round barn's theoretically cheaper construction cost. Having also lost all his horses in a barn fire, he believed a round barn would make any future evacuation easier. Timber was cut from a tract of linden trees about ten miles east of his farm. McCarty hired Horace Duncan to build the barn (McCarty, personal communications, Jan. 23, July 16, 1981). Having accepted Fraser's invitation to visit in late 1909 (*Knightstown Banner* Nov. 19, 1909), Duncan may have gone home as one of the few builders Fraser could confidently recommend to inquiring farmers as he sought to popularize the round barn.

Duncan's finished product, which cost $2,000, stabled forty horses (McCarty MSS). McCarty took advantage of Duncan's self-supporting roof to increase mow capacity, and added a one-story rectangular extension on the north side to stable additional horses. Over time, the round barn roof sagged and, by the mid-1950s, had to be braced internally with a large scaffold. Despite this failed roof, neither McCarty nor his son complained that the barn did not fulfill its original promise. In his continued enthusiasm for agricultural improvement, and in the prominence he achieved within the local farm community, McCarty typifies the round barn farmer.

About 1914, the Reverend Henry T. Biehler had a sixty-foot-diameter round barn built near Easton, Kansas, in Leavenworth County. On the western edge of the corn belt, the farm was on a relatively old claim; it had been in Biehler family hands since 1860, a year before statehood. Biehler, needing a barn and being an avid reader of farm journals, was especially impressed with one journal's mention of a round barn in Missouri. He also admitted to wanting a round barn simply because it was unusual, an occasional explanation given for the choice of nonorthogonal barns and one which cannot be dismissed despite the barns' usually overt rational appeal. Jim McGee, who operated a portable sawmill, moved his operation onto Biehler's property to cut walnut from the farm's wood lot. Asa Aaratt, not known to have built any other nonorthogonal barn, erected the structure to house and feed Biehler's work horses and mules. Roof-supporting posts and a dormered-mow access identify Aaratt's individualized approach, combining old and new techniques for round barns.

Aaratt's handiwork served its original purpose, albeit for a reduced number of animals, until it burned in 1978. By then, the barn had become a relic merely tolerated by Biehler's son, yet a sentimental favorite with local people of historical sensibilities (Pankratz and Wyma 1976; Kontowicz 1990).

THE DECLINE

Meanwhile, suspicion accumulated about the nonorthogonal barn's proported functional advantages, and this reduced its limited demand. Complaints surfaced in the same agricultural press which had helped spur rising demand, but the press should not be mistaken as the only agent of decline. Word-of-mouth probably led the way within the farming community (Colman 1968).

Limitations were known almost from the outset. Because the round plan was unfamiliar to the average builder and consequently more expensive to the buyer, Fowler and Stewart had promoted the octagon instead. By 1892, Stewart was willing to concede that a rectangular barn, despite disadvantages in capacity and cost, was good because of the relative ease of construction. From the start of the twentieth century, Joseph E. Wing, editor of *The Breeder's Gazette*, was an especially outspoken opponent of nonorthogonal barns. Wing claimed round barn mows were hard to fill (Wing 1902) and published a claim that their often wedge-shaped stalls were inconvenient compared to right-angle stalls (Wing 1905). A virtual litany of complaints mounted: Round barns let in too little light; required careful selection of lumber for construction; and did not vent silage odors well (Cottrell 1910; *Country Gentleman* 1912). Advocates like Benton Steele directly countered such claims by publicizing solutions. Thus, some nonorthogonal barns appeared with dormers for easier hay loading, and barn-equipment manufacturers produced circular hay tracks (Detraz and Steele 1903; Newlin 1918). A handful of barns with "oval" and "doughnut" plans, built in Douglas and Sibley counties, Minnesota, and Stephenson and Ogle counties, Illinois (fig. 10.9), only hint at the many remedies, most of which were probably attempted without publicity (Price and Sculle 1986; Sprengler 1990; Barbara Grover, director, Douglas County [Minnesota] Historical Society, personal communication, November 5, 1990).

Insurmountable problems in the round barn became undeniable, however. One was the waste of materials due to the need to cut certain members on an angle. One discontented builder perhaps exaggerated his claim in the *Ohio Farmer* (1906) that he built a small round barn that was six times more expensive than a rectangular barn would have been, and he was left with a "large two-horse wagonload of small blocks" (Shawver 1906, 3–67). Debate in the agricultural press suggests there was a practical range for the barn's diameter. One Michigan farmer reasoned that nothing less than a seventy-foot diameter would work (fig. 10.10) for labor-saving devices of manure removal and water supply (Wasson 1907). Someone else, who had observed more than fifty round barns, thought the two concentric rows of stalls in larger barns was cumbersome (Dacy 1916). And, a Nebraska farmer, who believed the round barn's advantages were limited to a structure with no larger than a sixty-foot diameter, built two attached round barns of 60 feet each for his large herd of cattle (Radford 1920). Functional limitations appear to have dictated size, regardless of theoretical arguments to the contrary. Most of the round barns observed by the authors range between fifty and seventy feet in diameter.

Debate and construction alike peaked in the 1910s. Perhaps one of the most convincing voices in the farming community was that of C. Doane, who had accumulated opposing evidence at the Maryland Agricultural Experiment Station after he left work with King in Wisconsin in 1898. He published his reasons against the round barn in 1912. Meanwhile, Frudden (1915) and Radford (1919) not only were vigorously advertising their nonorthogonal plans, but also contributed to the growing debate by their defenses in the agricultural press. Of course, Fraser's two bulletins in Illinois were the most elaborate advocacies in this decade, but even his conclusions turned from unqualified to conditional endorsement (Fraser 1910, 1918). By the end of the decade most of the commentary had turned negative. Several extensive articles reported more disadvantages than advantages (Dickerson 1918; Smith 1917; USDA 1919). The agricultural community was summing up forty years of experience.

The nonorthogonal barn's once-promising technology was eventually overwhelmed by superior technology. By the 1920s, the depressed farm economy induced great caution about technological innovation, although some farmers continued to take calculated risks. Most notably, the tractor began to be adopted widely (Fite and Reese 1973). A technology with mixed reports such as the nonor-

Fig. 10.9. Clear profile of an oval frame structure in Joseph Stengel's barn outside Mt. Morris, Illinois, in 1914
Photo: From authors' collection

Fig. 10.10. A. L. Wasson's barn, Gratiot County, Michigan, in three stages of construction in 1905. a. Balloon frame of the ninety-foot diameter barn; b. *Michigan Farmer* featured this barn in a series of articles (March–April 1906) and used this view to emphasize several techniques to strengthen a self-supported roof; c. V-shaped roof braces, visible at the upper edge, helped strengthen the barn.
Photos: Courtesy of Jefferson P. Arnold, 1905

thogonal barn, however, became an unreasonable risk in this tentative climate. As illustrated in a 1927 article, the last extensive summation on nonorthogonal barns, the increasingly scientific and industrialized values which had ushered in the barns judged them highly conditional assets and not the ideal (Fenton 1927). Later, mechanized technologies for saving labor were ill-fitted for nonorthogonal barns, thus rendering the structures obsolete (Starck 1983). Although a round dairy barn with many novel features at Rutgers University was reported as "experimental" in 1969, it seems to have won little attention since (Singley, Roberts, and Mears 1970).

CONCLUSION

Adoration has become the last vestige of concern. It began with Fowler's aesthetic, which found beauty in the round plan, and continued in the nonorthogonal barn's heyday (Crooker 1921). Farmers still are divided. Some owners fondly recall their nonorthogonal barn, while many dismiss it as an antiquated nuisance. Mostly, it is weekend motorists, agricultural sentimentalists, and round barn hobbyists who have salvaged unquestioned respect for the nonorthogonal barn. For them, nonorthogonal barns are nostalgic symbols of lost craftsmanship and relics of a mythic rural America, thus, ironically, they confer upon them a degree of acceptance never achieved in the barns' construction heyday.

ACKNOWLEDGMENT

The authors are heavily indebted to numerous individuals and organizations, including barn owners and county historical societies, unfortunately too numerous to name. Essential were the State Historic Preservation Offices (SHPOs) of the Midwest as well as in New York and West Virginia, whose files on nonorthogonal barns were made available. Long-time students of the nonorthogonal barns freely shared their knowledge: William Clark, Illinois; John Hanou, Indiana; Eric A. MacDonald and Jack Worthington, Michigan; Roy W. Meyer and La Vern J. Rippley, Minnesota; Joetta Davis Cornett, Missouri; Mary Ann Brown, Ohio; and Timothy L. Ericson, Wisconsin. L. Martin Perry, at the Kentucky SHPO, provided information on his North Dakota research. Steele's granddaughters, Coralie Tighe and Shirley L. Koch, shared family records. Sears, Roebuck, and Company opened its archives. Generous thanks are due especially to Lowell J. Soike, whose files were furnished the authors. Lastly, without the sterling service of William B. Tubbs, interlibrary loan officer, Illinois Historical Library, this chapter would not have been possible.

REFERENCES CITED

Akers, Charlene (director, Brown County [Minnesota] Historical Society). 1990a. Letter to Keith A. Sculle, September 7.

————. 1990b. Letter to Keith A. Sculle, August 20.

Alexander, John W. 1963. *Economic geography.* Englewood Cliffs, NJ: Prentice-Hall.

Baltensperger, Bradley H. 1985. *Nebraska: A geography.* Boulder, CO: Westview Press.

Beecher, Raymond (librarian, Greene County [New York] Historical Society). 1991. Letter to Keith A. Sculle, Feb. 2.

Benedict, F. M. 1897. A satisfactory round barn. *American Agriculturalist.* 54:621.

Bogue, Allan G. 1963. *From prairie to corn belt: Farming on the Illinois and Iowa prairies in the nineteenth century.* Chicago: University of Chicago Press.

Boss, Andrews. 1912, 4th ed. Minnesota. In Vol. 1, pp. 72–73, *Farms, cyclopedia of American agriculture,* edited by L. H. Bailey. London: Macmillan.

Calvert, Charles B. 1854. Essay on farm buildings. *The American Farmer* 9:369–71.

Colman, Gould P. 1968. Innovation and diffusion in agriculture. *Agricultural History* 42:173–87.

Cottrell, Fred R. 1910. A round barn in Kansas. *Breeder's Gazette* 57:834.

Country Gentleman. 1912. A round dairy barn. 77:21.

Crooker, Orin. 1921. The circular dairy barn—Some samples. *The Jersey Bulletin and Dairy World* 40:1599–1600.

Cultivator and Country Gentleman. 1884. Octagonal barns. 49:679.

Curtis, F. C. 1899, reprint 1973. An inexpensive round barn. *American Agriculturalist* 63:230.

Dacy, George H. 1916. Why I like a round barn. *Country Gentleman* 81(Ap. 16): 7.

Detraz and Steele. 1903. Round barn for ranchmen. *Breeder's Gazette* 43:424.

Dickerson, I. W. 1918. Round versus rectangular barns. *Wallace's Farming* 43:350.

Doane, C. 1912. Round barn handicaps. *Country Gentleman* 77(Sept. 14): 26.

Douglas, Nancy Belle. 1978. Centric barns in Rock County. National Register of Historic Places, unpublished nomination form, November 10.

Drury, John. 1955. *American aerial county history series.* Chicago: Loree.

————. 1956. *American aerial history series.* Chicago: Inland Photo.

Duncan, Horace. 1912. Letter to Dennis Severin, February 10.

Dunn, Walter S., ed. 1971. *History of Erie County, 1870–1890.* Buffalo, NY: Buffalo and Erie County Historical Society.

Farrell, Richard T. 1977. Advice to farmers: The content of agricultural newspapers, 1860–1910. *Agricultural History.* 51:209–17.

Fenton, Fred C. 1927. A round dairy barn. *The Dairy Farmer* 25(Aug.): 13.

Fite, Gilbert C., and Jim E. Reese. 1973, 3d rev. ed. *An economic history of the United States*. Boston: Houghton Mifflin.

Fowler, Orson S. 1853. *A home for all or the gravel wall and octagon mode of building new, cheap, convenient, superior and adapted to rich and poor*. New York: Dover Publications.

Fraser, Wilber J. 1910. Economy of the round dairy barn. *Circular 143*. University of Illinois, Agricultural Experiment Station Circular No. 143 (Urbana).

———. 1918. The round barn. University of Illinois, Agricultural Experiment Station Circular 230.

Freeport [IL] *Daily Bulletin*. 1901–1907.

Frudden, W. E. 1915. Is a round barn desirable? *Ohio Farmer* 135:4–92.

———. 1916. *Farm buildings: How to build them: A booklet of practical information for the farmer and rural contractor*. n.p.

Gebhard, David, and Tom Martinson. 1977. *A guide to the architecture of Minnesota*. Minneapolis: Univ. of Minnesota Press.

Genesee Farmer. 1854. Octagon barns. 15:119–20.

Grover, Barbara (director, Douglas County [Minnesota] Historical Society). 1990. Letter to Keith A. Sculle, November 5.

Hackett, John. 1978. Olof M. Titud round barn. Unpublished report in possession of Minnesota State Historic Preservation Office. (January).

Hanou, John. 1993. *A round Indiana: Round barns in the Hoosier state*. West Lafayette, IN: Purdue University Press.

Hart, John Fraser. 1972. The middle west. In *Regions of The United States*, edited by John Fraser Hart, 258–82. New York: Harper and Row.

Haworth, Paul Leland. 1915. *George Washington: Country gentleman*. Indianapolis, IN: Bobbs-Merrill.

Herman, Bernard L. 1987. *Architecture and rural life in central Delaware, 1700–1900*. Knoxville: Univ. of Tennessee Press.

Hood, Doris. 1971. *Fulton County's round barns*. n.p.

Hubka, Thomas C. 1984. *Big house, little house, back house, barn: The connected farm buildings of New England*. Hanover, NH: University Press of New England.

Jost, Larry T. 1980. *The round and five-or-more equal sided barns of Wisconsin*. Privately published, n.p.

King, F[ranklin] H. 1890. Plan of a barn for a dairy farm. Wisconsin University Agricultural Experiment Station Annual Report (Madison).

———. 1908. *Ventilation for dwellings, rural schools, and stables*. Madison: privately published.

Knightstown [IN] *Banner*. 1909. Nov. 19.

Kontowicz, Pamela J. (assistant administrator, Leavenworth County [Kansas] Historical Society). 1990. Letter to Keith A. Sculle, October 5.

Lampard, Eric E. 1963. *The rise of the dairy industry in Wisconsin: A study in agricultural change, 1820–1920*. Madison: State Historical Society of Wisconsin.

Marcus, Alan I. 1985. *Agricultural science and the quest for legitimacy: Farmers, agricultural colleges, and experiment stations, 1870–1890*. Ames: Iowa State Univ.

Marti, Donald B. 1980. Agricultural journalism and the diffusion of knowledge: The first half-century in America. *Agricultural History* 54:28–37.

McCarty, John. 1915. Response to questionnaire sent by H. E. Crouch, University of Illinois, College of Agriculture and Agricultural Experiment Station, Jan. 13.

McCarty, John. 1981a. Interview with Keith A. Sculle, January 23.

_____. 1981b. Interview with Keith A. Sculle, July 16.

Meyer, Roy W. 1986. Directory of round barns in Minnesota. Unpublished record. (September).

Newlin, J. J. 1918. Stewart likes round barn. *The Prairie Farmer* 90(July 13): 32.

Pankratz, Richard, and Cornelia Wyma. 1976. Biehler barn. National Register of Historic Places, unpublished nomination form, June 17.

Paullin, Charles O. 1975. *Atlas of the historical geography of the United States,* Plates 144 D-H, 145 A-H, and 146 A-B, E-F, and J-K. Westport, CT: Greenwood Press.

Price, H. Wayne, and Keith A. Sculle. 1983. The failed round barn experiment: Horace Duncan's experience as carpenter. *PAST—Pioneer America Society Transactions* 6:1–7.

_____ and _____. 1986. The 'doughnut' and 'oval' barns of Ogle and Stephenson Counties, Illinois: An architectural survey. *PAST—Pioneer America Society Transactions* 9:31–38.

Radford, Boyd C. 1920. Double round barns save time and cost. *System on the Farm* (December): 340–41.

Radford, William A. 1909. *Radford's practical barn plans.* Chicago: Radford Architectural.

_____. 1919. A round barn for the man who produces milk. *Power Farming.* 28:22.

Rankin, David. 1902. Feeding range cattle for beef. In *Practical farming and gardening,* edited by Willis MacGerald, 293–95. Chicago: Rand, McNally.

Robinson, Solon, ed. 1868. *Facts for farmers: Also for the family circle.* Vol. 1. New York: A. J. Johnson.

Rome, Adam Ward. 1982. American farmers as entrepreneurs, 1870–1900. *Agricultural History* 56:37–49.

S. S. S. 1910. A round cattle barn in Kansas. *Breeder's Gazette* 57:834.

Schafer, Joseph. 1992. *A history of agriculture in Wisconsin.* Madison: State Historical Society of Wisconsin.

Schlebecker, John T., and Andrew W. Hopkins. 1957. *A history of dairy journalism in the United States, 1810–1950.* Madison: Univ. of Wisconsin Press.

Sculle, Keith A., and H. Wayne Price. 1983. The round barns of Stephenson County, Illinois: The preliminary report. Paper presented to Pioneer America Society, Oct. 7, Macomb, IL.

Sears, Roebuck, and Co. 1914. *Modern Homes.* n.p.

_____. 1915. *Modern Homes.* n.p.

_____. 1916. *Modern Homes.* n.p.

_____. 1917. *Modern Homes.* n.p.

_____. 1918. *The Book of Barns.* n.p.

Shawver, John L. 1906. Round Barn. *The Ohio Farmer.* 110:3–67.

Singley, Mark E., William J. Roberts, and David R. Mears. 1970. Experimental circular dairy barn. *Agricultural Engineering,* 51(February): 78–79.

Sisson, O. S. 1897. Unique round barn silo. *American Agriculturalist* 61:434.

Smith, Robert H. 1917. Hole in the doughnut. *Country Gentleman* 82:396–97.

Soike, Lowell J. 1983. *Without right angles: The round barns of Iowa.* Des Moines: Iowa State Historical Department.

Sprengler, Waldo. 1990. Letter to Keith A. Sculle, Oct.

Starck, Peggy. 1983. *The barns of Winona County: A dying and vanishing tradition.* Chronicles, 2:2, pp. 5–8.

Steele, Benton. 1903. Many silos to be built. *Indiana Farmer.* 58(May 9): 9.

_____. 1904a. A circular barn. *Indiana Farmer.* 59(Jan. 9): 1.

_____. 1904b. Grouping, planning and general arrangement of farm buildings. *Indiana Farmer.* 59(Ap. 9): 1–2.

_____. 1905a. Farm dairy barn. *Indiana Farmer.* 60(Jan. 14): 7.

_____. 1905b. Circular barn for forty to eighty acre farm. *Indiana Farmer.* 60(Dec. 30): 1.

_____. 1906. Two Barns compared. *Indiana Farmer.* 61(Dec. 15): 5.

_____. 1907a. Silo construction. *Indiana Farmer.* 62(Aug. 24): 8.

_____. 1907b. Silo plans. *Indiana Farmer.* 62(Dec. 28): 5.

_____. 1908a. Rural architecture. *Indiana Farmer.* 63(Jan. 4): 1; (Jan. 25): 1; (Feb. 1): 1; (Feb. 15): 1.

_____. 1908b. Best barn for 160 acre farm. *Indiana Farmer.* 63(June 13): 3.

_____. 1908c. A round barn. *Indiana Farmer.* 63(Sept. 5): 7.

_____. 1909. Barn ventilation. *Indiana Farmer.* 64(Jan. 16): 1.

_____. 1915. A modern farm barn. *Dakota Farmer.* 35(Feb. 15): 230.

_____. Manuscripts in possession of Coralie Tighe and Shirley L. Koch, granddaughters of Benton Steele.

Stewart, Elliot W. 1876. An octagon barn. *Cultivator and Country Gentleman* 41:554.

_____. 1887. The octagon barn. *The Cultivator and Country Gentleman* 52:532.

_____. 1888, 4th ed. *Feeding animals: A practical work upon the laws of animal growth specially applied to the rearing and feeding of horses, cattle, dairy cows, sheep and swine.* Lake View: privately published.

_____. 1892. Barn for one hundred cows. *The Cultivator and Country Gentleman.* 57:812.

Taft, Lisa. 1976. Nutwood Place. National Register of Historic Places, unpublished nomination form, October 10.

Titrud, Albert O. 1910. The new barn at the Titrud Farm. *Minnesota Farmers' Institute Annual, Number 23.* St. Paul, MN: Webb Publishing.

U.S. Department of Agriculture. 1919. Comparison of round and rectangular barns. *Information Series No. 34* (October).

Wasson, A. L. 1907. Pointers on building a round barn. *Michigan Farmer* 50(Jan. 19): 50.

Wells, Wilson L. [1976]. *Barns of the U.S.A.* [San Diego: Acme Printing].

Whitson, A. R. 1912, 4th ed. Wisconsin. In Vol. 1, *Farms, cyclopedia of American agriculture,* edited by L. H. Bailey. London: Macmillan.

Whyte, Bertha Kitchell. 1950. Octagonal houses and barns. *Wisconsin Magazine of History* 34:42–46.

Wing, Joseph E. 1902. An octagon cattle barn. *Breeder's Gazette* 42:10.

_____. 1905. An Iowa round barn. *Breeder's Gazette* 45:273.

11

THE MODERN MIDWESTERN BARN, 1900-PRESENT

Glenn A. Harper and Steve Gordon

IN 1910, George Hyslop, a Henry County, Ohio, farmer, built what the *Toledo Daily Blade* proclaimed "the most scientifically constructed barn anywhere in the nation." A true "cow palace" in every sense, the so-called pagoda barn (named for its impressive pagoda-style roof designed by Toledo architect E. O. Fallis) housed state-of-the-art facilities. It featured crop storage, four 160-ton interior silos, a system for eliminating waste, and a comfortable environment for nearly 170 cattle, horses and hogs (*Toledo Daily Blade* Nov. 14, 1911, 11) (fig. 11.1).

And yet, just two years earlier and only about one hundred miles away, in Adams County, Indiana, Swiss Mennonites had built several post-and-girt, timber-frame, Sweitzer barns, continuing a tradition begun over two hundred years earlier by their Swiss ancestors (Neuenschwander 1986).

The Mennonite Sweitzer barns and Hyslop's pagoda barn, while not representative of early twentieth-century barn construction, do symbolize the collision of technology and tradition which characterized agricultural practices during this period. It is in this context that the development of the modern midwestern barn will be discussed.

If a single theme characterized twentieth-century barn construction, and agriculture in general, it was experimentation. Indeed, the period from 1890 to 1920 was marked by great innovation and experimentation in farm building design, especially in the Midwest. A corresponding farm modernization movement was encouraging agricultural scientists to test their new designs and products in the "real world" laboratory of the farm.

The declining condition of many farms fostered the modernization movement, but not enough for writer F. L. Marsh. In 1911, he complained to agricultural engineers that "a great stir [has been] made about farm machinery, but little said about farm buildings" (125). A post-World War I drop in farm prices aggravated the farm maintenance problem, and the Great Depression and the demand for raw materials during World War II only made things worse.

213

Fig. 11.1. A true "cow palace" in every sense, George Hyslop's barn housed state-of-the-art facilities, including crop storage, a system for eliminating waste, and a comfortable environment for nearly 170 cattle, horses and hogs.
Photo: *Landscape*, Vol. 22, Summer 1978

A federal farm survey revealed in 1934 that 700,000 farmhouses were, according to their occupants, beyond repair, and that more than two million farms needed new service buildings. Even more alarming, the survey showed, only one home in three had running water or a water pump, only one in four had electricity, and just one in ten had an indoor toilet and central heat (*American Builder and Building Age* 1943). A 1945 study of buildings on four-hundred Illinois farms indicated that the average age was forty-nine years, with no barns under twenty years old (Ekblaw 1945).

At the turn of the century, many midwestern farmers, especially those in the eastern part, were still building barns in the time-honored, traditional fashion. Materials were generally fabricated on site by the farmer himself or by local builders. These men were accustomed to erecting braced-frame, mortise-and-tenon barns using the *"scribe"* and *"square"* rules. With scribe rule barns, every piece of framing was uniquely fitted to the piece it joined. The joinery of square rule barns was laid out and cut so the framing did not need to be assembled until the barn was raised. Most barns were multipurpose structures, housing horses, cows, feed, and forage under one roof (Sheets and Kelley 1923; Parks 1923).

By 1910, however, a dramatic shift had taken place in the rural Midwest. The prototypical barn, although still two stories, was now a spacious, plank-frame structure built on a concrete or hollow tile foundation with an adjoining silo (fig. 11.2). Barn framing and interior plans had become more standardized. An optimum width of thirty-six feet provided the most economical use of lumber and allowed room in the basement for service alleys and a double-row arrangement of animal stalls (Webster 1908; White and Griffith 1916; Frudden 1918). Although a barn's length depended ultimately on the number of animals to be housed, the general-purpose midwestern barn, designed for a small farm by the United States Department of Agriculture in 1923, was a gambrel-roofed structure built to accommodate twenty cows and six horses. The barn included a bull pen and feed room on the first floor, with storage for hay, bedding, and grain above (Wooley 1946; Parks 1923).

What had occurred during the intervening decade to bring about the fundamental changes on many midwestern farms, in particular, the metamorphosis of the traditional farm barn? Several factors appear to have contributed to modern barn development, what one writer would ultimately refer to as "a revolution in the design of farm buildings" (McWethy 1947, 52). Factors include: (1) new framing systems and other innovative techniques for rehabbing old barns; (2) new construction materials; (3) the influence of the USDA and state agricultural colleges, especially their practical links with the farmer, the Agricultural Experiment Station, and the Extension Service; and (4) the impact of professional and popular agricultural journals, pattern books, mail-order catalogs, and other product dealer and manufacturer promotions.

Two conflicting schools of thought emerged on efforts to modernize the

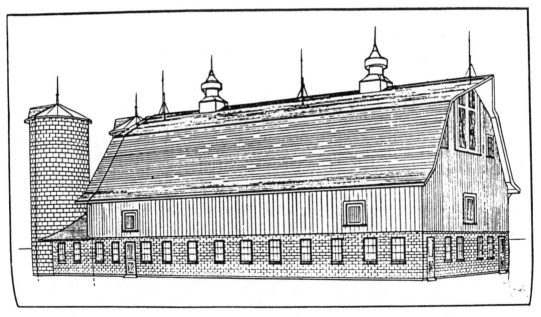

Fig. 11.2. By 1910, a dramatic change had taken place in barn construction. The prototypical barn was now a spacious, two-story plank-frame structure built on a concrete or hollow tile foundation, with an adjoining silo.
Source: Kansas Agricultural Experiment Station Bulletin 236, November 1925 p. 4

215

barn and its several agricultural functions: to remodel or rebuild the old barn, or to build an entirely new structure. Disagreements arose, not over the need and desire of every farmer to have a "clean, well lighted, well equipped, well ventilated and thoroughly insulated" barn (*Hoard's Dairyman* 1939, 177), but simply whether a modern farming operation could fit into a remodeled and renovated structure, or if it necessitated an entirely new barn. Argued the *Hoard's Dairyman*:

> It takes more intelligence to raise a building than to raze one. Don't tear down the old red barn—rebuild it for 50 years of additional service. (1939, 195)

This pointed statement is perhaps typical of the pragmatic attitudes of barn preservationists during the early twentieth century. Although a small percentage of people spoke philosophically and sometimes emotionally of the so-called passing of the barn (Allen 1914), few believed outdated structures should stand in the way of progress on the farm.

An Ohio State University extension specialist in agricultural engineering noted that timber-frame barns were rapidly being replaced by newer and more efficient types of framing (Twitchell 1921–22). Meanwhile, material manufacturers, who stood to gain the most from new barn construction, added their voice to the growing chorus of criticism regarding the "old red barn."

> We have seen the farm lighting system replace the kerosene lamp, the tractor take the place of the mule, and the gasoline engine supplant much of the manual labor of the farm. The time has come when the present, unproductive, unsafe, uninhabitable and costly-to-maintain buildings must give way to a new and better form of construction. (*Hollow Tile Farm Buildings* 1920, 2)

Having been criticized for their inefficiency and inability to meet modern agricultural needs, particularly those of the growing dairy industry, old barns also were derided for their vulnerability to nearly every kind of natural disaster. Hay-filled mows were viewed as highly combustible targets for lightning, and wood-frame barns were described as the major contributor to the annual fire loss. Furthermore, old barns were seen as extremely vulnerable to tornadoes and wind-storms (Witzel 1939; McWethy 1947). Although most farmers had managed to live with their old barns for decades, timber-frame barn critics became no less vocal.

There also were practical reasons for switching to plank-frame barn construction. Timber-frame barns, with their supporting interior bents or crossbeams, reduced the amount of space in the loft, created obstructions for the hay, and interfered with the hay carrier (*Hoard's Dairyman* 1939). In most standard timber-frame barns, a loaded hay carrier, which might weigh as much as half a ton, could not easily pass through the close-spaced tie beams. Moreover, tie beams forced the farmer to hoist the hay to the peak of the barn, requiring more time and often resulting in compacted hay (Wing 1898; Orange Judd 1903).

In the "modern" plank-frame barn, the roof itself was self-supporting or supported by purlins, which, in turn, were supported on specially designed, self-supporting trusses (fig. 11.3). Agricultural engineer J. L. Strahan established a classification of five such barn roof trusses, and clearly distinguished between these and what he called the "old" heavy timber-frame (Strahan 1918). The trussed barn, with its distinctive gambrel roof, could accommodate a radically different floor plan. It also eliminated the need for crossbeams, allowing for maximum use of the hay carrier. Indeed, improvements in the hay carrier and grapple forks had a profound impact on barn design, prompting farmers to modernize their haying operations, either by remodeling their old barns or by building new ones.

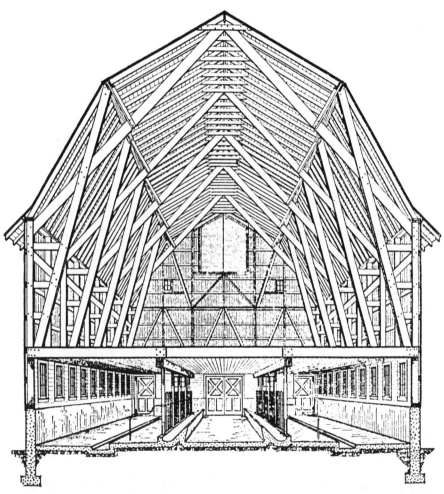

Fig. 11.3. In the "modern" plank-frame barn, roofs were supported by purlins which, in turn, were supported on specially designed, self-supporting trusses, or the roofs themselves were self-supporting.
Illustration: John Wooley, *Farm Buildings*, 1946, p. 249).

REBUILDING AND REMODELING

An essentially modern barn could be created by rebuilding or remodeling an older structure. Remodeling involved constructing a self-supporting roof over the lower portion of the earlier timber-frame bents. How many barns were remodeled in this manner is not known; perhaps thousands. Besides the obvious economy of a remodeled barn over a new one, the decision about whether to remodel or to build an entirely new barn was probably dictated by the essentially conservative nature of many farmers. Having relied for generations on their timber-frame barns, many simply were not ready to completely reject such a dependable building tradition. For them, remodeling or adding a plank-frame addition to an earlier timber-frame structure were acceptable alternatives. Even some tradition-bound Amish and Mennonite farmers remodeled their old Pennsylvania barns to incorporate the new, lighter-weight roof construction and expanded loft space. Today, these gambrel-roof barns, with their traditional bank or ramp and forebay, often conceal their true hybrid identity (fig. 11.4).

Despite the radical alteration of the barn created by the new, lighter-weight trussing systems, remodeling often involved other fundamental changes to the barn's appearance and function. For example, the focus of one plan for salvaging

Fig. 11.4. Remodeling a timber-frame barn usually involved constructing a self-supporting gambrel roof over the lower portion of the earlier timber frame bents. Even traditional Pennsylvania barns were remodeled in this fashion.
Photo: Glenn A. Harper and Steve Gordon

wooden farm structures was the construction of a new concrete base and concrete masonry walls, similar to those utilized in new barns. Since many old barns were considered unsanitary and structurally unsound, this plan also suggested removing all inside partitions and cutting off old siding, studs, and other vertical members (*American Builder and Building Age* 1943; Minot 1930). Other remodeling plans suggested incorporating the latest insulating and ventilating technology. Insulation was thought to save feed because cows burned less energy when housed in comfortable quarters, while proper ventilation was increasingly tied to laws governing the production of milk (*Hoard's Dairyman* 1939).

New Types and New Materials

Those promoting new barn construction believed that barns often required such extensive renovation that it was more economical and, ultimately, more efficient, to build an entirely new structure. The economy of materials and labor, as well as the design and aesthetic appearance of new barns, seemed to be the main selling points. Like those who espoused barn conversions, promoters of modern, lighter-weight balloon- and plank-frame construction nearly always focused on the opportunity for larger, unobstructed spaces in the haymow (Frudden 1918).

During the first years of the twentieth century, agricultural experiment stations, farmers' journals, and rural self-help guidebooks increasingly promoted the need for new, well-built, properly lighted, and well-ventilated barns. Farmers were advised to carefully select the proper site, floor plan, and building type before constructing barns and outbuildings (White and Jacobson 1925). "The right barn for the right farm" seemed good advice, since a poorly built "rule-of-thumb" barn, according to the *Farmers' Bulletin*, "all too often [was] a daily source of annoyance and wasted time and money" (Fish 1924; Marsh 1911; Kelley 1933). Arguably, a well-planned, well-built barn was as important to the health of the farmers' livestock as good feed and hygiene. Catchy slogans like "A good farm is worth good buildings" and "Fair barns that are well managed are better than good barns badly managed" were targeted to the average farmer who usually was his own architect and builder (Sherlock 1922, 88; Kelley 1933, 273). Readers of agricultural circulars and *Country Gentleman* were admonished to "build the farm on paper first" because "a bad building lasts for generations" (Radford 1918). The persistence of poor barn design prompted E. L. Seymour, a noted rural authority, to write in 1918:

> The tendency to follow the design of existing buildings in a neighborhood is no doubt the greatest hindrance to progress in barn construction. Defects are perpetuated and improvements ignored in copying the arrangement and construction of old barns, even if these have been found handy and durable. Farming methods are changing rapidly, and the old type of barn will soon be classed among relics. (366)

To reduce fire hazard, guidebooks advised farmers not to locate barns too close to the farmhouse, preferably no less than 100 feet, yet not too far as to make a long walk. Livestock and dairy barns built on a north-south axis received more direct sunlight and were generally cooler because the prevailing winds created a cross draft through the barn (White and Griffith 1916). Barns located on a high, well-drained site north and east of the farmhouse, with windbreaks to the northwest, were drier and utilized the summer's prevailing winds to carry offensive odors and insects away from the farm house (Betts 1920; Miller 1915). Bank barns were considered dark, damp, and difficult to ventilate, even if the forebay faced south and east, as was common. Farmers who continued to build bank barns were told to build a bridge to the second floor, instead of a dirt ramp, so light and air could enter the basement (Betts 1920).

Attention to sanitation was a central theme in the agricultural press, especially for dairy farmers producing certified milk. Fresh air, ample sunlight, and a clean, warm barn made for healthier animals, which, in turn, meant increased profits for the farmer (*Concrete on the Dairy Farm* n.d.; Hopkins 1920). Livestock, and dairy barns in particular, had to be kept clean and free of moisture and diseases, such as *bovine tuberculosis*. Feed alleys, stalls, gutters, and barn floors received increasing attention as part of what one advertiser referred to as the "Better Barn Building Movement" (*Building Age* 1920, 71). At a minimum, each cow was to have an equivalent of four square feet of window glass, and, when possible, wooden stanchions were to be replaced by swinging steel ones. Separate manure sheds or pits connected to the barn by litter carriers were to be located 100 feet from the barn and on the opposite side from the milk house (Frandsen and Nevens 1919; Parks 1923; LeClair 1917).

Because of its durability, easy on-site production, and fireproof and sanitary qualities, concrete had become a favored building material for barn foundations and floors by the end of the nineteenth century. The agricultural press, relying heavily on testimonial advertising, almost universally recommended concrete or hollow terra-cotta tile. A typical endorsement called for a concrete or hollow-tile basement wall with a concrete floor covered with cork brick or shiplap. Concrete was promoted as practically fire safe; even when fire did occur, the farmer suffered less financial loss because only the roof burned, leaving the remainder of the structure practically unharmed. Concrete also required no paint and was said to be rat proof (Ives 1920; Orange Judd 1903; *Building Age* 1919). Like concrete, hollow tile was advertised as fire resistant, "warm, dry and rat proof," (Durant n.d., 5) and easy to clean. However, hollow tile never challenged concrete's popularity, except where it was produced as part of a larger drainage-tile industry, such as in the Black Swamp region of northwest Ohio. The main disadvantages to hollow tile were its added expense and the need for skilled labor. Some observers also cautioned that the upper walls of a completely fireproof concrete or tile barn would likely crack from the intense heat of a haymow fire (fig. 11.5).

DEVELOPMENT OF PLANK-FRAME AND ARCHED-ROOF BARNS

The four decades from 1890 to 1930 were marked by a tremendous increase in farm productivity, including improvements in breeding, growing, feeding, har-

Fig. 11.5. Materials manufacturers, like the Hollow Tile Building Association, promoted their products as fireproof, sanitary alternatives to the traditional timber-frame barn. Although hollow tile never challenged concrete's popularity as a barn building material, this cover design from the association's 1920 promotional catalog illustrates the possibilities of tile on the farm.
Source: *Hollow Tile Farm Buildings*

vesting, and marketing. For example, Ohio statistics indicate that the widespread use of such farm machinery as corn binders, shredders and pickers, hay loaders, manure spreaders, and milking machines probably increased the crop acreage one man could handle from 25 to 50 percent (Falconer 1933). In Kansas, between 1914 and 1924, the number of farms selling butterfat rose from 28,000 to 60,000, while the value of dairy farms doubled (Fitch and Hillman 1925). Increased farm acreage, larger dairy herds, and the improvements in haying tools discussed in chapter 5 also contributed to greater farm productivity.

All of these changes increased the demand for larger interior spaces, making plank- and balloon-frame barns the preferred type for modern farm operations. At the same time, a diminishing supply of choice lumber forced many builders towards lighter, more economical methods of frame construction (Ives 1915). Plank frames required little skilled labor and could be built in less time with less lumber. A standard thirty-six-by-forty-eight-foot barn constructed of plank framing could be put up faster than, and required only half the lumber of, a conventional, braced-frame barn (Chamberlain 1902; Hickox 1899). Since every rafter was made to form a truss, no scaffolding was needed, and the trusses could be bolted and assembled on the ground or in the haymow. In essence, the truss created a self-supporting arch which, when completed, formed a rigid structure as strong or stronger than mortise-and-tenon framing (*Louden Barn Plans* 1914; Roberts 1918). Moreover, the size of the loft could be increased without building the barn higher at the plate or ridge (White and Griffith 1916). According to the *Ohio Farmer*, the substitution of plank for square timbers was the greatest advance made in barn framing during this period (Miller 1915).

The Midwest's leading proponent and builder of plank-frame barns was John Shawver (fig. 11.6). Deriding improperly built plank-frame barns as "guess work" frames, Shawver (1901) demonstrated how the strength of a barn frame depended less on the amount of lumber used and more on its method of framing. Each beam was to be only as large as needed to withstand the strain and was to be placed in its optimum position. In Shawver's truss, all inner bents were open arches which lacked the collar beams of a standard timber-frame barn. Since timbers were seldom thicker than two inches, planks could be doubled and tripled for added strength, while wire nails and three-eighth-inch spikes substituted for mortises and tenons (*Barn Plans and Outbuildings* 1903; Roberts 1918). Problems with end walls bowing out could be corrected by adding end braces (White and Griffith 1916).

Improved grapple forks, power hoists, and steel hay carriers further changed barn designs and made more efficient, labor-saving uses of the barn (Seymour 1918; Myers n.d.). Threshing floor space, which often consumed as much as one-third of the main floor area, was no longer needed since hay could be lifted through the hayloft door on a side elevation. A modern barn, designed in 1918 by Chicago architect William Radford, featured the use of wide feed alleys that extended through the center of the basement. Feed carriers suspended from metal tracks were employed to move silage directly from the silo into the feed alley, while chutes funneled hay directly from the mow to waiting livestock. Litter alleys,

....Rural....
Architecture

JOHN L. SHAWVER & BROS.
Architects and Builders
BELLEFONTAINE,   -   OHIO.
SIXTH EDITION 1908
Residence at Hazelton.   Long Distance Telephone

Fig. 11.6. John Shawver was the Midwest's leading proponent and builder of plank-frame barns. A carpenter-builder by trade, Shawver built hundreds of houses and barns in western Ohio and eastern Indiana.
Source: Courtesy David Kukuk

which ran behind the animals, allowed the farmer to remove the manure from the barn by metal litter carriers or manure spreaders (*Country Gentleman* 1917).

During the second quarter of the twentieth century, the gothic or arched-roof barn, with its laminated bents and glued arches, found considerable popularity among Midwest farmers. Framing for gothic barns was constructed either on the foundation, the mow floor, or the building plate. Most gothic barns were built from the mow floor up, resting on a glazed tile or concrete block basement. Two leading midwestern fabricators, G. N. Brekke, a Rock Island, Illinois, structural engineer, and Rilco Laminated Products Company of St. Paul, Minnesota, designed and manufactured gothic barn rafters for distribution to lumber retailers (Brekke 1937; *Ohio Farmer* 1948) (fig. 11.7). A fuller discussion of gothic roof framing appears in chapter 8.

A trend toward barn specialization and single-story construction began in the 1930s and accelerated after World War II. Government and university agricultural experts alike confidently predicted that the general-purpose wood-frame barn, nostalgically, and at times sarcastically, referred to as "the big red barn," would be replaced by five million gleaming buildings made of steel, aluminum, and treated wood (Witzel 1939).

Increased mechanization, especially after 1920, created new demands for implement storage facilities and altered traditional barn functions. Most farms changed from a dependence on draft animals to mechanical power, and farmers shifted from general-purpose farming to crop and animal specialization, which increased the demand for highly specialized equipment and facilities designed to

Fig. 11.7. The roof of this Clark County, Illinois, barn is constructed of Rilco ready-made laminated rafters. Built as a dairy barn in 1939, it was converted to a restaurant in 1976.
Photo: H. Wayne Price

meet these new production needs. In 1930, 61,000 combines were reported by the U.S. Census; in 1953, 918,000. One in six farmers already owned a tractor by 1932 (Williams 1987). In 1944, 14 percent of the nation's hay was harvested with windrow balers; by 1948, the figure was 46 percent (Cavert 1956). Ohio farmers surveyed in the 1950 Census reported having only 13,378 pickup bailing machines; by 1959 the number had risen to 41,809 (*U.S. Census of Agriculture: Ohio* 1959).

METAL AND POLE BARNS

The shift from loose to baled or chopped hay reduced the need for haymows as many farmers adopted the "loose-housing" or "loafing" system for housing cattle (Ashby 1957; Wooley 1946). University of Wisconsin agricultural scientists effectively argued that cows did not need stalls and would be more content if permitted to roam in and out of the barn at will. The theory, of course, was that a more contented cow would give more milk. Failure to house livestock properly not only could impair production, but also could pose a sanitary hazard (Giese 1949). The loose-housing theory resulted in construction of one-story, galvanized, all-steel barns to test the efficiency and economy of this type of dairy operation. The use of metal products in barn construction encouraged companies such as the Carnegie-Illinois Steel, Alcoa, and Reynolds Metals to get into the barn building-materials business. For the first time, even the word "barn" did not seem appropriate. The Reynolds company, for example, described its all-aluminum, factory-built barn as a "general utility building" (Carter 1956, 258).

Farmers began to rely less on conventional structures built by carpenters and more on engineer-prepared plans, manufactured materials, and factory-built, fireproof barns constructed of standardized components, trusses, panels, and frames. The importance of designing barns for the efficient flow of materials and the facilitation of labor-saving equipment was strongly supported by engineers and progressive farmers. Perhaps predictably, farm building designers even invented a one-building farm—a family size apartment built over a milking parlor—similar to the old-world concept of the housebarn. Fortunately, the kitchenette-efficiency approach to farm building design never gained wide acceptance (Hicks 1948; Carter 1957).

Despite the radical change in appearance, the all-metal farm building seemed to be the wave of the future. New milk-production codes, efforts to stop the spread of infectious diseases by housing animals in separate structures, and modern methods and machines for processing hay heavily influenced barn design. Research conducted by Purdue University indicated that separate, ventilated, metal hay structures with electric fans and concrete livestock barns reduced the threat of fire and removed dust and dirt from the milking barn. Farmers who experienced devastating losses from barn fires also were attracted to alternative materials such as steel and concrete (Anderson 1938; McMunn 1947a; Carter 1957; Schaffhausen 1939).

Although metal never surpassed wood as an inexpensive, lightweight material, some farmers, such as John Cole of Mulliken, Michigan, opted to build an all-steel barn. Comparatively light and rigid, the gothic-roofed framework was covered with twenty-two-gauge, corrugated, copper-alloy sheet metal (*Literary Digest* 1926). Other early metal-barn types, such as Quonsets, gained a notable measure of popularity among midwestern farmers immediately after World War II. One of the leading manufacturers of Quonset barns and sheds was the Great Lakes Steel Corporation of Detroit (fig. 11.8). Advertisements appearing in the *Ohio Farmer* during the late 1940s touted the Quonset's fireproof, rat-proof, sag-proof, and age-resistant qualities. Reinforced with "Stran-steel framing," the Quonset-36 model made an ideal two-row dairy barn, although Quonsets one hundred feet in length were built (McMunn 1947b).

The Quonset was just one of many attempts to prompt farmers into using materials other than wood for their barns. Corrugated metal and plywood often were suggested as coverings for wooden barn siding, and organizations such as the Asbestos Farm Service Bureau promoted the use of large asbestos-based cement boards for siding old barns (McMunn 1947b; *Ohio Farmer* 1946a, 1946b, 1946c, 1947). Despite the proliferation of modern barn products, some members of the agricultural press readily admitted that there was no universal building material (Giese 1949).

The modern concept of utilizing round poles as the principal structural support for farm buildings was initially developed by H. Howard Doane in the early 1930s. Doane, founder of Doanes' Agricultural Service of St. Louis, and Bernon George Perkins, his farm manager, devised a system of creosoted, pressure-treated poles as primary framing, with two-by-fours spaced four feet apart as sheathing material. Perkins' pole-building design concept, patented in 1953, significantly reduced the amount of lumber needed and could be erected in considerably less time than traditional wood-frame buildings. Further improvements in barn design, especially with lumber-rigid frames and their post-free interiors, were introduced in the early 1960s by engineers at the University of Illinois College of Agriculture. Both the single-story metal-pole barn and the lumber rigid frame could be fabricated by local lumberyards, local builders, and home labor (Doane and Perkins 1990; Ashby 1957) (fig. 11.9)

BEYOND THE BARN

Today's agricultural buildings bear little resemblance to their timber-frame or plank-frame predecessors. Perhaps for this reason, manufacturers seldom use the term *barn* in promoting their products. Instead, modern farm buildings are typically designed and identified according to their specific function, such as machinery storage or livestock housing. The traditional multipurpose barn simply is no longer necessary or practical. For example, loose or baled hay, which once required large amounts of barn space, now can be rolled and kept in the field. Concurrently, the increasing size and cost of farm machinery has necessitated an entire category of structures just for the storage of tractors, combines, and other farm equipment.

The prefabrication process that led to the development of the modern barn has evolved into the corporate mass production of standardized wood, metal, and fiberglass elements kept in large, year-round inventories. As a result, materials can be transported quickly to a building site and assembled into well-lighted, well-

Low-Cost...Easy-to-Erect
STRAN-STEEL BUILDINGS FOR THE FARM!

THE STRAN-STEEL
"Quonset 20"

Here is a 20'-wide steel building, available in various lengths to meet your needs, that gives you *steel construction at its best*. The sturdy, adaptable "Quonset 20" is fire-safe, rot-proof, sag-proof, termite-proof and age-resistant — "better from the ground up" — *yet it costs no more* than an ordinary building of comparable size.

We ask you to inspect the "Quonset 20" foot by foot and feature by feature, and see how much more value it offers for the money. The interior is clear-span, permitting full use of every inch of space. The framing is sturdy, efficient Stran-Steel arch-rib construction — uniform in quality and strength — with its patented *nailing groove* that permits ex-

terior covering and interior fixtures to be *nailed directly* to the framing members, simply and permanently. The siding and roofing are high-quality sheet steel, proof against wind, weather, fire and dry-rot . . . easy and economical to maintain.

Safeguard your farm profits and property with these stronger, longer-lasting, fire-safe buildings. *Tested and proved* in the tens of thousands of military "Quonsets" produced by Great Lakes Steel Corporation for the armed forces, the "Quonset 20," the larger "Quonset 40" and the "Quonset 24" are available now to meet your building requirements. For complete information, see your nearest Stran-Steel "Quonset" dealer, or write us direct.

GREAT LAKES STEEL CORPORATION
STRAN-STEEL DIVISION • PENOBSCOT BUILDING • DETROIT 26, MICHIGAN
UNIT OF NATIONAL STEEL CORPORATION

STRAN-STEEL

"Quonset 40"
Some quality features of construction and material in a 40'-wide Stran-Steel arch-rib building. Length to meet requirements—40', 60', 80', 100', etc. Free-rolling 12'x12' door, large windows and ventilating louvers in each end-panel — additional windows in sides if desired. Fire-safe, sturdy, adaptable to many uses.

"Quonset 24"
An ideal building for implement, auto, truck or farm produce storage. 24' wide by any length, in extensions of 12', the "Quonset 24" is available with or without front sliding doors or solid front panels. Walk-door and windows for end-panels, as well as solid steel interior partitions for any 12' section, are also available.

Fig. 11.8. Metal Quonset barns gained a measure of popularity among midwestern farmers after World War II. The Great Lakes Steel Corporation of Detroit was among the leading manufacturers.
Source: *Ohio Farmer*, January 19, 1946, p. 39

Fig. 11-9. Lumber-rigid frames, with their post-free interiors, were introduced in the early 1960s by engineers at the University of Illinois, College of Agriculture. Like its predecessor, the pole building, lumber-rigid frames could be fabricated by local lumber yards, local builders, and house labor.
Photo: Courtesy of Arthur Muehling, Cooperative Extension Service, University of Illinois

insulated, and weather-tight farm buildings. Perhaps the most marketable feature of contemporary agricultural buildings, from which those who seek to renovate old barns have taken their cue, is that they provide abundant amounts of single-story, clear span space. Manufacturers offer roof trusses which support clear spans as long as eighty feet and high clearance, all-steel, end and side wall doors with wide openings for easy machinery movement. Interiors can be lighted with ridge lights, sky lights, and eave lights, and a variety of natural and mechanical systems offer draft-free ventilation. Livestock housing is said to be designed for easy herd handling and even can be custom designed to match the farmer's "personal management style and to provide a healthy, productive environment" for the farmer and his animals. Even solar-heated livestock buildings are available, with heavy-duty fiberglass panels designed to collect and hold solar heat (Cleary Building Corporation, Verona, Wisconsin).

BARN IMPROVEMENTS, GOVERNMENT, AND THE AGRICULTURAL PRESS

The "Better Barn Building Movement" and the evolution of the modern midwestern barn coincided with a period of growing government involvement in the nation's agricultural industry and an increasingly visible and outspoken agricultural print media. Several important pieces of federal legislation were passed, including the Smith-Levy Act in 1914, which provided for the expansion of agricultural extension work under the direction of the state agricultural colleges, and the Smith-Hughes Act in 1917, which encouraged the teaching of agriculture in high schools. Later, the Research and Marketing Act provided funds for farm structures research and furthered the goals of the state cooperative programs (Falconer 1933; Giese 1949). State and federal publications, cooperative building plan services, and the agricultural press disseminated information on the location of farm buildings and better building design. The extension service departments of most agricultural colleges and college departments of rural economics or farm management, agricultural engineering or farm mechanics, and horticulture or landscape architecture also offered advice on the arrangement of farm building groups (Ives 1922; Ashby 1957; Lewis 1921). Across the Midwest the leading agricultural experiment stations published bulletins and circulars on a wide range of subjects, including silo construction, barn ventilation, farm home improvement, and farm building plans (Lewis 1921; Beattie 1909). By 1900, an average of four hundred bulletins and reports were being distributed to more than half a million addresses each year. Yet, according to Roy Scott, author of "Science for the Farmer," few farmers read such information because "book farming" had only a limited following (Scott 1974). Meanwhile, experiment stations may have had only indirect influence on ordinary farmers and farming practices until well after 1900, when methods of modern agricultural extension techniques were developed by county agents (Scott 1974, 218–220). As recently as 1949, some experts cautioned that agricultural research was of little value since the results were not made widely available (Giese 1949; Ekblaw 1945).

The University of Wisconsin Experiment Station offered nine barn plans, ranging from a general-purpose barn to a pioneer barn, and sent its free publications to all residents of the state. In Indiana, a 1921 circular reported "many calls are coming daily to the Experiment Station from farmers asking for assistance in planning their buildings." The Indiana farmers echoed the "great demand" at the U.S. Department of Agriculture "for information related to the construction of dairy buildings" (Lewis 1921, 3). The USDA's Division of Agricultural Engineers published its first list of farm building plans in 1923, and another list of nearly three thousand farm building and equipment plans was published in 1929 (Lyle 1931). After World War I, farmers could obtain free blueprints from the USDA or county agents (Sheets and Kelley 1923; Parks 1923; White and Jacobson 1925). Extension offices soon formed committees and published bulletins that exchanged information among the midwestern land-grant colleges (Parks 1923).

Despite the rapid increase in barn bulletins and circulars, some governmental agencies still may not have devoted enough attention to designing barns that met modern farming needs. For example, from 1887 to 1931, Ohio's Agricultural Experiment Station apparently published only one bulletin on barn design. Similarly, *Agricultural History*, the leading academic journal in the field, gave minimal coverage to the subject of barn and farm structures design (Whitehead 1977).

Where some state and federal agencies appear to have failed to adequately address the issue of modern barn design, carpenters and builders, and, later, private design companies and professional agricultural societies, apparently filled the need. Individual barn plans and descriptions had first appeared in the late eighteenth century. By the mid-nineteenth century, several publications, including G. Shaw's *Rural Architecture* (1843), *Stepens Book of the Farm* (1851), and Lewis Allen's *Rural Architecture* (1852), offered a few barn plans and discussed barn design within the larger context of farm planning. William Radford's architectural company and Orange Judd began publishing more complete plans and specifications for farm houses, barns, out-buildings, and other farm structures well before the turn of the twentieth century (*Harneys Barns* 1873). By the early 1900s, several companies were publishing detailed plans for every aspect of the modern farm. These included E. Powell's *Barn Plans and Outbuildings* (1903), Sanders Publishing Company's *Farm Buildings* (1907), and Radford's *Combined House and Barn Plans Book* (1908) and *Practical Barn Plans* (1907). Sears Roebuck and a company with the unlikely name of Chicago House Wrecking included several barn plans in their widely distributed house plan books.

All these later publications claimed that any individual who planned to erect a building of any kind could obtain a wealth of information for a small sum. Farm building-plan books not only provided plans for barns and outbuildings, but also expounded on a number of related issues, including the proper location of buildings, the best type of construction, and even the aesthetics of good farmstead design. For example, Orange Judd's 1911 publication noted the following:

> Barns can be pleasant objects and impart an impression of comfort and completeness upon all who see them. Their attractiveness will depend upon the symmetry and exterior finish of the buildings themselves, their grouping, the planting of shade trees, etc. The projecting cornice and cupola costs little but add much to the appearance of a building. (xvi)

In an attempt to keep up with the latest in agricultural sanitation concerns, some plan books also discussed such issues as ventilation. Orange Judd (1911) promoted the very latest in ventilation technology, the F. W. King system, which controlled the inflow and outflow of air through ventilating tubes regulated by dampers. Some companies, such as Jamesway Manufacturing, peddled their literature in the popular agricultural journals of the day. With such eye-catching appeals as, "I got this part of my barn free with Jamesway service," and "Get Jamesway plans first and save money," this company invited readers to write for a free book, *What We Should Know About Each Other*, and to consult a Jamesway serviceman about their barn problems (*Ohio Farmer* 1923, 77) (fig. 11.10). After rural electrification, Jamesway even broadcast a radio program titled: *Jamesway Barn Warming*, billed as a half-hour of fun and entertainment.

Detailed drawings and plans for modern barns increasingly appeared in trade journals. *Building Age*, a leading national trade journal, published several articles during the 1910s featuring barn plans and framing and construction details. The American Society of Agricultural Engineers regularly published articles on farm improvement and barn planning. The ASAE addressed such long-range farm

"I Got this part of my Barn Free with Jamesway Service"

Fig. 11.10. The James Way Manufacturing Company was a leader in farm-building plan books. Using eye-catching slogans, like the one in this advertisement, James Way urged readers to write for their free book and to contact a James Way serviceman with their barn problems.
Source: *Ohio Farmer.* 1923. (January 6) 16.

design issues as standardization in farm construction and designs for permanent farm buildings, arguing that buildings should be designed so they could easily be converted to a variety of uses (Fowler 1913; Cartwright 1929; Giese 1949).

CONCLUSION

Throughout the rural Midwest, the impact of the post-1900, modern barn is visually evident. Countless gambrel-roof, plank-frame structures dot the landscape, though such forms were nearly nonexistent before 1900. These structures vividly reflect the construction technologies and scientific farming practices which brought about dramatic changes in American agriculture after the turn of the century.

At the same time, an impressive number of nineteenth-century timber-frame barns is still present on the landscape. Did the owners of these barns, despite an avalanche of propaganda, seldom feel compelled to abandon or alter this traditional building technology; or, did economics play a role in their decision? Further study may confirm that fewer new and remodeled barns are found in areas where agriculture, even in the early twentieth century, was already in decline.

Equally telling, at least in terms of their effect on the appearance of historic rural landscapes, are the ever-increasing numbers of single-story, wood and metal, prefabricated agricultural buildings. Like the ranch house, their domestic suburban equivalent, these structures are ushering in a homogeneous leveling of the landscape. Their horizontal appearance is in stark contrast to the perpendicular orientation of earlier generations of barns. Nor do these modern agricultural buildings engender much in the way of design or architectural aesthetics. In fact, except for an occasional gambrel roof and their rural location, there is little to distinguish these utilitarian structures from similar buildings constructed in urban areas for commercial use. The uniform design of such modern agricultural structures has led one author to predict "a national rural landscape of repetitious buildings" (Carlson 1978, 33).

Perhaps the ultimate tribute to the generation of technicians, engineers, and builders who fostered the development of the modern barn can be found in the growing efforts to rehabilitate and renovate many older timber-frame structures (see chapter 13). Many of these projects, like the new, factory-built agricultural buildings they compete with, focus on the need for more clearance or obstruction-free space. For example, Dave Ciolek, a licensed builder from Bridgeport, Michigan, has helped save more than two hundred old barns by removing low lofts and posts and installing a truss on each crossbeam for roof and side wall support. The triangle-shaped trusses bear the load formerly carried by vertical posts (Creager 1988). This system, like the self-supporting trusses of the plank-frame and remodeled timber-frame barns of the early twentieth century, creates larger amounts of open space for hay and machinery storage or for a variety of modern uses. Both the concept of and the justification for the modern barn appears to have come full circle. Undoubtedly, early twentieth-century barn designers and builders such as John Shawver would be impressed.

REFERENCES CITED

Allen, Lewis. 1852. *Rural architecture.* New York: Saxton.

Allen, Lorraine Anderson. 1914. The passing of the barn. *Suburban Life* (August) 77, 85.

American Builder and Building Age. 1943. An immediate farm job: Rebuilding old barns. (January): 50–51.

Anderson, Earl D. 1938. New barns for new conditions. *Agricultural Engineering* 19(March): 117–18.

Ashby, Wallace. 1957. Fifty years of development in farm buildings. *Agricultural Engineering* 42(June 1957): 426–32, 459.

———. 1917. Barn planning. *American Society of Agricultural Engineers, Transactions* 10(2): 22–34.

Beattie, W. R. 1909. Comforts and conveniences in farmers homes. *Yearbook of the United States Department of Agriculture,* 345–46. Washington, DC: Government Printing Office.

Betts, M. C. 1920. Planning the farmstead. [United States Department of Agriculture] Farmers' Bulletin No. 1132, 1–23. (August).

Brekke, G. N. 1937. Bent, glued rafters make strong barns. *American Builder* 59(May): 74.

Building Age. 1919. Dairy barn and manure pit on modern farm. 41(April): 140–41.

———. 1918. How a dairy barn and silo were planned for convenience. 40(February): 285–87.

———. 1920. Advertisement for national manufacturing company. 42(November 1920): 71.

Carlson, Alvar W. 1978. Designating historic rural areas. *Landscape* 22(Summer): 29–33.

Carter, Deane G. 1956. Factory-built farm buildings. *Agricultural Engineering* 37 (April): 258–60.

———. 1957. Farm building trends. *Agricultural Engineering* 38(June): 433–35.

Cartwright, Frank P. 1929. The need of standardization in farm construction practice. *Agricultural Engineering* 10(4): 116.

Cavert, William L. 1956. The technological revolution in agriculture, 1910–1955. *Agricultural History* 30(1): 18–27.

Chamberlain, W. I. 1902. A model grain and livestock barn. *Fifty Seventh Annual Report of the Ohio State Board of Agriculture,* 645–51. Springfield: Springfield Publishing Company.

Cleary Buildings Livestock Housing. Verona, Wisconsin. (Advertising brochure).

Concrete on the dairy farm. n.d. Chicago: Portland Cement Association.

Country Gentleman. 1917. 82(March 31).

The Courier (Findlay, Ohio). 1980. Unique barn fulfills dream. (August 1): 83.

Creager, Ellen. 1988. Sprucing up works from the inside out. *Detroit Free Press* (July 7): 1, 33b.

Curtis, J. O., and E. L. Hansen. 1959. Lumber rigid frames for farm buildings. Univ. of Illinois, College of Agriculture Circular 812, 1–12.

Dairy Farmer. 1927. The gothic roof. (January 15): 20.

Doane, H. Howard, and Bernon George Perkins. 1990. Pole frame buildings. *Frame Buildings* (April). Unpublished MMS.

Durant, E. G. n.d. *Hollow building blocks, their manufacture and uses, past, present and future.* Bucyrus, OH: American Clay-Working Machinery Company.

Ekblaw, K. J. T. 1945. The postwar farm structures situation. *Agricultural Engineering* 26(April): 149–55.

Falconer, J. I. 1933. *Twenty years of Ohio agriculture.* Ohio Agricultural Experiment Station (Wooster).

Farm buildings. 1913. Chicago: Breeders Gazette.

Farm buildings. 1911. Chicago: Breeder's Gazette.

Farm buildings. 1907. Chicago: Sanders Publishing Company.

Fifty-year Index to Personnel and Publications of the Ohio Agricultural and Experiment Station. *Ohio Agricultural and Experiment Station Bulletin.* 1932. (April): 501.

Fish, N. S. 1924. Building the dairy barn. Wisconsin Agricultural Experiment Station Bulletin No. 369 (August): 1–31.

Fitch, J. B., and V. R. Hillman. 1925. Dairy buildings for Kansas. Kansas Agricultural Experiment Station Bulletin No. 236 (November): 1–45.

Fowler, E. S. 1913. The design of permanent farm buildings. *American Society of Agricultural Engineers, Transactions* 7(December): 106–17.

Frandsen, J. H., and Nevens, W. B. 1919. Dairy barn and milk house arrangement. Nebraska Agricultural Experiment Station Circular No. 6 (October): 1–28.

Frudden, W. E. 1918. A frame that is well adapted to large barns. *Building Age* 40(June): 285–87.

Giese, Henry. 1949. Farm structures—A forward look. *Agricultural Engineering* 30(December): 565–68, 571.

Harneys barns, outbuildings and fences. 1873. New York: Orange Judd Company.

Hickox, C. H. 1899. Barn plans. *Ohio Farmer* 95(April 6): 294.

Hicks, Clifford B. 1948. The old red barn is vanishing. *Popular Mechanics* 89(5): 137–42.

Hill, George G. 1901. Practical suggestions for farm buildings. United States Department of Agriculture Farmers' Bulletin No. 126: 1–47.

Hoard's Dairyman. 1939. Don't tear down the old barn. (March 25): 177–95.

Hollow tile farm buildings. 1920. Chicago: Hollow Tile Building Association.

Hopkins, Alfred. 1920. *Modern farm buildings.* New York: Robert McBridge.

Ives, F. W. 1915. Large barn and straw shed. *Ohio Farmer* 135(February 20): 244.

———. 1920. Economy of the plank frame barn. *Ohio Farmer* 146(November 27): 634–35.

_____. 1922. Locating farm building groups. *Ohio Farmer* 149(March 11): 281.

Justice, J. L. 1917. Some hints on modern barn construction. *Ohio Farmer* 140(September 15): 209-10.

Kelley, M. A. R. 1933. A study of 100 dairy barns in Wisconsin. *Agricultural Engineering* 14(October): 271-73.

King, M. L. 1910. Hollow clay blocks for farm buildings. *American Society of Agricultural Engineers, Transactions* 4(December): 47-56.

LeClair, C. A. 1917. Handling dairy-farm manure right. *Country Gentleman* 82(December): 6, 37.

Lewis, Frank C. 1921. Farm buildings. Indiana Agricultural Experiment Station Circular No. 100 (January).

Literary Digest. 1926. An all steel barn. (September 11): 23.

Louden Barn Plans. 1914. Fairfield, IA: Louden Machinery Company.

Lyle, S. P. 1931. Coordinating building plan service. *Agricultural Engineering* 12(October): 378-80.

Marsh, F. L. 1911. The principles of barn framing. *American Society of Agricultural Engineers Transactions* 5(December): 116-30.

Mayer, I. D., and J. H. Hilton. 1943. The construction and operation of an experimental dairy barn. Indiana Agricultural Experiment Station Bulletin 483 (May): 1-16.

McMunn, E. W. 1947a. Here's a barn 'Built for the future.' *Ohio Farmer* 199(February 15): 5.

_____. 1947b. Quonsets come to the farm, as barns, sheds, and utility buildings. *Ohio Farmer* (August 2): 14-15

McWethy, John A. 1947. The big red barn is doomed. *Science Digest* 22(July): 52-55.

Midwest plan service catalog. 1991. Ames, IA: Midwest Plan Service.

Miller, H. P. 1915. Barn building. *Ohio Farmer* 135(April 10): 519.

Minot, Charles. 1930. Fewer cows, better barns. *Ohio Farmer* 165(May 3): 598.

Myers, F. E. & Bros. n.d. *Catalogue and price-list of pumps, pipe, hose, cylinders and fixtures, haying tools, hay carriers, hay forks, pulleys, grapples, etc.*, Dayton, OH: Troup Manufacturing Company.

Neuenschwander, Albert. 1986. Interview with Glenn Harper.

New barns from old. 1929. Des Moines, IA: Meredith Publishing Company.

Ohio Farmer. 1918. Concrete barns. (February 12): 43.

_____. 1917. Hints on modern farm building. (September 15): 209.

Ohio Farmer. 1903. The Ohio experiment station. 4(21): 381-82.

_____. 1913. The dairy: An old barn made new. 132(September 20): 242.

_____. 1923. (January 6): 16; (January 20): 77.

_____. 1946a. (January 19): 39.

_____. 1946b. (February 2): 37.

_____. 1946c. (October 19): 12.

_____. 1947. (August 16): 15.

_____. 1948. (February 7): 33.

Orange Judd Company. 1903. *Barn plans and outbuildings.* New York: Orange Judd.

_____. 1911. *Barn plans and outbuildings.* New York: Orange Judd.

Parks, K. E. 1923. Dairy barn construction. United States Department of Agriculture Farmers' Bulletin No. 1342 (October): 1–22.

Powell, E. 1903. 2d ed. *Barn plans and outbuildings.* New York: Orange Judd Co.

Radford, William A., ed. 1907. *Radford's practical barn plans.* Chicago: Radford Architectural Company.

———. 1908. *Radford's combined house and barn plan book.* Chicago: Radford Architectural Company.

———. 1918a. Build the farm on paper first. *Country Gentleman.* 83(January 12): 14.

———. 1918b. Plans for a modern barn. *Country Gentleman* 83(February 2): 12–13.

Rhode, C. S., and W. A. Foster. 1937. Building and remodeling dairy barns. Illinois Agricultural Experiment Station Circular No. 478 (October): 1–27.

Roberts, H. Armstrong. 1918. *The farmer his own builder.* Philadelphia: David McKay.

Robinson, Guy A. 1915. A good rebuilt barn. *Ohio Farmer* 135(May 29): 726.

Schaffhausen, J. F. 1939. Trends in one-story barn construction. *Agricultural Engineering* 20(December): 467–68.

Scott, Roy V. 1974. Science for the farmer: Comment. In *Farming in the Midwest, 1840–1900,* edited by James W. Whitaker, 215–20. Washington: Agriculture History Society.

Seymour, E. L. D., ed. 1918. *Farm knowledge,* Vol. 3. New York: Doubleday, Page.

Shaw, G. 1843. *Rural architecture.* Boston: Dow.

Shawver, John L. 1901. Plank frame barns. *Farmer's Guide* 13(January 12): 19–20.

Sheets, E. W., and M. A. R. Kelley. 1923. Beef-cattle barns. United States Department of Agriculture Farmers' Bulletin No. 1350: 1–15.

Sherlock, Chesla C. 1922. *Modern farmyard buildings.* Des Moines, IA: Homestead Company.

Stepens book of the farm. 1851. New York: Saxton.

Strahan, J. L. 1918. Barn roof design. *American Society of Agricultural Engineers, Transactions,* 57–75.

Toledo [OH] *Daily Blade.* 1911. Henry County has model barn. (April 6): 294.

Twitchell, H. P. 1921–22. *Braced rafter barn framing.* Ohio State University, Extension Service Bulletin, 7(8).

United States Department of Commerce. 1961. *U.S. Census of Agriculture, Ohio, 1959: Agriculture,* vol. 3.

Webster, Edward H. 1908. Designs for dairy buildings. United States Department of Agriculture, Bureau of Animal Industry, Circular 131 (March): 287–308.

White, Frank M., and Clyde I. Griffith. 1916. Barns for Wisconsin dairy farms. Wisconsin Agricultural Experiment Station Bulletin No. 266.

White, H. B., and M. G. Jacobson. 1925. Barns. Minnesota Agricultural Extension Division Special Bulletin No. 98. (August): 1–24.

Whitehead, Vivian B., comp. 1977. *Agricultural history: An index, 1927–1976.* Davis: Univ. of California Agricultural History Center.

Williams, Robert C. 1987. *Fordson, Farmall, and Poppin' Johnny: A history of the farm tractor and its impact on America.* Urbana: Univ. of Illinois Press.

Wing, Joseph E. 1898. The "Open center," barn frame. *Ohio Farmer* 93(March 23): 233.

Wooley, John C. 1946. *Farm Buildings.* New York: McGraw-Hill.

Witzel, S. A. 1939. The one story dairy barn. *Agricultural Engineering* 20(10): 395–98.

12

MIDWEST BARN DECOR

David T. Stephens

WHEN ASKED THE color of a barn, many people will answer, red. But, are barns always red? A scan of the Midwest landscape reveals the presence of other colors, even multiple colors on barns. Some barns also sport graphic images—names and dates, animals and advertisements, even murals. Lest the wrong impression be given, the typical midwestern barn *is* painted a single color, roofed in a different color, and neither the barn nor its roof is adorned by graphics or other decoration. Midwestern farmers are supposedly a traditional lot, and one would expect the decor of their buildings to reflect a conservative bent. The traditional mindset suggests barns should be functional and not works of art. Fortunately, not all barns fit the stereotype.

Barns offer an inviting surface for artistic display, a canvas which may be utilized in many ways. Some use it for self-expression and others as an extension of their egos. Folklore surrounds the painting schemes for some barns. Advertizers frequently employ barns in publicizing their products or services, providing a modest income supplement for the barn owners. Others use barn walls for spreading religious or political messages. The results are graphic and polychromatic additions to the rural landscape.

Because some farmers mimic their neighbors' initiative, one can often find distinct regional variations in barn decor. Sometimes the process turns into a game of one-upmanship as neighbors try to outdo each other. This chapter examines some of the variations of decoration found on midwestern barns.

COLOR AND BARN PAINTING

Why are barns painted at all? Many early barns were unpainted. The October 10, 1874 *Ohio Farmer* noted a double benefit from painting farm buildings. "In the first place no expenditure of time and money pays better than the application of good linseed oil and lead to weather boarding to make it more durable, and in the second place no expenditures of equal amount can so much enhance the value of the whole premises" (*Ohio Farmer* 1874, 225). Given the nature of human vanity, one could add the desire to reflect the success of the owner as another reason for painting.

Obviously, a single color is most economical. However, not all farmers wanted a monochrome format. Why increase the costs by using multiple colors or adding graphics? The answer apparently lies in farmers' desires to make their barns different from those of their neighbors, just as residents of post-World War II housing developments planted shrubs and painted their houses in different colors to distinguish them from otherwise similar neighboring properties. In the late nineteenth century, as barn types began to be standardized and ready-mix paints became more widely available, farmers faced the same problems as today's residents of modern tract housing. All barns had the potential to look alike because significant architectural modifications were not practical. Since it did not make sense to deviate from successful designs, one available option was to use color for differentiation.

As settlers made their way to the Midwest, some Easterners already were painting barns. Circumstantial evidence suggests that many barns were decorated in the 1830s in eastern Pennsylvania (Yoder and Graves 1989). Professional barn painters were in the state by 1850 (Stoudt 1945). However, on the frontier, barn painting was not given a high priority. Barn painting in the Midwest was rare until after the Civil War. The impetus for painting occurred with the development in the 1880s of ready-mixed paints. By the 1890s, plan books were listing the cost of paint or suggesting painting schemes (Sanders 1893).

The initial color of midwestern barns was usually either red or white. If red, Midwesterners were probably following the lead of Europeans and Easterners (Janik 1990; Arthur and Witney 1972). As early as 1860, red "paint"—a mixture of animal blood, lime and linseed oil—had been applied to a barn near Philadelphia (Howard 1951). In time, Venetian Red, a red iron oxide and the pigment known as "barn red," became the coloring agent. The practice of painting barns red was in the cultural baggage of settlers reaching the Midwest from southeast Pennsylvania. Another migrant stream to the Midwest, that of New England, had a red or Spanish brown barn tradition (Stilgoe 1982, 168).

On the other hand, a strong case can be made to suggest that most early barns in the Midwest were painted white. Kocher notes that whitewash was the earliest form of paint in America (Kocher 1928, 278). Early issues of the *Ohio Cultivator* contained several items about making whitewash and using it to preserve houses, fences, and farm outbuildings.

An 1864 article in *The Weekly Ohio Farmer*, the *Cultivator's* successor, set forth the available options for painting buildings: The cheapest protection was whitewash, the next economical was a mineral paint using cheap oil, and the best and most expensive, a combination of linseed oil and white lead. White lead also was used to produce a white wall covering. *The Weekly Ohio Farmer* declared that, "when mixed with linseed oil," white lead "forms a coating on wood as hard as iron" (274). By 1872, however, Midwesterners had a cheaper alternative, even to white lead paint. That year, two Ohio paint jobbers, Henry R. Sherwin and Edward P. Williams, were selling "Venetian red," a pigment ground in oil, for only eight cents a pound, while their price for white lead was fourteen-and-a-half cents a pound (Patricia S. Eldredge, pers. comm., Sept. 4, 1991).

It would appear that simple economics determined the early practice of painting barns red. Other factors included red's landmark attributes during the frozen brown and white months of winter and its pleasing contrast with green fields and white farmhouse in the summer (Howard 1951). Red also may have been the occasional color of choice because, in winter, it absorbs more of the sun's rays than white does (Sloane 1954).

The possibilities for other colors on barns emerged with the development of ready-mixed paint. The first can of ready-mix was offered for sale in 1880 by Sherwin-Williams (Eldredge 1983). In 1887, the company suggested that Rockwood Red, a moderate red brown, trimmed in Rockwood Dark Olive, a grayish olive, was a nice choice for a barn. Its 1907 *Dealer's Price List* indicated the availability of three different types of paint for barns, roofs, fences, and outbuildings: (1) Commonwealth Barn Red, a "bright economical red" that, according to Eldredge (1991), may have been the first paint specifically manufactured for barns; (2) red and brown Roof and Bridge Paint; and (3) Creosote Paint, available in twelve shades. Clearly, red was the most available color, at least through Sherwin-Williams.

Given the short durability of paint and the rigors of the midwestern climate, little evidence survives of the earliest barn painting practices in the Midwest. We can glean some insights into later years, however, from Trewartha's 1948 study of the regional characteristics of American farmsteads and from observations I made during field work in 1991.

Although the states included in the two studies are not the same, and despite forty years between the two samples, some general trends in color preference are evident. Red is likely to be found on the barns of Michigan and Wisconsin, and while still important, has been surpassed by white, which is especially prevalent on the barns of Ohio and Illinois. Farmers' upholding of traditions and their connections to New York and New England help to explain this color preference. Apps and Strang (1977) note that barn color was not an issue in Wisconsin: The barn was painted red because red paint was cheaper than white, lasted well, and provided a pleasing contrast to the white farmhouse.

Little variation occurs in the percentages of unpainted barns between 1948 and 1991. A distinct concentration of unpainted barns occurs in the western and southern parts of the Midwest. In some areas the lack of paint on barns might be attributed to a tradition of poverty. Since painting involves an outlay of money, unpainted barns are likely to be in regions where money is hardest to come by (Glass 1986). But, it is said that in southern Illinois, farmers are proud of the fact that their barns have never been painted (Sculle 1991; Price 1991). In Missouri's Little Dixie, houses are usually painted, while barns are not (Marshall 1981). Writing about German settlement in Missouri, van Ravenswaay (1977) confirms that many barns have never been painted.

Barns come in many colors, but deviations from white, red, or combinations of the two are rare. The color preferences for midwestern barns are ranked as follows: white, red, yellow, gray, green, and blue. Among multicolored barns, red with white trim accounts for nearly one-fifth of all barns. White with green trim and white with black trim are the next most common combinations. These last two trim combinations show no regional concentration, yet are prone to cluster, as are many other decorating schemes.

BARN DECORATIONS

Barn decoration literature suggests that Pennsylvania Germans were responsible for the creation of most American barn art (Beck and Webb 1977). Not surprisingly then, one of the most widely recognized barn decorations is a circular hex sign. The best-known hex signs are found in southeastern Pennsylvania, although their origin can be traced to European folk art (Yoder and Graves 1989). Much speculation surrounds the significance and meaning of these circular designs, but their primary aim appears to be decorative or, in the Pennsylvania Dutch vernacular, "chust for nice" (Shoemaker 1956, 68).

Hex signs painted directly onto barns become increasingly rare as one moves westward in the Midwest. Outside eastern Ohio, hex signs generally are not painted directly on the barn, but on circular boards affixed to the barn wall. The source of these signs is the hex painters who market their art to tourists through outlets in Pennsylvania Dutch country (Yoder and Graves 1989, 18). In recent years a modern circular symbol, the "happy face," has begun to appear here and there on midwestern barns, conveying a positive and upbeat message.

Advertising has provided particularly well-known graphic additions to the barn. Barn walls indeed were some of the nation's first billboards, with ads placed to be visible from both roadside and railroad (Taylor 1978). Meramac Caverns, a tourist attraction in Missouri, once was widely advertised from the sides of barns along major highways throughout the Midwest. In Wisconsin, signs for Miller Beer and King Midas Flour frequently adorned the sides of barns. National products such as Coca Cola, Hires Root Beer, and Burma Shave often used midwestern barns as advertising space.

About 1950, firms began to stop this practice (Apps and Strang, 1977). The creation of the interstate highway network and the restrictions associated with the Highway Beautification Act drastically reduced barnside advertising. So powerful is the tobacco lobby, however, that the familiar Mail Pouch sign was granted an exemption from the restrictions of the Highway Beautification Act (Reisler 1988). Amended section 131 of this Act allows an exemption to the ban on highway advertising for "signs lawfully in existence on October 22, 1965 determined by the State and subject to the approval of the Secretary (the Secretary of Transportation) to be landmark signs including signs on farm structures" (*United States Code: 1988 Edition*, 1989, 1110). Now, though, perhaps, due to the surgeon general's warning, tobacco ads are becoming a rarity. The messages of national firms are quickly fading from the side of the barn, although a few local companies continue to announce their products and services on the occasional barn (fig. 12.1).

Without doubt the most common barn advertisements were those associated with tobacco companies; Red Man, Bull Durham, and Mail Pouch are among the best known (fig. 12.2). Their origin, in West Virginia, predates the automobile. In the 1890s, the Blochs, two Wheeling brothers who created Mail Pouch chewing

240

Fig. 12.1. The sign for the Overpass Motel, five miles away from this Randolph County, Indiana, barn, is typical of numerous local advertisements adorning midwestern barn walls
Photo: D. Stephens, 1991

Fig. 12.2. *Mail Pouch* signs (this one in Hardin County, Ohio) are among the most common decoration on midwestern barns.
Photo: A. G. Noble, 1992

tobacco, hired a crew of painters to lease space and to paint advertisements on farmers' barns (Paris 1991). In time, Mail Pouch and other tobacco products were advertised on thousands of barns throughout the Midwest. One account suggests that in their heyday, the 1960s, ten thousand Mail Pouch signs on barns dotted the landscape from New York to Kentucky (Reisler 1988, 67). From 1946 until 1970, three crews covered nine states painting the signs (Griffin 1991). In 1988, however, just one thousand Mail Pouch signs were estimated to have survived (Reisler 1988). The last Mail Pouch sign painter retired in 1990. Since 1946, Harley Warwick reportedly had painted and repainted more than 22,000 barns in nine states (Paris 1991).

Barn advertising is found mostly along major highways. Little would be gained by placing them on a rural backroad. Tobacco ads also are far more common close to tobacco country, and rarely occur west of Wisconsin and Illinois.

The largest and most distinctive regional concentration of a type of midwestern barn decor is associated with trim paint. The origins of this form may be the Pennsylvania Dutch.

> Once the prevailing red color of the boarded forebay was established, the use of limited areas of white lead paint or whitewash was resorted to. Openings were lined in white or edge trimmed in narrow bands. The simple rectangular outline was softened and transformed with arched or triangular forms. (Dornbusch 1956, XXI)

In the Midwest, painted arches have been studied by Beck and Webb (1977), who delineated the parts of Michigan, Indiana, and Ohio where the practice most commonly occurs. Within these areas, at least 10 percent of the barns had painted arches and, within the core, 25 to 40 percent had decorative arches (fig. 12.3). Observations within these areas in 1991 suggest the practice is still very common, although its frequency has diminished. Painted arches also are found in eastern Ohio.

In the Beck and Webb (1977) study, the most frequently observed form was one in which a rounded arch is contained within the margins of the door. Two other variations exist: one has a teardrop symbol extending downward from the top portion of double arched doorways; the other has decorative borders along the top and sides of the door with convex filled-in corners (fig. 12.4). Most of these barns were red and the arches were white. Both in the original study and in my later observations, white barns with green arches were the major color scheme variant.

The most common decorative element added to midwestern barns is some combination of date and the name of the farm or owner. Sometimes, the farm's breed of stock also is noted on the barn. The East Coast antecedents for these kinds of decoration may be the brickwork houses of New Jersey, the datestones of southeast Pennsylvania houses, or the dated slate roofs of New York and Vermont's Slate Belt. The form, size, and placement of these informational items vary. Analysis of farm names painted on barns would make an interesting study. Many have a physical connotation such as "hill" and "valley," or are related to

242

Fig. 12.3. The double-painted arch, such as this one in Elkhart County, Indiana, is the most typical decorated door form
Photo: D. Stephens, 1991

Fig. 12.4. The convex corners variation of the painted arch, Adams County, Indiana. In most cases, the corners are filled in.
Photo: D. Stephens, 1991

weather or climate, such as "Sunny Acres." The date is most likely the year the farm was acquired, not the year the barn was constructed.

Several generalizations may be made about the names and dates painted on barns. First, if you see one in an area, you will probably see several more. Second, named and dated barns are rarely encountered off highways and are likely to be closer to towns. Third, the lettering of names varies in size in direct proportion, perhaps, to the size of the ego of the barn's owner. This latter statement is pure speculation on my part.

BARNSCAPES AND MURALS

Another decorative addition to the barn is often a graphic depicting livestock (fig. 12.5). Shoemaker (1956) refers to these as barnscapes, farm scenes, farm animals, or domesticated fowl painted on the forebay fronts of barns. This form is found in all parts of the Midwest, but there appears to be a distinct geography of species. Horses are often on barns in "horsey" country, i.e., affluent suburban counties, while cows of course are highly correlated with dairying regions. Pigs are only occasionally seen, most likely in areas of the corn belt that specialize in hog production. Sheep, poultry, and crops other than apples are rarely seen.

Midwest barn owners frequently display a sense of history and patriotism. In 1976, some were stimulated to decorate their barns for the Bicentennial with the date, a prominent American flag, or a red, white, and blue color scheme. No apparent pattern to the distribution of this brand of national boosterism exists.

Perhaps the ultimate barn decoration is the barn mural (fig. 12.6). Antecedents for this practice are found in Europe. In Bavaria and Austria, especially, murals are painted on both houses and barns (Janik 1990). Unfortunately, due to the rigors of weather, murals tend to last only about ten years and often are not renewed (Byers 1989). In the early 1970s, Michigan barn murals gained national acclaim when Douglas Tyler decorated several barns near Detroit. Among his subjects were the Mona Lisa, a Geisha, Paul Revere, and copies of portraits by Raphael and Piero della Francesca (*Horizons* 1976).

Wisconsin has even more barn murals. The Dairyland Graphics Program of the mid-1970s, partially funded by the National Endowment for the Arts, financed the painting of murals on twelve barns throughout the state. The purpose was not so much to attract attention to barns, but to increase public awareness and appreciation of art (Nelson 1975). These were not the first murals on Wisconsin barns, however. The barn muralist extraordinaire was Frank Engebretson, who, between 1914 and 1958, painted more than one hundred barn murals in the area around Broadhead. Three of his barn murals remain today. One, near Woodford, spans 150 feet and is eighteen feet tall. Englebretson's work was chronicled in such publications as *Life, Country Gentleman,* the *American,* and the *Christian Science Monitor.* The price for one of his creations was about $150 for a large barn (Marx 1963). The cost to restore two murals on a farm near Broadhead in the late 1980s was $13,000. At this price, it is not surprising that barn murals are not widely popular today.

Fig. 12.5. The cow and lettering on this Stark County, Ohio, barn leave little doubt that Holsteins are bred on the farm
Photo: D. Stephens, 1991

Unfortunately, given the changing nature of midwestern agriculture that renders old barns obsolete, and the rising cost of painting and decorating, the rural midwestern landscape will be far less colorful in the future. Barn art will continue to fade from the scene. Another element of midwestern barn decor that also is endangered is roof art.

ROOF ART

Roofing on midwestern barns passed through an evolutionary cycle from wooden shingles to metal, slate, and, finally, asphalt shingles. Although metal roofs are sometimes painted, slate and asphalt shingles of various colors are used more often to place an artistic signature on a barn. During the last ten years, I have examined hundreds of decorative-slate barn roofs (Stephens 1982, 1984, 1987; Stephens and Bobersky 1983, 1985). More than 750 decorative-slate roofs can be found on Midwest barns. Outside the Midwest, fewer than fifty decorative-slate barn roofs have been documented. (These occur in New York, Pennsylvania, and Vermont in proximity to slate deposits.) A new genre, the decorated asphalt shingle roof, occurs less often than slate, but it reflects the continuance of the tradition and the farmer's desire to give the barn roof a unique signature.

During the late nineteenth and the early twentieth centuries, slate was the preferred roofing material throughout much of Ohio. Slate was not applied as frequently to barns farther West, and rarely was used beyond Indiana and Michigan. The locations of quarries and slate's high transportation cost explain the geographical limitations. The slate used to roof midwestern barns was quarried primarily in Maine, Vermont, New York, and Pennsylvania. In the late 1880s, slate emerged as a competitive roofing material. An 1899 issue of *The Ohio Farmer* reported on a contest that had solicited letters on the best materials for roofing barns. Twenty papers were received. "A large majority of the writers favored slate first" (411). Three of the six best papers in the contest were from Ohio, two from Indiana, and the other from Michigan. A square of roofing slate was more expensive in Michigan and Indiana than Ohio. In Jefferson County, Ohio, for example, the cost of a square of slate was $4.40, but in Indiana, a roofer reported the cost to be $6.00, and in Michigan, the price varied from $5.00 to $7.00 (*Ohio Farmer* 1899, 411). The differences in price were a reflection of transportation costs. With increasing distance from the quarries, slate could not economically compete with alternative roofing material.

Most slate roofs are either of two colors. Instead of red or white, as are barn walls, slate roofs are usually green or gray. In addition to green and gray, slate can be black, blue, purple, or red. Variations in the mineral content of slate produce color differences. The color generally indicates its source area. Gray slate is found in New York, Pennsylvania, Vermont, and Virginia; black in Maine, Maryland, and Pennsylvania; green and purple in New York and Vermont; and red only in New York (National Slate Association 1926). On occasion, slaters and, more recently, roofers working with asphalt shingles use variations in colors to create decorative patterns in the roofs of barns and other structures. Some designs are simple, taking the form of colored bands, names, or dates. Others are far more intricate, depicting flowers and even livestock.

Several caveats concerning the data on decorative slate barn roofs should be noted. Not every decorated-slate barn roof in the Midwest has been identified. However, enough of the Midwest has been examined to suggest that few decorated-slate barn roofs occur outside the area identified in fig. 12.7. Old photographs and interviews suggest that many decorative-slate barn roofs had disappeared before the inventories were begun, especially in areas around major cities.

As barns disappear, so, of course, do their roofs. Indeed, loss of integrity of the roof is usually the first step in the destruction of the entire barn. I know of at least thirty decorative barn roofs that have disappeared in the last ten years, and the rate of attrition is increasing, as is that of entire structures (Noble and King 1989). Field observation of roofs can be hindered by vegetation, frost, snow, and sun angle. In some cases, additions to the barn obscure part of the date, or repairs to the roof render letters, numerals, or designs illegible. Finally, decoration is not always located on the roof slope facing a road.

The distribution of decorative slate roofs in the Midwest (fig. 12.7) is related to several factors, including the location of railroads, the quality of farmland, the type of farming, and the affluence of the barns' owners. The role of the railroad was crucial to the development of the slate roofing industry. "It was not until the

Fig. 12.6. The work of Frank Engebretson has been restored on this Green County, Wisconsin, barn
Photo: D. Stephens, 1991

middle of the nineteenth century that the use of slate seems to have become general" (Delaware and Hudson Company 1929, 374). Railroads provided a means of transportation for the product from mine and quarry and greatly widened the market for slate (Delaware and Hudson Company 1929).

Slate is a very heavy, durable roofing material. A square of slate shingles can range in weight from six hundred pounds to nearly a ton. Thickness of the slate is the critical factor in determining weight. A modest-sized barn having thirty squares of standard three-eighths-inch slate shingles would require, at a minimum, nine tons of roofing material. Once the slate reached a local rail siding, there was then the problem of moving nine or more tons of shingles by horse and wagon to the barn site. Comparison of the distribution of decorative-slate barn roofs and an early twentieth-century railroad map reveals that almost all such roofs were located within five miles of a railroad (Stephens 1987). Nevertheless, many areas well-served by railroads in the Midwest lack decorative slate barn roofs.

In the late nineteenth century, the cost of a slate roof in Ohio compared favorably with other forms of roofing. Farther West, slate was decidedly less competitive (*Ohio Farmer* 1899). Crafting a decorative-slate roof involved more expense than a plain slate roof. A skilled slater was needed, and different colors of slate had to be obtained in the required quantities. Because decorative-slate roofs tend to be on substantial farmsteads and on barns that are larger than others in the surrounding area, it is safe to conclude that a slate design was not for the poor

247

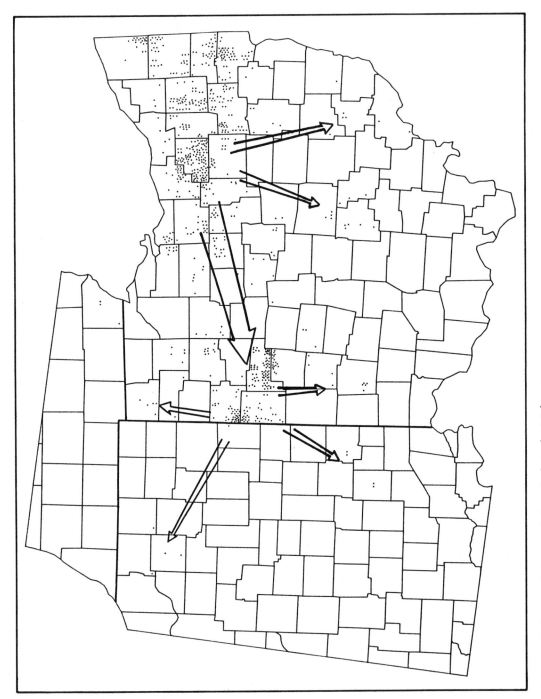

Fig. 12.7. Diffusion of decorated slate roofs in the Midwest

farmer. This notion is reinforced when the occurrences of such roofs are compared with glacial and soil maps (Stephens and Bobersky 1985). In the Midwest, few decorative-slate barn roofs occur south of the glacial boundary where the land is less suited to farming. Neither are they generally found in areas having poor quality soils. Again, not all glaciated areas with good soils have such roofs.

Decorative roofs are most likely to be associated with dairying, as opposed to grain or special crop farming. In Ohio, the two largest concentrations of such roofs are found in areas identified by Noble (1975) and Stephens (1990) as dairy regions. The same also holds true in Indiana and Michigan. The extensive roof surfaces created by the need to store large amounts of hay in dairy barn lofts provided slaters with an ideal place to display their handiwork. Decorations occur on a variety of barn types: English, Erie shore, German, raised three-bay, three-gable or three-end, and Wisconsin.

Little ethnic connection can be demonstrated. The backgrounds of the settlers differ in the two Ohio areas where the greatest concentrations of decorative slate roofs occur. Northeastern Ohio's early ties are to the British Isles and New England, while western Ohio has a strong Middle Atlantic and German component. An analysis of the names found inscribed on roofs shows no dominance by any particular group. The Welsh were most connected to the quarrying of slate in the eastern United States, but there is no evidence to suggest that they were the carriers of the decorative-slate barn roof idea to the Midwest.

DATED SLATE ROOFS

The most common decorative feature of slate roofs is a date. Most dates fall between the years 1880 and 1920 (fig. 12.8). A common assumption is that roof dates indicate the date of barn construction (Noble 1974; Schuler 1984). However, interviews with owners and examinations of tax records and building techniques reveal this assumption to be false in most instances. A more plausible explanation is that the dates coincide with the time of remodeling and/or reroofing of the barn. Some rooftop dates have other meanings for owners, such as the year a farm was acquired. Most roof dates coincide with a significant change in the agriculture of the eastern part of the Midwest. Agricultural statistics from Ohio counties where slate roofs are found show a rapid and steady rise in the number of milk cows and in the volume of milk production. Barn construction was in response to the increased demand for milk and milk products and the need to accommodate additional stock, straw, hay, and other feedstuffs. The distinctive three-gable or three-end barn type identified by Noble and Korsok (1977) in Columbiana County, Ohio, dates from this period. The barn frequently sports a slate roof, a favorite place for slaters to add decorative signatures.

The decorative-slate roofing era for midwestern barns began in the late 1870s and was ending by the time of World War I. Slate during this period was a commercially viable barn roofing material in the Midwest. Again, this discussion must be tempered with the knowledge that the greatest attrition in rooftop dates probably has been among those roofs of earliest times.

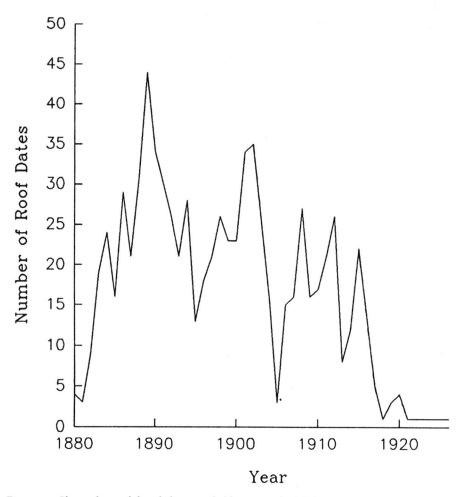

Fig. 12.8. Chronology of dated slate-roofed barns in the Midwest

The earliest dates, while interesting, are suspect for several reasons. The dates of 1837, 1860, 1869, and 1870 found on barns in the Ohio counties of Mercer, Stark, Montgomery, and Hancock, respectively, mark a period before or just after rail links were being established to the eastern slate-producing regions. It is questionable whether slate would have reached these areas, especially in the year 1837. The color of these roofs, green with gray or black designs, also raises some questions. The only source of green slate is the slate belt of western Vermont and eastern New York, which had no regular rail service until 1852 (Bonham 1981). Also, these dates are earlier than the oldest-known slate-roof barn dates in Vermont and eastern New York, the hearth area for the practice of working dates into slate roofs. It is unlikely that the practice would have begun in Ohio and then spread eastward toward the slate deposits. Given such facts, it is doubtful that slate roofs were applied at those early times to barns in Ohio. Those early dates may indicate when the farmstead was acquired or some other significant time in a family's history. The most recent date, 1926, on a barn located in Crawford County, Ohio, was well after asphalt shingles and metal had become the most common roofing materials for Midwest barns and marks a time when slate was no longer an economically viable roofing material for barns.

Plotting roof dates also provides insights into the economic climate of the times and the competitiveness of slate with other roofing materials. Figure 12.8 shows the cyclic nature of the barn roofs' dates. The peak years were in the late 1880s, early 1890s, and the first few years of the twentieth century. The Panic of 1893 apparently affected the activities of roof daters. Later, a noticeable decline in roof dating coincides with the outbreak of World War I. These patterns identify the rise and decline of slate production in the United States. By the end of World War I, slate had lost its competitive position as a roofing material for barns, although it continued to be used on other, more expensive structures until the 1930s.

The practice of dating roofs did not start in the Midwest, but in the eastern slate-producing region. Eastern New York and western Vermont have slate-roofed barns with dates from the 1860s and 1870s. No antecedents for the practice have yet been discovered in Europe, although slate roofs are widespread there. The idea might be a variant of the date stones associated with early German settlement in Pennsylvania. Date stones were carved stones worked into the walls of buildings showing builders' names and construction dates (Diffenderffer 1905). Many of the dates are from the 1700s. Another possibility is that the dated roof is an outgrowth from the dated, patterned brickwork houses. Love (1955) suggests that dates and initials in the brickwork of houses were known in the late seventeenth century along the Hudson River. These are not improbable antecedents, as dates found on houses with slate roofs tend to be earlier than those found on barns (Stephens 1984). On the other hand, it is also quite possible that dated roofs are an independent invention not related to house dating. At least one dated log barn has been found in the Midwest (see fig. 2.1).

DIFFUSION OF DATED ROOFS

Mapping the early dates offers some insights into the probable pattern of diffusion for decorative slate roofs. Based on evidence from railroad maps linking the Midwest to slate producing regions, accounts concerning the construction of prominent Midwest public buildings with slate roofs, the appearance of advertisements for slate materials and professional slaters in city directories, and the listing of "slater" as an occupation in manuscript censuses, little slate made its way into the Midwest until the late 1870s and early 1880s. Slate barn roofs with dates before 1885 are concentrated in northeastern Ohio, suggesting the dated-slate barn roof first appeared there. Further evidence comes from early dates found on slate-roofed houses, commercial buildings, and farm outbuildings in that region (Stephens 1987).

Two Ohio areas are the most likely places for the first appearance of the dated slate roof in the Midwest. Southern Mahoning and northern Columbiana counties have the largest existing cluster of early dates on barns and other buildings. Summit and Stark counties may be an alternative source area. Unfortunately, the suburban expansion of both Akron and Canton has destroyed many early roofs that may have helped support the thesis. One of these two areas undoubtedly served as the point of initial introduction to the Midwest. Early rooftop dates on the limited number of structures discovered in western Pennsylvania, generally precede 1885 and, thus, further support this argument.

Some very intriguing questions remain about how the dated-roof practice made its way to the Midwest and about the route of diffusion. No trail of dates across New York and Pennsylvania to Ohio has been found. The most likely scenario involves relocation diffusion: An eastern roofer brought the practice to eastern Ohio as a part of his cultural baggage. Who and when remain a mystery.

Using the variation in dates, some conclusions can be drawn about the probable path of diffusion of roof dating in the Midwest (see fig. 12.7). The practice moved rapidly from northeast Ohio across the Western Reserve, reaching western Ohio and then scattering to eastern Indiana and southeast Michigan by the 1890s. Apparently, people, or at least their ideas, were highly mobile by the late 1880s. Most dated barns in western Ohio have dates from the 1890s and the twentieth century.

These diffusion routes are confirmed by the spatial patterns of other roof decorations. Once the date had been placed in the roof, it was not long until other features were added. On ever-bigger barn roofs, room remained for other features. Farmers personalized the roofs with their initials or had their names in bold letters worked into the slate (fig. 12.9). What better way to trumpet success and

Fig. 12.9. Initials and a date, like these on a barn in Columbiana County, Ohio, are the most typical slate roof decorations
Photo: D. Stephens, 1985

prosperity than to emblazon one's name in eight-foot-high letters across the roof of a newly built or remodeled barn? Sometimes the roof included both names and dates, but as the practice moved westward, the date was usually omitted and the size of the name made larger. The concentration of personalized roofs in western Ohio and the limited number in the Mahoning-Columbiana hearth area supports the notion of their spread across the Western Reserve to western Ohio. Another inference from the map is the propensity of personalized roofs to cluster. Clustering may reflect attempts to outdo, or a least copy, one's neighbor, or the skill of a particular slater.

Comparisons of names on barns and those on mailboxes suggest that most personalized barns are no longer owned by the family identified in the rooftop. Given the custom of identifying farms by the names of their early owners, new owners may have been reluctant or economically unable to remove or change the rooftop signature. Today, the cost of slate and slate-roof repair is a significant deterrent to modifying the roof to reflect the name of a new owner.

A variant of the personalized roof is one that proclaims the farm's name, much like the common signature painted on barn sides. Fairview is the most frequently encountered farm name on a slate roof. Other additions to the roofs include geometric borders and various designs. The rosette, often a feature of barn hex signs, is frequently found on roofs in eastern Ohio, but is rarely encountered westward.

The roof also became a place for advertising breeds of livestock. In Ohio, Medina County has a large gambrel-roofed dairy barn with the owner's name, a date, and the words, "PUREBRED HOLSTEINS." In Auglaize County, Hereford cattle are advertised in a complex slate-roof design. That roof, unfortunately, is rapidly deteriorating.. It reads, "KOLEPIN AND MORGAN, BREEDERS OF HEREFORD CATTLE, 1903." Even it pales in comparison to a roof in Fairfield County (fig. 12.10). It contains a rosette; the owner's name, *T. B. Reese*; the name of the roofer, *S.W. Walker*; the date, *1888;* and a representation of a thoroughbred racehorse, which served both as decoration and an advertisement for the breeder (Hothem 1979). Such complex roofs were the exception, not the rule, but they may have served as models for some modern decorative roofs.

Asphalt Shingle Roofs

The artistry associated with the decorative slate roof did not disappear with the demise of slate. It persisted on the modern asphalt-shingled roof, which is found throughout the Midwest. Field investigation reveals that the most pervasive modern decorative type is the asphalt-shingled roof that has been personalized. Apparently, printing one's name in eight-foot letters across the top of a barn is not too gauche for many modern farm owners. Since the cost of transporting roofing material is not a major consideration with asphalt shingles, the modern decorative roof is found in all parts of the Midwest. However, it is most likely to occur in those areas already having decorative slate roofs. The quality of these roofs varies; some roofers obviously had limited skills, while others had considerable skills.

Fig. 12.10. The ultimate in decorated slate barn roof, Fairfield County, Ohio
Photo: Jim Reedy, 1992

Very few dates are found on modern roofs. The earliest known date on an asphalt-shingle roof is 1955. Given the life expectancy of asphalt shingles, it is unlikely that earlier dates will be found. As with barn painting, the Bicentennial seems to have stimulated activity. Several roofs are dated 1976.

Roof decoration holds considerable appeal for owners of modern horse barns as a means of advertising themselves and their stock. The modern, one-story stable is one of the most common barn types having a decorated roof. Horse farms, with four-board, white fences, are more often showplaces than working farms, so it is not surprising to find such roofs associated with them. One horse farmer in Stark County, Ohio, has boldly labeled his barn roof with the word, "PEGASUS." In the same county, a stable roof notes that the farm specializes in "ARABIAN HORSES."

In at least two midwestern locations, one near Canton, Ohio, and the other around Rochester, Indiana, the modern decorative barn roof reaches its most complex form. In the Canton area are several asphalt-shingled roofs with dates, personalizations, and breed advertisements. The most elaborate of these, appearing on both sides of a gable roof on a one-story barn, contains the head of an Angus bull, the words, "Bunker Black Angus," and the farm's brand.

Around Rochester, Indiana, the Sherriff-Goslin Roofing Company, and in particular, its roofer, Tom Rentschler, is responsible for several attention-getting roofs (Selz 1990). The company already had done several dated and personalized roofs by 1983, when Rentschler began a new phase of shingle artistry by working the design of a horse into a roof. It wasn't long until Rentschler had requests for other animals, as well as fruits, field crops, and tractors (fig. 12.11). Rentschler is a busy roofer, adding his animal and agricultural designs to some thirty roofs each year (Selz 1990). One of his best-known jobs is a round barn roof that sports four different animals: a cow, a pig, a chicken, and a sheep (Karst 1989). In all likelihood, the initial model for such modern pictorial roofs was a horse applied to a slate roof in 1888 in Fairfield County, Ohio.

CONCLUSION

What conclusions can be drawn about the decor of midwestern barns? First and foremost, most midwestern barns are not decorated. This chapter often has emphasized the exceptions rather than focusing upon the rule. What is obvious is that midwestern barn decor was greatly influenced by southeast Pennsylvania and, to a lesser degree, by New England. A distance decay function also appears to have been at work. Barns in the western portion of the Midwest are less likely to have decorations than those in the eastern section, although Wisconsin is a notable exception.

The color of barns is changing. Red, once dominant, is giving way to white. There is less decoration on barns today. The decline is due to several factors. First is the disappearance of old barns (1880–1930) that were more likely to have been decorated than newer barns. Second, economically pinched farmers are less likely to spend money to make their barns distinctive. Third, the increased regulation and the advent of the interstate highway have made barn advertising less attractive. As a result, the midwestern farmscape is becoming less varied and less interesting.

Fig. 12.11. In Fulton County, Indiana, this rooftop Holstein, one of the largest cows in the world, is the work of roofer-artist Tom Rentschler
Photo: D. Stephens, 1991

255

REFERENCES CITED

American Magazine. 1954. Does your barn need painting. 157(February): 59.

Apps, Jerry, and Allen Strang. 1977. *Barns of Wisconsin.* Madison, Wisconsin: Tamarack Press.

Arthur, Eric, and Dudley Witney. 1972. *The barn: A vanishing landmark in North America.* Toronto: M. F. Feheley Arts Company.

Beck, Robert L., and George W. Webb. 1977. Barn door decorations in the boundary junction area of Indiana, Michigan and Ohio: The case of the painted arch. *Professional Paper No. 9.* Terre Haute, Indiana: Department of Geography and Geology, Indiana State University: 3–12.

Bonham, John. 1981. *The economic impact of the slate industry in the Slate Valley: 1850–1900.* Grandville, NY: The Slate Museum.

Byers, Ellen. 1989. Portfolio: Murals. *Wisconsin Trails* 30(January/February): 26–33.

Christian Science Monitor. 1942. Outdoor gallery: Beautifying the barnyard with murals. (October 17): 14.

Delaware and Hudson Company. 1929. The sheltering stone. *Delaware and Hudson Company Bulletin* (December 15): 373–76 and 382.

Diffenderffer, F. R. 1905. Date stones, with examples. *Papers read before the Lancaster County Historical Society,* ix. No. 12. 1905. 359–85.

Dornbusch, Charles H., and John K. Heyl. 1956. *Pennsylvania German barns.* Allentown: Pennsylvania German Folklore Society, 20.

Eldredge, Patricia S. 1983. Paint capital of the world. *Western Reserve Magazine* 10 (July–August): 55.

Glass, Joseph W. 1986. *The Pennsylvania culture region: A view from the barn.* Ann Arbor: UMI Research Press.

Griffin, Velma. 1991. The last mail pouch painter hangs up his brush. *Farm and Dairy.* (May 23): 7.

Horizons. 1976. And now edifying the edifice. (Summer): 80–83.

Hothem, Lars. 1979. When slate was great. *AAA Newsletter.* Cleveland: Cleveland Auto Club.

Howard, Robert W. 1951. The red barn—An American epic. *Think* 17(June): 13–14.

Janik, Carolyn. 1990. *The barn book.* New York: Gallery Books.

Karst, Judith. 1989. They're farming in the round. *Farm and Ranch Living* 12(October/November): 22–23.

Kiefer, Robert. 1972. An agricultural settlement complex in Indiana. *Annals of the Association of American Geographers* 62(September): 487–506.

Kocher, A. Lawrence. 1928. Color in early American architecture with special reference to house painting. *Architectural Record* 64(October): 278–90.

Love, Paul. 1955. Patterned brickwork in southern New Jersey. *Proceedings of the New Jersey Historical Society* 23(July): 182–208.

Lichten, Frances. 1946. *Folk art of rural Pennsylvania*. New York: Charles Scribner's Sons.

Life. 1942. Wisconsin barn art: Huge pastoral scenes brighten 100 farmsteads. (September 28): 56–58.

Marshall, Howard Wight. 1981. *Folk architecture in Little Dixie: A regional culture in Missouri*. Columbia: Univ. of Missouri Press.

Marx, Jill Moore. 1963. Wisconsin's unique barn murals. *Wisconsin Tales and Trails* 4(Summer): 9–12.

National Slate Association. 1926, reprint 1977. *Slate Roofs*. Fair Haven, VT: Vermont Structural Slate Company.

Nelson, Bill. 1975. Barn art. *Wisconsin Weekend* 21(November 26): 6

Noble, Allen G. 1974. Barns and square silos in northeast Ohio. *Pioneer America* 6(July): 12–21.

———. 1975. The agriculture of Ohio. In *Ohio: An American heartland*, edited by Allen G. Noble and Albert J. Korsok. Columbus: Ohio Geological Survey Bulletin 65.

——— and Deborah Phillips King, 1989. Here today, gone tomorrow—Determining the disappearance rate of agricultural structures in Pike County, Ohio. In *The old traditional way of life: Essays in honor of Warren E. Roberts*, edited by Robert E. Walls and George H. Schoemaker, 272–82. Bloomington, IN: Tricksler Press.

——— and Albert J. Korsok. 1977. Barn variations in Columbiana County, Ohio. *East Lakes Geographer* 12:98–111.

Ohio Farmer. 1874. Preservation of farm buildings. (August 27): 225.

———. 1899. Roofing barns. (November 30): 411.

Paris, Jay. 1991. The signs of Harley Warwick's times. *Ohio Magazine*. (February): 23–26, 59–62.

Price, Wayne. 1991. Telephone interview with author, August 23.

Reisler, Jim. 1988. Forty years of barns: The last of the barn painters is still going strong. *Americana* 16(March/April): 66–67.

Sanders, J. H., comp. 1893. *Practical hints about barn building*. Chicago: J. H. Sanders Publishing Company.

Schuler, Stanley. 1984. *American barns: In a class by themselves*. Westchester, PA: Schiffer Publishing Company.

Sculle, Keith. 1991. Telephone interview with author, August 20.

Selz, Sharon. 1990, Shingle minded about agriculture: Roofing ex-farmer's really right on top of things. *Farm and Ranch Living* 12(February–March): 40–41.

Sherwin Williams Paint Company. 1887. *Color applied to architecture*.

———. 1907. *Dealer's price list*.

Shoemaker, Alfred L., ed. 1956. *The Pennsylvania barn*. Kutztown: Pennsylvania Folklife Society.

Sloane, Eric. 1954. *American barns and covered bridges.* New York: Funk & Wagnalls.

Smith, Elmer T. 1965. *Hex signs and other barn decorations.* Lebanon, PA: Applied Arts.

Stephens, David T. 1982. Dates in the roof. *PAST-Pioneer America Society Transactions* 5:1–7.

———. 1984. Ohio's dated and personalized slate roofs. Paper presented at Annual Meeting of the Association of American Geographers, Washington DC.

———. 1987. The dated and personalized slate roofs of northeast Ohio. Paper presented at Annual Meeting of the Association of American Geographers, Portland, OR.

———. 1990. Agriculture. In *The changing heartland: A geography of Ohio,* edited by Leonard Peacefull. Needham Heights, MA: Ginn Press.

Stephens, David T., and Alexander T. Bobersky. 1983. Dated slate roofs of Columbiana County, Ohio. *PAST-Pioneer America Society Transactions* 6:9–17.

——— and ———. 1985. Some notes on Ohio's decorative slate roofs. Paper presented at Annual Meeting of the Pioneer America Society, Cape Girardeau, MO.

Stilgoe, John R. 1982. *Common landscape of America, 1580 to 1845.* New Haven: Yale Univ. Press.

Stoudt, John Joseph. 1945. The decorated barns of eastern Pennsylvania. 15, Plymouth Meeting, PA: Mrs. C. Norman Keyser.

Taylor, Fannie. 1978. Rural murals. *Wisconsin Tales and Trails* (Winter): 27–30.

Trewartha, Glenn T. 1948. Some regional characteristics of American farmsteads. *Annals of the Association of American Geographers* 38(September): 169–225.

United States Code: 1988 Edition. 1989. Vol. 9, Title 22—Foreign Relations and intercourse through Title 25—Indians. Washington DC: Government Printing Office.

van Ravenswaay, Charles. 1977. *German settlements in Missouri: A survey of vanishing culture.* Colombia: Univ. of Missouri Press.

Velie, David. 1942. Country art. *Country Gentleman* (November): 2.

Weekly Ohio Farmer. 1864. Preservation of farm buildings (August 27): 274.

Yoder, Thomas, and Thomas E. Graves. 1989. *Hex signs: Pennsylvania Dutch barn symbols and their meaning.* New York: E.P. Dutton.

13

PRESERVING THE MIDWESTERN BARN

Hemalata C. Dandekar and Eric Allen MacDonald

THE BIG RED, or white, barn is a readily recognized cultural icon, perhaps because many Americans share a relatively recent agrarian heritage and identify with the family farm it symbolizes. To many, the family farm and the traditional values associated with farm families have come to represent the antithesis of modern urbanism, which has often been blamed for many of the social problems confronting our nation. Agriculture, and agricultural structures, have shaped the image many Americans have of the Midwest. Picturesque barn scenes are featured on greeting cards, calendars, and posters, and farm architecture is even represented in children's toys (fig. 13.1). Agricultural settings frequently appear in television and magazine advertisements and are used to evoke a sense of security, stability, wholesomeness, or honesty.

Despite the romantic imagery and fondness which many Americans hold for barns, these structures are rapidly disappearing from the midwestern countryside. Some are being bulldozed, along with the rest of the farmstead, to make way for new housing developments, shopping malls, or office centers. Many more are sinking slowly into the earth as years of neglect and weather take their toll. New "subrural" landscapes are emerging as suburban-style residential and commercial development infiltrates rural lands and renders alien the existing traditional farm structures. The causes of this decline are varied and numerous, and the prognosis for stemming it doubtful. What is encouraging, however, is that more people now recognize that, as barns disappear, a valuable part of our heritage is lost (Carlson 1978; Dandekar and Bockstahler, 1990).

National and local preservation groups, in a shift from focusing primarily on "high-style" or monumental buildings, are beginning to identify barns and other agrarian structures as cultural resources worth saving (Fedelchak and Wood 1988; Stokes et al. 1989). The preservation of vernacular buildings and historic rural landscapes recently has become a major thrust of the federal government's National Register of Historic Places program. The National Trust for Historic Preservation launched a Rural Conservation Project in 1979, and in 1987 co-sponsored with the magazine *Successful Farming* a "Barn Again!" program to encourage farmers

Fig. 13.1. Fisher Price's "Little People Farm" is found in many American homes, urban or rural. Prominently featured is the big red barn and silo. This toy may give young minds a lasting impression of farm life as it was in 1940s.

to rehabilitate their barns (Humstone 1988). The Barn Again! program continues to receive considerable media attention across the country. In addition, rural conservation efforts in several states are specifically addressing the problem of preserving barns.

Preserving the midwestern barn is a daunting task. Unfortunately, the responsibility falls primarily on farmers, individuals engaged in an industry widely recognized as being under duress (Ball and Beatty 1986; Davidson 1986; Brodner 1987). Barn owners, even if they value their barns and are inclined to preserve them, face many challenges of a technical and institutional nature. If their dilemma is to be eased, strategies for barn preservation and reuse must be designed and implemented. Preservation options must be cost effective. Such preservation strategies must address both the nature and quality of the barn as a material artifact and the larger system or context in which the barn exists.

A strictly traditional preservation approach that seeks to create a museum by freezing the structure in a selected time frame will not be widely successful. Modifications that allow barns to shelter nontraditional farming activities, but which make the structures commercially viable, must be accepted. Strategies should attempt to save barns and any cluster of surrounding agricultural buildings by exploiting the social and economic systems at work in the community and region.

Preservation action at the scale of the individual barn could be encouraged by making changes in local and regional regulations and by providing technical assistance to barn owners. In developing effective and appropriate barn preservation strategies for a specific region, the following three questions might be answered: Why are barns being lost? Why should barns be preserved? What are the evaluation and identification issues in preserving barns?

WHY ARE BARNS BEING LOST?

Across the Midwest, barns and other traditional farm structures are vanishing from the landscape (fig. 13.2). Asking why is a crucial first step toward identifying potential strategies for stemming the decline. The many factors that contribute to the big barn's disappearance in the Midwest can be organized under three trends: (1) urbanization; (2) innovations in farm technology; and (3) the spread of corporate farming and agribusiness.

Near growing cities, many barns are lost to urban sprawl. The most noticeable effect of this trend is a zone frequently called the urban fringe where agricultural land is in transition to low-density residential and commercial strip uses. The image of a picturesque farmstead being bulldozed to make way for more suburban sprawl raises the popular conscience and often spurs rural preservation efforts. The underlying destructive nature of urbanization often is less overt than that of the bulldozer, but more insidious in the extent of its impact on barns.

A host of problems accompany the process of urbanization. The characteristics of good quality farmland—land that is flat, well-drained, and easily accessible—also make it attractive for urban development. As a result, much of the farmland lost to urbanization is of above-average quality. Barns are allowed to decay on farmland that has been removed from production for land speculation purposes.

261

Fig. 13.2. Barns on an abandoned Finnish farm outside Ontonagon, Michigan

Tax policies that set rates on property according to its "highest use" encourage the idling of farmland and its sale to developers and land speculators. Increases in real estate taxes, which occur as a result of the maintenance or rehabilitation of barns, further encourage neglect.

A related problem, termed "the impermanence syndrome," occurs when farmers see agricultural land in their community being developed for other uses and come to believe that their land will inevitably be developed, too. This expectation may lead farmers to defer long-term improvements or maintenance of capital facilities such as buildings (Lockeretz 1989; Berry 1978).

Although the decline of barns in the urban fringe is of great concern, the number of barns lost in "suburbanizing" areas is much lower than the number being lost in more remote rural areas. Across the Midwest, more barns are disappearing due to neglect than to bulldozers. Two interrelated trends contribute to this loss: changes in agricultural technology and changes in the agricultural economy that have redefined the scale and scope of farming in the Midwest (fig. 13.3).

Technological changes have historically influenced almost every aspect of farming, including how barns are used. Most barns in the Midwest were built in the nineteenth or early twentieth century, before the widespread mechanization and specialization of agriculture. When these buildings were built, many farms

Fig. 13.3. Giant metal storage containers dominate this farmstead and its traditional barns in southeastern Michigan.

depended primarily upon human and animal power and raised a variety of crops and livestock. As farming practices changed and new technologies were introduced, the big barns were modified to meet new needs. (See chapter 8 for a discussion of this process.)

In almost every farm enterprise, the increased use of heavy machinery has diminished the usefulness of older buildings. Door openings in traditional barns are often too small for the new, larger equipment, and the heavy post-and-beam structure of many barns is too difficult to maneuver around. Old structures may have difficulty meeting sanitation and safety requirements for livestock operations, and electrical and plumbing systems are often inadequate. The huge round bales produced by modern mechanical hay balers have rendered the haylofts of many old barns useless, since these bales can be left outside through the winter, or stored in open shelters. Many older barns were built for specific functions that are no longer needed today, such as sheltering horses. The trend toward specialized production and monocropping has resulted in farms on which few animals are reared and need shelter (Dandekar and Schoof 1988).

To compound these problems, the big barn often becomes a liability to farmers because property taxes are levied on it, even if unused. Thus, old barns are viewed by many farmers as unsuitable for modern agricultural practices and as a financial liability. They believe that rehabilitation of old structures for modern uses is usually not possible, and when it is, it is more complicated and more expensive than building anew. The lending policies of financial institutions also frequently reflect this idea, even though numerous barn rehabilitation projects have proven successful and economical (Humstone 1988; Johnson 1988).

The higher costs of production associated with modern, high-tech farming have affected the scale of agriculture. For decades, the average size of farms in the United States has increased, while the total number of farms has decreased. Small farmsteads have been consolidated into large holdings, as family farms are replaced by corporate farms. Large farm operations purchase smaller farms for the value of their land, not their buildings. As a result, the buildings are razed, or the farmhouse is rented and the barns and other outbuildings allowed to decay (Dandekar 1989).

WHY PRESERVE BARNS?

Many reasons exist for conserving barns and older farm buildings. These reasons encompass individual psychological factors and social, cultural, and economic needs. Barns are tangible reminders of our cultural heritage; they speak about the past; they contribute to the aesthetic quality of the local landscape, and, in some cases, promote local tourism; and old barns are not terminally obsolete, but are significant nonrenewable resources which can be useful and productive when put to a variety of other uses.

Barns are visible reminders of our agrarian heritage. At the personal level, the structures on a farmstead often hold a special meaning for family members whose ancestors built and used them. Barns, and other farm buildings, can be tangible links to a family's past. Barns also may be important in reinforcing a rural community's cultural identity and local sense of place. Perhaps one of their most important contributions is in providing a tangible connection with a past lifestyle, one to which popular culture has given a patina of nostalgia and embodied with nobility and virtue. Preservation of old barns and other traditional structures and landscape features provides a community with a sense of continuity. Many such structures are community landmarks. Such is the case with a polygonal barn in Hastings, Michigan. In interviews authors of this chapter conducted with area residents, this large and unusual barn surfaced as a focal point of their cognitive maps. Significant barns often become such mental landmarks for succeeding generations.

Barns and rural landscapes should be preserved for what we can learn from them. As the essays in this book demonstrate, barns can communicate information about past cultures, technologies, values, and ways of life. Through their form, their geographic distribution, and their relationship with the land and other man-made structures, barns reveal information about the social and economic development of rural regions, communities, and the people who built them.

We know we can learn from the past. We also should recognize that the past can tell us much about the future. For example, the study of historic vernacular environments can reveal how people solved design problems by modifying the environment. The study of vernacular building processes has the potential to influence the way we shape environments today, to help us create more humane, culturally meaningful places for people to live (Hubka 1986; Domer 1989, 56). The buildings and landscapes of the past represent a wealth of design precedents and a source of ideas for the future.

264

There is an important utilitarian reason for conserving old barns. Many offer large open spaces that can be efficiently exploited for new farm uses such as livestock shelter, repair shops, or storage. For farmers, the rehabilitation of older farm structures *is* a viable alternative to new construction. Rehabilitation can be less expensive and require less capital outlay since it can be done in stages ("pay as you go"), and barn owners can often do much of the necessary work themselves. In localities where continued farm use is not a viable alternative, barns can be successfully adapted for a wide range of other purposes. Old barns should be viewed as resources with the potential for increased economic and utilitarian value.

Old barns represent a nonrenewable material and cultural resource, and should be valued as such. The quality and size of timber used to build them are no longer widely available. The technical knowledge and skills needed to design and construct them are disappearing as old barn builders die and young builders are no longer trained in the art. Conserving existing barns and returning them to productive use therefore makes good environmental sense.

SOME PROBLEMS OF IDENTIFING AND EVALUATING BARNS

Not long ago, preservation activity was viewed as obstructionist, the work of a few fanatics aiming to impede growth and progress. However, citizens and public officials have increasingly come to appreciate the role historic places play in enhancing the quality of life in their communities. Preservation is coming to be recognized as a way to manage change in human environments (Stovel 1987; Fitch 1990). For preservation to be successful in the rural Midwest, it must be reconceptualized, largely because much of the midwestern environment is a *vernacular* environment.

The notion that preservation only involves artifacts associated with major events, persons, or monumental architecture leads many people to believe that more humble artifacts are not really "historic" or "significant," and that they are therefore not worthy of preservation. It is clear that focusing preservation efforts on "significant" artifacts, as defined by these criteria, leaves out many vernacular artifacts, including most barns. Yet, vernacular buildings, including barns, *are* culturally significant. A more holistic approach to preservation is needed which allows for multiple definitions of significance and for enough flexibility to preserve the nature or essence of the artifact.

Most vernacular buildings are utilitarian in nature, built by ordinary people using local customs, knowledge, and materials (Heath 1988). The typical midwestern barn is no exception. Most barns have been constantly added to, altered, rebuilt, and remodeled throughout their history. They are the products of many individuals, generations, ideas, and social and economic changes. The sense of evolution communicated through vernacular environments is what makes them meaningful. Their significance is often local, highly personalized, and, in many cases, subconscious. The aesthetic criteria for the conservation of folk and vernacular buildings and landscapes should reflect the nature of vernacular artifacts (Stovel 1987). The preservation criteria should treat them as dynamic, utilitarian artifacts meant to serve a purpose and to adapt and change as circumstances require.

In some cases it may be entirely appropriate to preserve a vernacular building in a "pure" state, for example, in dealing with an exceptionally rare, intact vernacular artifact for pedagogic value, or in maintaining a certain visual character in an area for economic or social reasons. To achieve wide-scale preservation, the strategy must be sufficiently flexible and dynamic, and it must embrace change.

ALTERNATIVE APPROACHES FOR PRESERVING BARNS

In considering which strategies would work to preserve the barns in a particular region, aesthetic and pedagogic concerns must be balanced with utilitarian concerns such as cost and efficiency.

Preservation at the micro-scale level, i.e., that of individual barns and barn owners, can be encouraged through technical assistance. Even with incentives, preservation will not happen if barn owners lack the technical expertise needed to rehabilitate and maintain their buildings. Conversely, providing technical assistance without offering economic incentives or protection through zoning and other measures, will not encourage owners to invest in their buildings.

An ideal way to preserve large barns is to preserve the economic and social system—small-scale, diversified, family farming—that produced and depended upon them. Since this system, with few exceptions, no longer exists today, the buildings it needed, such as the big barns, have become redundant. Ideally, the productive *unit*, the small-scale, diversified, family farm, should be saved. Barn preservation would thus be a natural outgrowth of building strong farm communities. This solution would preserve the dynamic utilitarian quality of barns, as well as the larger, rural cultural system of which they are a part.

A large farm is not always more efficient than a small one. Small farms also may have substantial ecological advantages over large ones, partly because of the more intensive care the small farmer gives his or her land.

If a regional or local planning strategy is oriented toward preserving the small-scale, diversified, family farm, older barns would be maintained because they would still be needed for functions similar to those for which they were built generations ago. This approach could enhance the conservation potential of other buildings and landscape elements such as hedge rows and windbreaks. Nationally, some efforts to establish green belts around urban areas have promoted the concept of family farming. Establishing urban-rural linkages that enable the family farmer to sell products direct to retailers is part of this approach (Dandekar 1989). Such an arrangement could make farming on smaller land holdings more profitable (Lockeretz 1989).

Some well-known techniques useful in preserving old barns and farmland include performance zoning (Porter, Phillips and Lassar 1989; Stokes et al. 1989), cluster development and open space zoning (Yaro et al. 1988; Stokes et al. 1989), local historic district and design review ordinances (Stokes and Getty 1979; Stokes et al. 1989; McClelland et al. 1990; Hall 1991), recognition programs (Humstone 1988; Poll 1990), tax policies (Stokes and Getty 1979; Miner 1980; Stokes et al. 1989), minimum-lot-size subdivision rules (large lot zoning) (Stokes and Getty 1979; Miner 1980; Stokes et al. 1989), agricultural zoning (Toner 1984; American Farmland Trust 1987; Stokes et al. 1989), agricultural districts (Miner 1980; American Farmland Trust 1987; Stokes et al. 1989), right-to-farm laws (Stokes et al. 1989), conservation/preservation easements (Watson 1982; Diehl and Barrett 1988; Stokes et al. 1989; Ward and Benfield 1989), and purchase or transfer of development rights (Stokes and Getty 1979; Miner 1980; American Farmland Trust 1987; Stokes et al. 1989). Implementation may depend on the existence of state-level enabling statutes, so the situation necessarily varies from state to state (Bushwick and Hiemstra 1987). The design and implementation cattle of measures such as these should be approached with caution in order to avoid unanticipated, negative side effects. For example, rural residents may strongly oppose land-use regulations if they are difficult to comply with, are implemented capriciously, or do not reflect the community's values. Local opposition or poor design of any regulatory or incentive device may actually hinder the preservation effort in the long run.

One effective barn-preservation strategy is to find ways to extend the viability of a traditional barn on an existing farm, or to make it useful in a farm-related enterprise. Adaptation for new uses is in keeping with the historical utilization of barns. Most earlier barn adaptations were relatively small, incremental changes, usually to meet new requirements of "modernizing" the farm operation. For example, when farmers in Michigan turned from wheat to dairy production, they needed to modify the basement areas of the barn to house animals, as well as to build silos to feed the cows year-round. Change also occurs as a result of evolution in building technology, for example, the shift from heavy timber to increasingly lighter-frame structures discussed in chapter 8. Innovations in farming technology include the construction of silos and their placement relative to the barn (Dandekar and Savitski 1989). The displacement of horses by tractors required changes in the size of door openings and more navigable ramps and other access to the barn (for other changes see chapters 5 and 11).

Barns also changed as a result of regulatory legislation intended to improve the quality and safety of farm production. For example, sanitation considerations on dairy farms resulted in mandated standards for lighting, ventilation, and requirements that specified elements of the processing plant be constructed of concrete and steel. A separate milk house had to be built and was often attached to one of the external walls of the barn.

In this same vein, current adaptations can be experimented with in the effort to preserve a barn. Several examples of how big barns have been adapted for productive use in small-scale, diversified agriculture, or in large-scale agribusiness, are provided in the Barn Again! booklet (Humstone 1988) and in a research bulletin issued by North Dakota State University's extension office (Johnson 1988). Johnson (1988) provides some excellent examples of ways in which old barns of various configurations can be successfully and economically rehabilitated for farm uses. These include swine farrow and nursery, cattle feeding, machinery repair, grain storage, seed cleaning and storage, dairy calf housing, ewe housing, lambing, and poultry. Agriculture-related uses, such as horse stables and training spaces, farm produce markets, and cottage industries such as cheese factories and spinning or weaving shops, also have been successfully housed in traditional barns.

Use of large barns to shelter activities that are far removed from original functions is another crucial preservation strategy. In rapidly urbanizing areas, continuing a farm or farm-related operation may not be viable, yet the large volume and usable area that a barn encloses offers excellent shelter for a number of commercial and social activities. In continental Europe and the United Kingdom, where protecting historically significant structures is a tradition, there are many successful examples of conversions of farm complexes to art galleries, studios, residences, showrooms, and production facilities.

U.S. barn conversions are not as widespread, yet have been more far ranging in terms of function. Barns have been converted into reuse as churches, community theaters, farm museums, local museums, commercial markets, farm produce markets, storage facilities, light industrial production, workshops, boutiques, stores, professional office space, restaurants, artist studios, art galleries, health clubs, and sports facilities (fig. 13.4).

Nevertheless, the further a new usage is from the original barn function of commodity storage and animal shelter, the more complicated the technical issues related to rehabilitation. Conversion to residential uses may be the most problematic, because of stringent requirements for health and safety. Furthermore, a barn-to-house conversion can make a dramatic impact on the building's exterior. Barns usually have few openings other than the big doors, and most homeowners want lots of windows. Other exterior features of a house, such as chimneys, can drastically alter the appearance of a barn. And, while heavy timber may be aestheti-

Fig. 13.4. Unique agricultural structures such as this round barn in Spring Green, Wisconsin, frequently become well-known local landmarks and have the potential to become symbols of community pride and to attract tourists.
Photo: I. Vogeler

cally appealing, it presents problems in concealing wiring or plumbing, and in installing insulation. Barns are large, making for large living spaces, but they are expensive and certainly not for everyone.

STRUCTURAL AND ARCHITECTURAL DESIGN CONSIDERATIONS

The chronological, structural, and architectural evolution of the midwestern barn has implications for the most suitable adaptive reuse. The evolving structure and spatial organization of midwestern barns reflected cultural, economic, and technological transformations in the agriculture of the Midwest. An understanding of the evolution of barn types is useful in identifying the most significant structural and aesthetic aspects of a particular barn. This enables the designer to both preserve and exploit these characteristics to their fullest advantage when designing reuse.

The *structure* of a barn may be its most important characteristic. The structural frame may largely determine new uses of a barn. When contemplating reuse possibilities for old barns, a classification of their structure is useful. The Michigan Farm Project Phase II research team recently reviewed extension bulletins and publications of the agricultural experiment stations of the midwestern states, and the Canadian Province of Ontario, to identify the structure types that were being promoted for barns during the period 1880 to 1940. This search produced a barn structure typology which reveals the spatial potential of six major types of structures (fig. 13.5). Over time, the volume of space enclosed under the roof became increasingly unobstructed by structural members (see chapter 5 for a detailed discussion). This increasing openness was a result of changes in the nature and quality of available construction materials, particularly wood, evolving support technologies and designs for trusses and ribs, and demands for more open unobstructed space for mechanical reasons (see chapter 11).

Heavy timber barns may present the greatest challenge for reuse. The bulky structural members often get in the way of large modern machinery or equipment, reduce the clear headroom available if intermediate floors are installed, and make the space less usable for storage. Modifying the structure can be difficult because of the weight and thickness of the posts and beams. Modification needs to be done in consultation with a structural engineer and with appropriately large construction machinery at hand. Modifications to the frame must be designed so that the integrity of the structure is not threatened. However, there is great reward which comes with successful conversion. The structure of a heavy timber-framed barn is often its most distinguishable and remarkable feature. It is very expensive to replicate and the large timbers used in the old construction often are no longer available. The heavy timber frame can be a great aesthetic asset when barns are adapted for reuse in nonfarm functions such as retailing. Whenever possible, a reuse design should keep intact the major structure of the barn.

Lighter-frame structures are more easily adapted for farm use. However,

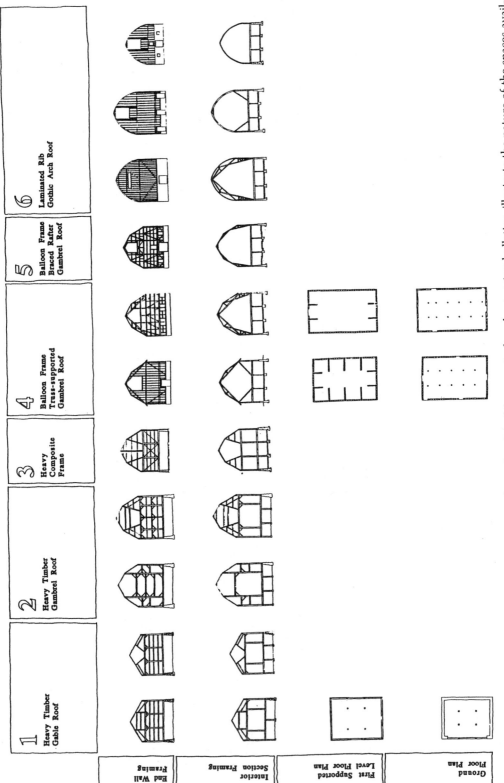

Fig. 13.5. The structure prototypes of the midwestern barn, developed from agricultural extension bulletins, illustrate the nature of the spaces available for reuse in different types of barns. The chronological development is of increasingly open plans and lighter frames.

they have their own problems. Making significant additions to such buildings can be more challenging than to heavy timber ones. On these barns, the structure is often more susceptible to localized failure, and since the complete shell provides structural stability, such failure can quickly lead to the collapse of the entire building.

Scholars of material culture have developed typologies of barns based not just on form, but also on the massing of the buildings, the size, style, and location of openings, construction materials and methods, and minor decorative features (see chapter 1). The texture of the external skin of the barn, the massing of the barn form, the fenestration, door locations and size, and the ornamented details and joints provide the barn with a specific identity. For these reasons, in adaptive reuse, it may be important to maintain the visual appearance of barns as much as possible. Structural changes may have little effect on the visual presentation of the building, yet make all the difference in making the building useful again.

The design elements that give a barn its aesthetic appeal need to be understood and treated with sensitivity. Barn siting and relationship to surrounding landscape and ancillary structures, such as earthen bank or ramp, silo, sheds, milk house, farmhouse, and barnyard should be considered. Other issues concern barn volume and roof line and what can compatibly fit with the rectangular gable structure, with the roof lines of the gambrel or arch, with round or banked barns, and those with cantilevered lofts of various configurations. There, too, are issues of what kinds of modifications different structures, such as heavy timber, light wood trusses, and laminated beams and rafters, will accommodate. The nature and appearance of the materials—wood, stone, metal, or concrete—also must be respected. Decorative features such as cupolas, weather vanes, lightning rods, and dormers must be considered, as must painted decorations and the size and shape of ventilators and louvers. Types of windows and doors, their placement, number, and size may be significant. Finally, the existing condition of the building, its maintenance, the evidence of current and past use, and its evolution are all factors to be reviewed in the design process.

The location of the barns and the category of reuse (figs. 13.6 and 13.7) are additional factors that need to be addressed. When human habitation is involved, especially in urbanized areas, increasingly stringent building codes and zoning restrictions may be encountered. Issues of insulating, fireproofing, and safe access have to be addressed. Design solutions must incorporate ways to preserve essential aesthetic attributes of the existing construction. Modification should involve appropriate materials and shapes. Heating and ventilation strategies for new usage must be designed. A rehabilitated and adapted barn needs to conform to the governing codes so that permission to occupy is obtained and the structure is rendered insurable. The more barn adaptation and reuse involves human occupation, the more stringent will be the technical standards to be met and the more expensive the cost of making these changes.

Figure 13.6 is a decision-tree diagram incorporating a range of functions that might be considered when developing an adaptive reuse strategy for barns in a region. A community might decide to have a multiple-pronged effort which would include saving some excellent barns in a more traditional preservation ef-

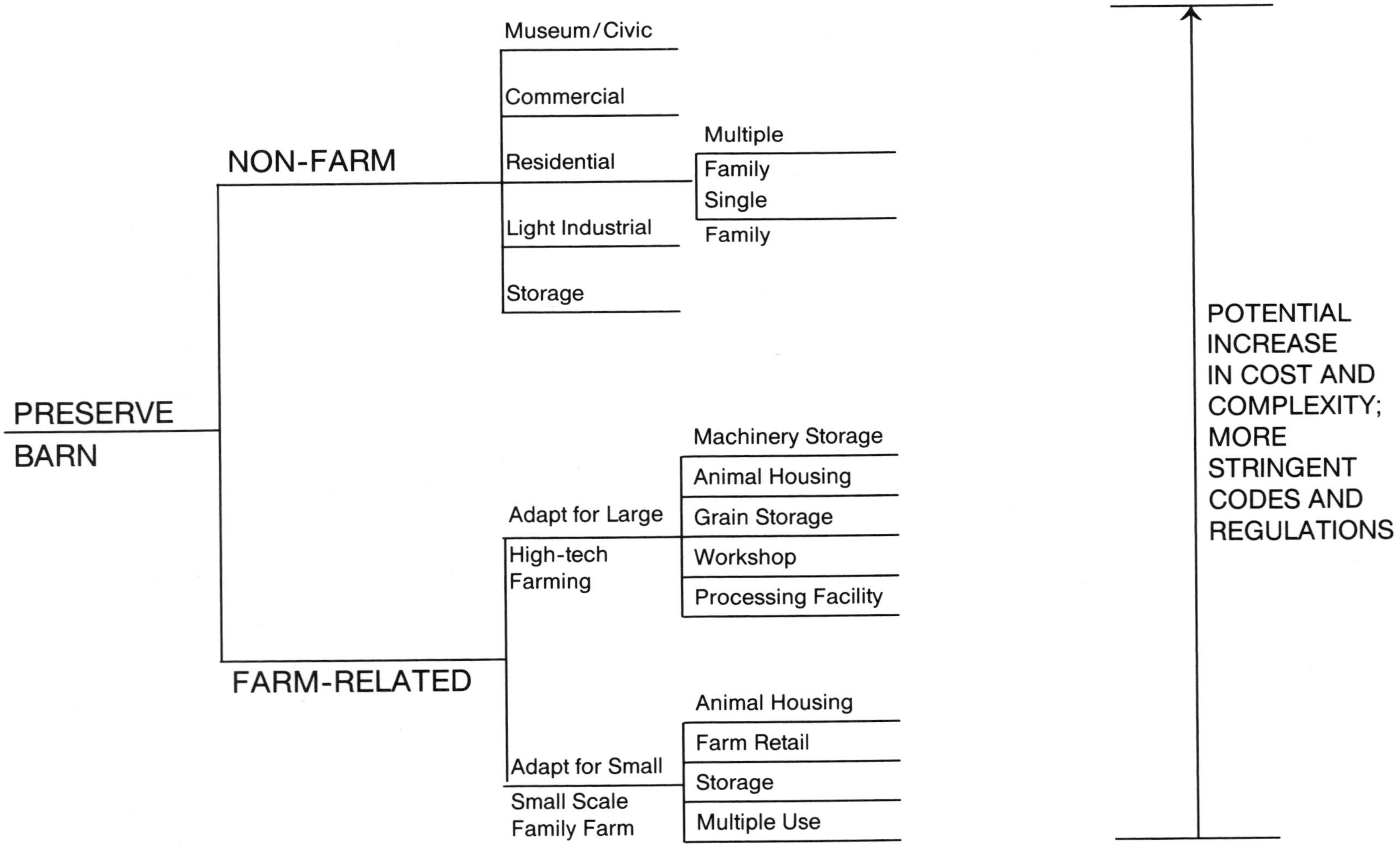

Fig. 13.6. Possible functions for barn reuse offer opportunities for an array of preservation strategies.

fort. It also might create a scenic or historic district to protect the composite elements of a traditional farmscape and thus create an area where other kinds of economic development strategies become viable. For example, tourism and related services might flourish in such an area. In other areas, the strategy might encourage some tax abatement for adaptive reuse of traditional barns for modern farming or for commercial use in other functions.

State and Local Legislation for Barn Preservation

Private rehabilitation of barns for continued use can be encouraged by legal frameworks at state and local levels. Specific measures depend upon the local context and the goals of the effort. For example, in urbanizing areas, the preservation strategy might focus on encouraging intensive farming of the remaining open land, *and* encouraging adaptation of barns for nonfarm, residential or commercial uses. In areas close to urban centers, direct-marketing of produce and promotion of tourism could be the components of such a strategy. In more remote rural areas, diversified family farming and rehabilitation for continued farm use might be the underlying objectives of a preservation strategy (fig. 13.7).

Ideally, a preservation effort is based on a comprehensive inventory of a community's resources, and an analysis of the threats that those resources face. Determining the state of small-scale family farming, inventorying land use and land ownership, and evaluating the quality and integrity of existing barns help identify problem areas and generate creative solutions. A survey of residents is useful so that preservation measures will reflect community goals and values. With this information in hand, specific preservation techniques can be tailored to both the nature of the barn resources in an area and the underlying cause of their decline.

Where to Get Information and Assistance

Several publications on barns and rural conservation provide general information about approaches and options for barn preservation. One important source of information for individuals and communities alike are State Historic Preservation Offices (SHPO). SHPOs carry out state-wide survey and preservation planning programs, review and prepare nominations to the National Register of Historic Places, and review applications for federal rehabilitation income tax credits.

The National Trust for Historic Preservation is another good source for preservation information. Its Barn Again! program may be of interest for those considering a farming use of their barns. The American Farmland Trust (AFT) is an organization devoted to preserving valuable but threatened farmland, and to promoting ecologically responsible farming techniques. AFT has completed several successful conservation projects in the Midwest. Many local land trusts or land conservancies make saving farmland a priority. Any local planning board or Cooperative Extension Office should be able to provide individuals with information on

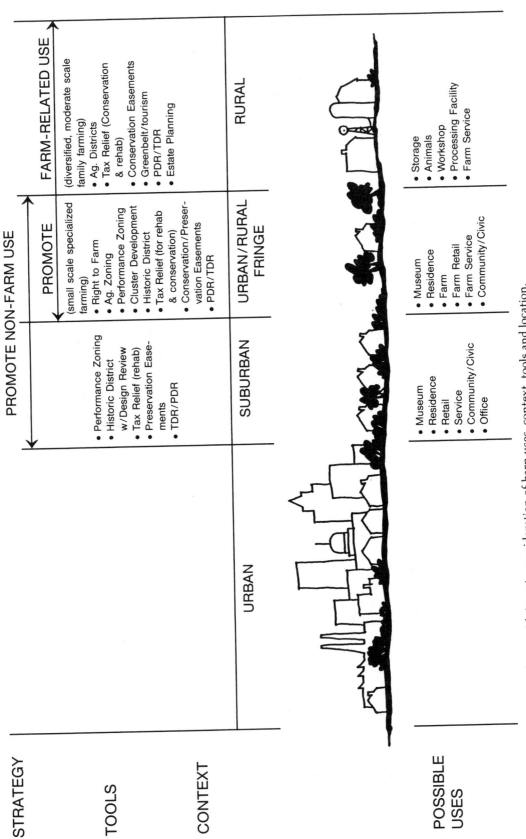

STRATEGY

PROMOTE NON-FARM USE | FARM-RELATED USE

TOOLS

- Performance Zoning
- Historic District w/Design Review
- Tax Relief (rehab)
- Preservation Easements
- TDR/PDR

PROMOTE

(small scale specialized farming)
- Right to Farm
- Ag. Zoning
- Performance Zoning
- Cluster Development
- Historic District
- Tax Relief (for rehab & conservation)
- Conservation/Preservation Easements
- PDR/TDR

(diversified, moderate scale family farming)
- Ag. Districts
- Tax Relief (Conservation & rehab)
- Conservation Easements
- Greenbelt/tourism
- PDR/TDR
- Estate Planning

CONTEXT

URBAN | SUBURBAN | URBAN/RURAL FRINGE | RURAL

POSSIBLE USES

- Museum
- Residence
- Retail
- Service
- Community/Civic
- Office

- Museum
- Residence
- Farm
- Farm Retail
- Farm Service
- Community/Civic

- Storage
- Animals
- Workshop
- Processing Facility
- Farm Service

Fig. 13.7. Preservation strategies must integrate consideration of barn uses, context, tools and location.

active local conservation programs. Some research and review of the existing literature on barns might be helpful to local barn-preservation efforts in the inventory, identification, and evaluation phases. Academic organizations that may be useful to communities wishing to learn more about barns include the Vernacular Architecture Forum (VAF) and Pioneer America Society (PAS). VAF publishes some of its annual conference papers in book form, as well as prepares a quarterly newsletter and bibliography. PAS publishes the quarterly journal, *Material Culture* and the proceedings of its annual conference in *P.A.S.T.—Pioneer America Society Transactions.*

CONCLUSION

Action at the local and state level to preserve the barns of the Midwest is crucial. The demise of traditional barns on the midwestern landscape need not be inevitable if local communities, hand-in-hand with state and national institutions and governments, take a positive and flexible stand for preservation. This chapter has provided some guidelines to help communities think about their specific barn resources and to contemplate alternative options for preservation. Issues that affect this consideration, such as the location of the barns, the nature of the surrounding economy, the functions that are viable within the barn structure, and the technical and financial issues of alternative barn uses, are critically important. The overarching message of this essay is that there is not one all-encompassing barn-preservation strategy that will be successful in all contexts, but rather that each individual and community must develop their own particular strategy.

We must start the preservation effort at any and every scale. We encourage a broad and flexible interpretation of preservation strategies rather than a more traditional, purist historic preservation approach, because we are convinced that this has more promise of obtaining the broad-based preservation effort needed if barns are to remain a tangible and viable element of our future landscape.

REFERENCES CITED

American Farmland Trust. 1987. *Planning and zoning for farmland protection: A community based approach.* Washington: American Farmland Trust.

Ball, Heather, and Leland Beatty. 1986. Blowing away the family farmer. *Nation* 242(January 18): 44–46.

Berry, David. 1978. Effects of urbanization on agricultural activities. *Growth and Change.* 9(3): 2–8

Bleznick, Susan R. 1991. Midwestern vernacular: Charles Moore's TINOVA headquarters rephrases agrarian form. *Inland Architect* 35(4): 54–55.

Brodner, Steve. 1987. Plowed under. *Progressive* 51(May): 35–40.

Bushwick, Nancy, and Hal Hiemstra. 1987. How states are saving farmland. In *Sustaining agriculture near cities,* edited by William Lockeretz. Ankeny, Iowa: Soil and Water Conservation Society.

Carlson, Alvar W. 1978. Designating historic rural areas: A survey of northwestern Ohio barns. *Landscape* 22(3): 29–33.

Dandekar, Hemalata C. 1989. *Michigan Farms Project: Phase I report.* Lansing: Michigan Department of State, Bureau of History.

_____ and Mary Bockstahler. 1990. The changing farmscape: A case study of German farmers in southeast Michigan. *Michigan History* 74(2): 42–47.

_____ and John A. Savitski. 1989. The silo: A century of experimentation on the Michigan farm. *Chronicle: The Quarterly Magazine of the Historical Society of Michigan* 25(3): 2–5.

_____ and Dan Schoof. 1988. Michigan farms and farm buildings: 150 years of transformation. *Inland Architect* 32(1): 22–27.

Davidson, Osha Gray. 1986. The rise of the rural ghetto. *Nation* 242(June 14): 820–21.

Diehl, J., and T. S. Barrett. 1988. *The conservation easement handbook.* San Francisco: Trust for Public Land.

Domer, Dennis. 1989. The old and the new of vernacular architecture: A review essay. *Journal of Architectural Education* 42(4): 45–46.

Fedelchak, Marilyn, and Byrd Wood. 1988. *Protecting America's historic countryside.* Washington: National Trust for Historic Preservation.

Fitch, James Marston. 1990. *Historic preservation: Curatorial management of the built world.* Charlottesville: Univ. Press of Virginia.

Hall, Donna. 1991. The role of local planning in the preservation of historic districts, *Small Town* 21(4): 12–24.

Heath, Kingston W. 1988. Defining the nature of vernacular. *Material Culture* 20(2–3): 1–8.

Hubka, Thomas. 1986. Just folks designing: Vernacular designers and the generation of form. In *Common places: Readings in American vernacular architecture,* edited by Dell Upton and John Michael Vlach, 426–32. Athens: Univ. of Georgia Press.

Humstone, Mary. 1988. *Barn again!: A guide to rehabilitation of older farm buildings.* Washington: National Trust for Historic Preservation.

Johnson, Dexter W. 1988. *Using old farm buildings: Agricultural research report No. 88–1.* Fargo: North Dakota State Univ.

Lockeretz, William. 1989. Secondary effects on midwestern agriculture of metropolitan development and decreases in farmland. *Land Economics* 65(3): 205–16.

McClelland, Linda, J. T. Keller, G. P. Keller and R. Z. Melnick. 1990. *Guidelines for evaluating and documenting rural historic landscapes.* Washington: U.S. Department of the Interior, National Park Service.

Miner, Dallas D. 1980. The role of government in shaping the rural landscape. In *New directions in rural preservation,* ed. Robert Stipe, 83–89. Washington, D.C.: U.S. Dept. of the Interior.

Poll, Christine M. 1990. That darn barn. *Preservation Forum* 4(2): 4.

Porter, Douglas R., Patrick L. Phillips, and Terry J. Lassar. 1989. *Flexible zoning: How it works.* Washington: Urban Land Institute.

Stokes, Samuel, and Joe Getty. 1979. *Rural conservation: Information sheet No. 19.* Washington: National Trust for Historic Preservation.

Stokes, Samuel N., A. Elizabeth Watson, Genevieve P. Keller, and Timothy J. Keller. 1989. *Saving America's countryside: A guide to rural conservation.* Baltimore: Johns Hopkins Univ. Press.

Stovel, Herb. 1987. Managing change in vernacular settings. *Association for Preservation Technology Bulletin* 19(3): 4–6.

Toner, William. 1984. Ag zoning gets serious. *Planning* (December): 20–24.

Ward, Justin R., and F. Kaid Benfield. 1989. Conservation easements: Prospects for sustainable agriculture. *Virginia Environmental Law Journal* 8(2): 271–92.

Watson, Elizabeth A. 1982. *Establishing an easement program to protect historic, scenic, and natural resources: Information sheet No. 25.* Washington: National Trust for Historic Preservation.

Yaro, Robert, R. G. Arendt, H. L. Dodson and E. A. Bradec. 1988. *Dealing with change in the Connecticut River Valley: A design manual for conservation and development.* Amherst: Univ. of Massachusetts, Center for Rural Massachusetts.

14

IN PRAISE OF
"EUERLASTYNGE BARNES"

Jack Matthews

BARNS ARE metaphors of houses, tangible whipboard models of where we live as humans, as projected upon the lifestock that surrounds us, day and night, summer and winter. To the extent they are houses, they are conceived to correct the outer world's bad weather and to domesticate sleet and snow and the ferocity of sunlight into an interior darkness, stability, and peace. Simple in conception and design, the barn is nevertheless the essence of artifice; and yet, to the extent it is the creation of *Homo Faber*, it is natural.

It is a shadow cast in the glaring sunlight of modernity; a pocket against the harsh winds that numb fingers and freeze thumbs; a cove of dry warmth against all the cold drizzle of February. It is a projection of human need, thrown like a cloth over the heads of dumb animals, creatures we've bred to satisfy both appetite and comfort. Thus it is a monument to the anthropomorphosis of cows and horses, and the heaven of hay.

And yet, it is essentially practical—a corral with a roof over it and the sides boarded up. A little world that enables us to find our horses when we need them; a place to feed and milk cows when the snow is piled knee-deep against the slabs of whipsawed oak, turned gray by the silent snow of time. If you close the barn door when you leave, upon your return you will find all you left behind. But even in the days and hours of your absence, it remains warm enough for horses and cows.

As a small boy I climbed up into those primitive attics, palpating the slopes of pungent hay in the lofts, little mountains that snored like paleozoic beasts under the great rafters, and those dark rafters themselves stretching as straight as latitudes across the roof's sky, a striated welkin hovering over all the fragrant roominess beneath. I speak of years packed into minutes, along with all the various silences of dust. I speak of one of the barn's town cousins, the feed store owned by my grandfather, Sam Matthews, in the small southeastern Ohio town of Vinton, and I speak of standing stock-still to marvel at the warm dry shower of wheat dust flecking the shafts of sunlight with their small and silent drift.

As with all the things of this world, they exist in dreams as well as sunlight. Where are the country lanes that lead to those Dream Barns? What dirt tracks bordered by a dark thick wall of osage orange trees, known as hedge apples, can you walk along, seeing the dark shape of the barn lurch into view and rock back and forth with each step, as you approach? What ghostly animals are kept there? And who will hear the clang of buckets on hot summer evenings, when it's milking time, and there is no other sound except for the starlings and swallows fluttering busily in the high eaves, thumping like a myriad little hearts, their wings flipping like the leaves of an old book fanned by a scholar fatigued with much reading but always and insatiably hungry to know more?

Such barns are the settings for scenes I'll never write about in my stories and novels, and will therefore never appear in those books which, in the wrong nature of things, will never be read. Those ghostly publications are more than I can imagine, for the barns they contain shelter all the animals of darkness—a class not limited to cattle and horses and sheep, but inclusive of ourselves. Those untold vessels are scenes of first love making—acts which take place in structures created for that element of creation—or, as we say of all us mammals, of procreation. So it is no wonder that the animals within us, our oldest selves, giving voice to the old Adam we can't help but remember, are lured into those earthy mystic Edens made of hard oak and walnut and cherry, as if they were the finest carved furniture of Sheraton or Hepplewhite, but unvarnished and smelling of hay and the rich perfumes of manure and ammonia from the ripening urine in the stalls.

Not even poetry can embody those austere embodiments in words. Not even "poetic prose" is sufficient, for it constantly leaves the hard physical reality of that which it wants to celebrate. And yet, it works the opposite way, too—from the other direction. The gray and worn old flagstone that the heavy quivering doors grind against shimmer with possibility. If you can't see that shimmering, wait until it lasts into your memory, and you cannot but help see the transformation. The Barn of our Past is a redolence, a nostalgia for a world that never was, and is therefore the most powerful evocative we can know.

So the poetry extends even unto this, the most prosaic, the most practical, of devices to clothe animals in a warm darkness made of wood. The barn is a box smelling of horses and cattle and hay, contained in them like living jewels in a treasure chest. And there is a society of barns, an elite, scorning the drab functionalism of corncribs, chicken houses, and sheds for plows and harrows. This is known by obversion, for how else could we understand the pungent grassy desuetude of barns in their abandonment?

As barns are vivid and specific in their use, so there are people who are specific to them, who know them in their hearts and belong with them, just as there are people who can speak to horses with their hands, gestures, and bodily aura. I have known men of this sort, and think of the Dunham brothers in Delaware County: shy, lean, hard-working, modest men with a slow and enduring passion for doing things right; I speak of Jim, Cecil, and Dwight, surely all dead by now—

or "gone to the barn," which is as good and homely a metaphor as any. When he heard of Hemingway's death, Gary Cooper used it, saying, "I didn't think he'd get to the barn before I did." But having said it, the shy movie actor—a barn person, beyond any doubt—would not have long to wait before he, too, followed his friend and reached the barn in his own way, as all of us have to do it.

I was surprised by Gary Cooper's metaphor, and found it felicitous, but later discovered that it had not been his private invention, but rather a figure of speech over four hundred years old, having lived in virtual secrecy, the way metaphors do underneath the sounds we make when we talk. I am thinking of an old book, attributed to Thomas Gascoigne, titled *The Myroure of Oure Ladye*, and published either in 1520 or 1530 (The Oxford English Dictionary cites 1520; however, the British Museum catalog does not list it at all, while the National Union Catalog cites the 1530 edition as the earliest), in which the following sentence occurs: "Aungels myghte gather them in to euerlastynge barnes."

The barn is a mythic presence, a familiar darkness looming at the edge of the mind's vision, which is only right and natural, for the barn is a projected mind, a place for storage—although that inner barn contains far more animals than we have domesticated. In remembering "the little clay fossil heads" he made as a boy, the anthropologist Loren Eiseley (1987) referred to the barn where he stored them as being more than a barn, his mind (131).

Being a mind, it is a natural habitat for memory, and I can remember milking time on hot summer evenings at my Uncle Ray's farm. This was Ray Grover, my mother's older brother, who lived in Gallia County, near Sam Matthews' Vinton. I can still hear the inimitable sounds, the clopping of cows' hooves, the strong ripping sound of milk squeezed hard into galvanized buckets, the shuffling and snuffling of cows, rolling their great walled eyes as if in dumb alarm at so much being pulled out of their bodies.

I remember our barn in Delaware County, on a farm whose house was built in 1821, and where, in the servant's quarters in back, an old black woman named Sarah Brandy died at the age of 125 years, having years before been a servant in George Washington's household. I remember stowing hay in the barn. I remember swinging the hay fork out from its pulley under the eave to gouge and pluck great clumps of hay, half as large as Volkswagons, to send them swinging ponderously into the loft.

I remember shooting rats with my .22 as they scurried up and down the walls of the corncrib, the barn's poor little country cousin. I remember a 115-pound boy from a neighboring farm horsing 100-pound bales of hay off the loading wagon, as hard-working and tireless as any big man could imagine. Then I remember evenings when I read the stories of Poe by lamplight and later walked the moonlit swamps at night on the shores of Old Alum Creek, returning through the apple orchard, the trees tangled with suckers, and past the barn to the house.

The barn and house are still waiting for me at the bottom of a lake, for they were flooded by the Alum Creek Reservoir, a project designed to preserve water and to provide bass fishing for lonely men and women who know little or nothing about barns, and to that extent and in that dimension are condemned to lead cold and sterile lives.

280

Since we are essentially symbol-using creatures, it is only natural that the familiar things of our lives gather unnatural meanings. I find this mysterious, for when something is invested with symbolic meaning, it is given access to all the enigmas of otherness. Thus, in the creation of a symbol, there is the familiarization of something necessary, but precisely as it becomes familiar, it estranges itself by acquiring remote and symbolic power.

Thus, that most humble, useful, and—to the common mind—most prosaic of structures, the barn, has acquired familiarity because of its utilitarian function. But, with the advent of familiarity, it began to alienate itself through the countermovement of the symbol. The paradox being that, the more secure it became in common, everyday life, the more it began to accumulate those dimensions of abstraction and distance implicit in symbols.

How can this be known? Or how measured? In one way, by everyday locution and popular metaphor, merging even into cliche. Thus, the nickname of the radical element of the Democratic Party gave us *barn burner*, a term still available for any sort of fomented public agitation. Then, too, there is *barn stormer*, referring first to nineteenth-century actors, then to daredevil pilots after World War I, and, finally, through metathetic association, becoming *brainstorming*, referring to the most active sort of committee action. Whoever misses the message implicit in this vital function or the image of the barn is impoverished of insight and couldn't hit the barn door with an apophthegm.

Such symbolic fecundity is only appropriate, for the barn itself is an instrument of growth and abundance. Where else can we store the plentitude of the earth except in those great bucolic and equine warehouses? What else have we built with such a wondrous appetite for our rich harvests? If we were cattle, they would be our first stomachs.

"And bursts the crowded Barns with more than promis'd Gains," Dryden wrote in his translation of Virgil's *Georgics*. Georgics is from the Greek, and means "farmer"; it is compounded of *geo*, or earth, and *erogen*, or work. The author of *De Re Metallica*, which Herbert and Lou Hoover translated in 1912, was Georgus Bauer, whose Latinate name was Agricola; if he had kept the German part, his full name translated into English would have been "Farmer, Farmer, Farmer," which is thrice signified and about as bucolic as you can get.

It is significant that barns are so little noticed in an increasingly urban world. As the institution of the family farm disappears, it carries the barn with it. Those vast, roomy structures on large corporate farms are not really barns at all; they are grain warehouses and silos, high-tech descendants of the homely old barn. Their aluminum sidings are no more appropriate for covering barns than vinyl plastic would be for the skin of a horse or steer.

Still, barns have not entirely disappeared; we still see them leaning under the burden of time, their Mail Pouch signs fading in the rain. They have turned into things whose primary function is to provide images for the majority of people, who see them standing in the weeds as they drive on Interstate Highways, listening to vulgar music on their radios and the fast patter of disc jockeys . . . all of them people who are exiled from barns, therefore deracinated.

In Don DeLilo's novel, *White Noise* (1986), there is an amusing passage about "the most photographed barn in America." In this scene, Murray, a displaced New Yorker and professor of popular culture whose specialty is Elvis Presley, tries to explain the inner meaning of this barn phenomenon:

> "No one sees the barn," he said finally.
>
> A long silence followed.
>
> "Once you've seen the signs about the barn, it becomes impossible to see the barn."
>
> He fell silent once more. People with cameras left the elevated site, replaced at once by others.
>
> "We're not here to capture an image, we're here to maintain one. Every photograph reinforces the aura. Can you feel it, Jack? An accumulation of nameless energies."
>
> There was an extended silence. The man in the booth sold postcards and slides.
>
> "Being here is a kind of spiritual surrender. We see only what the others see. The thousands who were here in the past, those who will come in the future. We've agreed to be part of a collective perception. This literally colors our vision. A religious experience, in a way, like all tourism."
>
> Another silence.
>
> "They are taking pictures of taking pictures," he said.
>
> He did not speak for a while. We listened to the incessant clicking of shutter release buttons, the rustling crank of levers that advanced the film.
>
> "What was the barn like before it was photographed?" he said. "What did it look like, how was it different from other barns, how was it similar to other barns? We can't answer these questions because we've read the signs, seen the people snapping the pictures. We can't get outside the aura. We're part of the aura. We're here, we're now."
>
> He seemed immensely pleased by this. (12)

"What was the barn like before it was photographed?" This satire is possible only in an age of compulsive communication; an age when seeming has pre-empted all sense of being; a media drunk age when people will take pictures of anything if other people are taking pictures of it. And an age when the noble simplicity of the barn has been lost, so that it has become no more than an image, something to make other images from, something to look at and find "quaint" or "charming."

But there is something else behind that image, and it is important that we remember what it was; or at least imagine it. Because no barn was ever made simply to be looked at or to provide a cosmetic embellishment for a country house. The essential seriousness of barns gives them an unmistakable dignity, one which connects us to the animals we have domesticated for our use. Behind that image, and even behind its usefulness, the barn is an artifact which, like all of our most honest inventions, mirrors us in what we have done and what we are.

REFERENCES CITED

Eiseley, Loren. (Kenneth Hever, ed.) 1987. *The lost notebooks of Loren Eiseley,* Boston: Little Brown.

De Lilo, Don. 1986. *White noise.* New York: Penguin Books.

15

REFLECTIONS

Hubert G. H. Wilhelm and Allen G. Noble

IN 1950 a German teenager came to the United States as a rural ex-
change student. His destination was a farm in Sangamon County, in central Illinois. He had spent six years in practical training on a number of European farms,
both small and large, in preparation for a career as a farm manager. Today, even
after almost half a century and a change in profession (now a settlement geographer and cowriter of this chapter), his impressions of the first day on that farm
south of Springfield remain vividly imprinted on his memory. He can recall the
flatness of the land, fields of corn, few trees, and long, straight roads and adjacent
fences; the white, box-like house which set back from the road on a grassy front
yard; and the red farm buildings, including an old threshing barn and a corncrib,
whose functions became known only later on.

To his surprise, this farm of several hundred acres was worked by only four
people, the "old man," his son, and two "hired hands." The field work was done
not by horses, as in Europe, but with shiny red International Harvester tractors.
The main crops were corn, soybeans, wheat and oats, and of course, hay, to feed
the farm's herd of Angus beef cows. Several hundred Hereford feeder calves,
which arrived one day by railroad from Montana, were turned out into the harvested corn fields and later penned in a concrete feedlot next to the old barn and
the silo. Of course, there were pigs of all sizes and shapes, many of them scaveng-
ing in the cow pastures.

The farm still had a few chickens, but they were sold during the year, as
was the only cow, the "in-house" milk supplier. What a culture shock: a farmer
having to rely on the in-town store for basic food items! (By the way, the above-
mentioned milk cow was indirectly responsible for the teenager's abrupt introduction to the rectangular land survey system. One day, while returning from milking
at the "home place," an obligatory ninety-degree road turn was forgotten and the
novice driver, in a 1950 green Ford with a bucket of milk on the rear seat, ended
up in a roadside ditch.)

Along with the disappearance of the last vestiges of midwestern subsistence

284

living came the removal of the old, red threshing barn that year. It was replaced with a "modern" gambrel-roofed hay and cattle barn, built from plans dropped off by a traveling sales representative. There was no wall on the lower level of the barn facing toward the south, so cattle and hogs could seek shelter from the adjacent feedlot area. The north side of the barn abutted the old, concrete silo which, a few years later, was replaced with a new, blue Harvestore. A lot of changes during a single year, but, in retrospect, typical of a region whose very existence depended on "keeping up with the times."

The preceding chapters represent a premier undertaking: the comprehensive treatment of a long-overdue subject, the midwestern barn. The two elements, *Midwest* and *barn*, are inextricable related, forming the underpinning of a people's spatial perception of the American heartland—neither East nor West, but rather in the center, where the combination of level land, fertile, dark, and grass-covered soils, ideal climate, and usually abundant water, offered—to all those who dared to settle there—a panacea.

The barn is a symbol of work, surpluses, income, thrift, and risk-taking. It is, in other words, the embodiment of a people's economic worth. To use Calkins and Perkins' analogy from chapter 3, the barn is the "farmer's bank." In America, and especially in the Midwest, with its specialized, commercial agriculture, the barn's image and function translated into extraordinary architectural forms, often appearing like veritable castles on the rural landscape.

The Midwest is an American mindset as well as a geographic region. True, its borders are, at best, fuzzy (see chapter 1). Where it begins and ends often depends on where one comes from. It is, however, that part of the country where American agriculture "came of age," where traditional land uses and forms responded to new challenges. Most important among those challenges were the rise of interior cities and rail links, the connectivity of the rural farm population with local towns and cities, the economic interdependence of farm and city, the growth of extraregional population concentrations as markets, an ever-increasing standard of living and related dietary expectations (i.e., America's steak-hamburger culture), and, not least, major world events, especially World Wars I and II.

To most Americans, the midwestern farmstead probably represents the epitome of up-to-date agriculture; its buildings are modern and functional and representative of the region's scientific approach to agriculture. This view is true, but only to a point. For one thing, it implies homogeneity within a very large region, one that is actually quite disparate from place to place. These differences are the result, as has been shown, of contrasting settlement traditions. There are environmental differences, too, especially of terrain and climate, which effected contrast in human responses. Perhaps, most important, especially when considering the contemporary agricultural patterns in the Midwest, are distance from sources of transportation and markets.

To an Iowa farmer, who relies heavily on animals, particularly hogs, the humorous reference to the crop rotation of a central Illinois farmer as "corn, soybeans, Florida," is a rather cruel joke. It all comes down, of course, to basic geographic principles, the location of markets and distance. The Illinois farmer is close to a number of places, particularly Peoria, Decatur, and Chicago, where he can sell his corn and soybeans. The Iowa farmer, in contrast, lacks much of this locational benefit and, therefore, must rely on a higher value product than corn and soybeans. By feeding his corn to animals in order to achieve parity in profit, the Iowa farmer must, of course, "stay down on the farm" to care for his cattle and hogs, while his Illinois compatriot may enjoy the warmer climes.

A book on the midwestern barn is by any measure a huge undertaking. The reader who has assiduously worked through all the chapters may be left with more questions than answers. This, of course, is good, because opportunities are opened up for further research and discussion, verification of facts, and, likely, new conclusions. On the other hand, it should now be clear that the midwestern barn is not just a simple, white, rectangular building with a gabled roof. Instead, it is a farm building with a complex material culture-history, conditioned by agricultural land use and economy, and above all, by scientific principles and modern technology.

As the barriers to westward migration fell, American migrants and foreign immigrants alike converged onto the country's central parts, guided by the spirit of manifest destiny and the paths of natural routeways, and drawn by the unfailing attraction of cheap and plentiful land. There were New Englanders and Easterners, including large numbers of Pennsylvania-Dutch, and, of course, Southerners, especially Virginians, who came by way of the hills of Appalachia and the rivers of Kentucky. The immigrants were a varied lot, but prominent among them were the Scots-Irish and the Germans. They all carried their own distinctive cultural baggage, including building traditions.

Within the time period of little more than a generation, however, these traditions would give way to new influences. In part, these resulted from acculturation, but, more importantly, were caused by urbanization and industrialization, and the impact which these processes had on agriculture.

The rise of midwestern cities happened in close alignment with the development of the rural hinterlands. As the urban centers consumed the raw materials of the farm, so did the countryside come to rely on the cities' manufactured wares. This economic interdependence triggered unheralded change in the landscape, and the barn, in all its mutations, became a most visible part of these alterations.

In a brief essay published in the journal *Landscape* (1962), Carl Sauer, one of America's foremost chroniclers of the human-made landscape, painted an eloquent picture of the settlement changes wrought by the occupance and development of America's interior. The idea of the "Middle Border," which he borrowed from Hamlin Garland's *A Son of the Middle Border* (1917),

> . . . was the wide, advancing wave of settlement that spread over the plains south of the Great Lakes and north of the Ohio River. . . . Its advances made Cleveland, Toledo and Chicago northern gateways. At the south, it gave rise to border cities such as Cincinnati on the Ohio, St. Louis at the crossing of the Mississippi, and Kansas city on the great Bend of the Missouri. . . . Although it did not begin as such, this became the peopling of the prairies, the founding and forming of the actual Midwest. (3)

The core of this region was the isolated family farmstead with its traditional Federal-style two-story, one-room deep house also known as I-house because of its prevalence in Indiana, Illinois, and Iowa or, later, "folk-Victorian" house, a barn and several smaller outbuildings, loosely arranged according to the dictates of the rectangular land survey. The farmstead was surrounded by a grid-like pattern of fences, remnant wood lots, and fields, whose division represented adherence to a four-year rotation of corn, wheat, oats, and clover.

The farmstead was socially and economically integrated with a nearby country church and a more distant town whose railroad-related facilities and activities offered the all-important linkage to the "outside world." That linkage would be greatly enhanced later on by the addition of the telegraph, rural mail delivery (RFD), rural electrification, the telephone, and hard-surfaced highways. The automobile completed the integration of farm and town, leading to what Peirce Lewis has characterized as the "metropolitanization" of the American farmer and countryside (1983, 33).

In contrast to the Old World and, for that matter, earlier settlement areas in the eastern parts of America, the rural landscape of the Midwest soon reflected the strong interdependence of town and country. Farms became production facilities for specific staples and animals demanded by an ever-growing American and world-wide market. Here, in America's heartland, agriculture truly changed from "a way of life" to "a way of making a living." The nostalgic picture of the Middle Border farm, sitting square on its quarter section, strongly relying on home-produced items, and taking the "Mason jar" approach to life and living, was, indeed, short-lived.

The twentieth century brought significant changes in this country and throughout much of the world. Formidable strides were made by the combination of science and technology to respond to World War I and, afterward, to effect economic stabilization. American agriculture, especially midwestern agriculture, was an important benefactor of these advances, and the rural, built-up landscape came to reflect these changes. The earlier, more traditional houses often were replaced with modern "Sears and Roebuck" types that featured interior plumbing and central heating. Older barns and other farm buildings were altered to accommodate tractors and new machinery, and farmers often turned to cheaper building materials.

An appropriate characterization of this "new" agriculture and its implications for the built-up landscape comes from the writings of J. B. Jackson, perhaps America's best-known student and chronicler of cultural landscapes. He notes that,

> the kind of modification which the modern farmer undertakes is entirely different; different not only in scale but in purpose; for its purpose is to create an entirely new and artificial setting for his work. The ultimate aim is man-made topography, a man-made soil, a man-made crop, all part of a new production process. (Cited in Zube and Zube, 1977, 1)

287

It is no accident of history that the American land-grant college system and its related emphasis on technical education, and the country's annual county and state fairs, had their fullest development in the Midwest. These institutions greatly contributed to and encouraged changes among the region's farm population. The age-old adage that "the farmer's dumbest son inherits the place, while the other sons are sent to school to learn a profession" was turned around. From then on, midwestern farming was to be placed in the hands of those best prepared for it.

Did this mean that those tried and true buildings of grandfather's era no longer had a place in this new American region, the Midwest? Well, yes and no. Several chapters in this book have reminded us that settlement of the Midwest began at a time which permitted traditional, nonspecialized agriculture, with its strong reliance on subsistence, to become well established.

We must remember, too, that early settlers came from different regions of America and Europe and many relied on time-honored practices, including those of ethnic architecture. For example, the ancient art of log construction survived throughout the timber-rich areas of the Midwest, especially its southern borderland along the Ohio River. Here, southern settlers already well-versed in log construction techniques took advantage of the forests and helped diffuse the log-building tradition. As was pointed out in chapter 2, many a log cabin, crib, or barn survive in the more distant and isolated parts of the Midwest. Neither should the influence of log construction on the development of the American corncrib and its likely close cousin, the three-portal barn (see chapters 2, 4 and 9, and Noble 1984), be discounted.

Perhaps, the most widely distributed barn in the Midwest is the three-bay English barn. It receives comprehensive treatment in Chapter 3 under the partial and well-deserved title of "threshing barn." Its ancient roots are in both continental Europe and the British Isles. In America, the three-bay barn became the barn of choice among the majority of early settlers. It fit very well into the small-scale, mixed agriculture of New Englanders and others from the Middle Atlantic area.

Furthermore, and to a large measure because of, its full-frame construction, the three-bay barn was the kind of building that could be relatively easily adapted. Plank or balloon framing was substituted for its original, hand-hewn, heavy frame, in raising and extending it, or in adding a new kind of roof. Another modification which produced a conspicuous landscape form was the raising of the barn above a solid stone, brick, or concrete foundation, thus adding a basement level. Because the additional area of the structure invariably was devoted to livestock housing, this raised barn gained popularity most readily in those areas of the Midwest which were shifting over to dairying from an earlier crop emphasis.

All of these changes happened to this nondiscript farm building. Chapters 5, 8, and 11 are primarily concerned with the modernization of the midwestern barn, especially in structure and function. However, the form of these new barns, including rectangular plan and gabled roof, continued to be based upon and to resemble closely their ancient ancestor, the English three-bay barn.

The subject of surviving traditions in the Midwest would be ill-served without an additional comment or so about the Pennsylvania-German barn. Here was a structure which changed hardly at all during its long diffusion route from the rolling Piedmont country of Pennsylvania and Maryland into the plains of the Midwest. Admittedly, there were fewer and fewer of these barns built west of Ohio, but to this day, travelers, especially on Route 40 or Interstate 70, marvel at these "barnyard castles" of bygone days with their conspicuous second-story overhangs or forebays and "banked" lower level. (Of course, in the level lands of the interior, "banking" this barn was replaced by using an earthen ramp.)

Simply because the terrain no longer suited the traditional way of building did not automatically mean that one altered the building accordingly. In general, human culture is conservative, and it was especially so among the Germanic settlers from the East, who were not a people inclined to change because it was the thing to do. Because the barn survived both time and space, it has been possible to trace its diffusion paths. Robert Ensminger (1980–81, 1983, 1992) has provided an excellent record of the "Pennsylvania barn," including identifying its source area as eastern Switzerland. Thus, to refer to the barn as Pennsylvania-German is only partially correct, but it does represent the fact that the majority of its builders west of the Appalachians were of Pennsylvania-German background (see chapter 4).

Both the English and the Pennsylvania-German families of barns ideally served their builders' farm practices, which centered on growing small grains, especially wheat and oats, and keeping livestock, particularly dairy cows. Because "form follows function," traditional regional land uses strongly influenced barn forms. The corn, tobacco, and livestock agriculture of Southern settlers required crib-type barns, with loft storage for hay (see chapter 2) and tobacco sheds (see chapter 7).

In time, midwestern farmers did change in response to shifting economic influences and modified their barns to accommodate these changes. A major alteration was effected when machine farming, with the increasing importance of corn and soybeans, replaced hand and horse cultivation of the small grains. The old threshing barns were recycled as storage and implement sheds, while corncribs mushroomed.

To the north, around the Great Lakes and its urban centers, the singular importance of dairying fostered a barn architecture that emphasized space for animals, hay, and straw. The silo complemented the barn and became an integral, and ubiquitous element of the dairy landscape (see chapter 6). Agricultural specialization has left its imprints on the built-up farm landscape of the Midwest. Surprisingly, traditional forms often could be readapted to the new land uses without major modifications. Again, for example, old threshing barns sometimes became hay barns with the simple addition of a gambrel roof and milking stanchions.

The round, octagonal, and oval barns of the Midwest are perfect examples of the interrelation of land use, science, and technology (see chapter 10). They, however, represent an extreme of that integration. In the final analysis, practical midwestern farmers preferred rectangularity (orthogonal plan) to the rounded and angled creations of scientific thinkers. Their rejection was based primarily on economic considerations, not on the old folk fear of the "devil hiding in the corners of the barn."

The Midwest, however, is richer for the presence of these magnificent farm palaces. Needless to say, many of these and other older barns today are threatened by age and by simply having outlived their intended purpose. We can only hope that future preservation efforts will become more affordable and, therefore, commonplace in rural America (see chapter 13). Unfortunately, largely because of the dispersed settlement pattern of American farmers, barn preservation may never warrant the same attention and scope as other historic buildings in urban locations.

Let us, therefore, conclude with an appeal for the creation of an outdoor museum or theme park of the midwestern farmstead. It should be similar in format to the splendid Old World Wisconsin museum operated by the Wisconsin Historical Society, but with the emphasis on an American New World: the midwestern farmstead—its past, present, and future. Such a theme park could become a national center from where state, community, or individual efforts to restore and preserve barns are coordinated. To this day, rural structures have not received the attention from preservationists granted urban buildings. This reflects the dispersed, individualistic nature of American farm settlement and our preoccupation with stylish buildings instead simple, functional ones. But, what better structure than the barn to tell America's story of the variety in its ethnic and regional traditions, environmental characteristics and land uses. Even in the country, the house changed in response to changing technologies and fashions. The old barn, however, remained—sturdy in its construction and symbol to an ever more tenuous past. Yet, time and changing agricultural practices have overtaken the old barns and their days are numbered. A theme park would not only permit an overview of all the various kinds of midwestern barns, their construction and function, but could also be an important link in a nation-wide effort to bring preservation to the countryside.

REFERENCES CITED

Ensminger, Robert F. 1980–81. A search for the origin of the Pennsylvania barn. *Pennsylvania Folklife* 30(2): 5–71.

————. 1983. A comparative study of Pennsylvania and Wisconsin forebay barns. *Pennsylvania Folklife* 32(3): 98–114.

————. 1992. *The Pennsylvania barn: Its origin, evolution, and distribution in North America.* Baltimore: Johns Hopkins Univ. Press.

Garland, Hamlin. 1917. *A son of the Middle Border.* New York: Macmillan and Company.

Lewis, Peirce. 1983. The galactic metropolis. In *Beyond the Urban Fringe: Land Issues of Non-Metropolitan America,* edited by Rutherford H. Platt and George Macinko, 23–49. Minneapolis: Univ. of Minnesota Press.

Noble, Allen G. 1984. *Wood, brick, and stone: The North American settlement landscape.* Vol. 2, *Barns, and Farm Structures.* Amherst: Univ. of Massachusetts Press.

Sauer, Carl. 1962. Homestead and Community on the Middle Border. *Landscape* 12(1): 3–7.

Zube, Ervin H., and Margaret J. Zube, eds. 1977. *Changing rural landscapes.* Amherst: Univ. of Massachusetts Press.

INDEX